Looking Beyond
Suppression

D0114919

Looking Beyond Suppression

Community Strategies to Reduce Gang Violence

Edited by Erika Gebo and Brenda J. Bond

LEXINGTON BOOKS
Lanham • Boulder • New York • Toronto • Plymouth, UK

Published by Lexington Books
A wholly owned subsidiary of Rowman & Littlefield
4501 Forbes Boulevard, Suite 200, Lanham, Maryland 20706
www.rowman.com

10 Thornbury Road, Plymouth PL6 7PP, United Kingdom

British Library Cataloguing in Publication Information Available

Library of Congress Cataloging-in-Publication Data

The hardback edition of this book was previously cataloged by the Library of Congress as follows:

Looking beyond suppression : community strategies to reduce gang violence / edited by Erika Gebo and Brenda J. Bond.
    p. cm.
  Includes index.
  1. Gangs. 2. Violence—Prevention. 3. Communities—Social aspects. I. Gebo, Erika. II. Bond, Brenda J.
  HV6437.L66 2012
  363.32'17—dc23
  2012010700

ISBN 978-0-7391-5016-0 (cloth : alk. paper)
ISBN 978-0-7391-9061-6 (pbk. : alk. paper)
ISBN 978-0-7391-7655-9 (electronic)

♾️™ The paper used in this publication meets the minimum requirements of American National Standard for Information Sciences—Permanence of Paper for Printed Library Materials, ANSI/NISO Z39.48-1992.

Printed in the United States of America

28,04   363.32
             Loo

Acknowledgments

The editors and contributors would like to thank the Massachusetts Executive Office of Public Safety and Security for their support of these projects, individually and as a whole. We would all like to send a special thank you to James Stark and his predecessor, Keith O'Brien, for their tireless work in advocating for funding, promoting collaboration between sites and researchers, and encouraging the project.

The editors would like to thank the Suffolk University College of Arts & Sciences Dean's Office for supplying financial support for our wonderful Research Assistant, Andrea Blasdale, who made sure our i's were dotted and our t's were crossed. We also would like to thank the Suffolk University Sawyer Business School's Institute for Public Service who provided financial support for completion of the project. Erika would like to thank Lawrence, Adelaide, and Phebe who gave up some of 'our' time to allow this to come together. Brenda would like to send a special thanks to Lowell Police Department friends and colleagues who continue to serve as enthusiastic partners.

CHAPTER 3—Laurie Ross and Ellen Foley would like to acknowledge the invaluable assistance of Nimesh Dhungana and Zaliah Zalkind, their research assistants on this project. They are also grateful for the insights, knowledge, and support of their community partners at the Worcester Police Department, Boys and Girls Club of Worcester, Worcester Youth

Center, and Worcester Community Action Council—particularly Sgt. Miguel Lopez, Yesenia Maysonet, Ron Hadorn, Roberto Diaz, Hilda Ramirez, Priscilla Holmes, and Todd Smith. We also want to express our respect and admiration for the young people living in Worcester.

CHAPTER 4—Erika Gebo and Kim Tobin would like to thank all the Springfield Shannon Partners who work passionately and diligently with the youth of the City.

CHAPTER 5—Sean P. Varano and Russell Wolff would like to thank the support of the many members of the H.O.P.E. Collaborative in the City of New Bedford who have directly and indirectly aided in the completion of this project. Special thanks in particular are extended to Chief Ronald Teachman (Retired), Chief David Provencher, Michelle Roderick, Dráe Perkins, Cheryl Robert, Robert McPherson, and Deirdre Lopes. They also acknowledge the dedication and hard work of the street outreach workers in the City of New Bedford with whom they have the privilege of working. Their dedication and passion made this work possible.

CHAPTER 6—Brenda J. Bond, Nicole Rivers-Kustanovich, and Erin McLaughlin would like to extend special thanks to Jennifer Ball, formerly of the Lowell Police Department; Tom Lombard, Robin Smith, and Meghan Ferriera of the LPD's Crime Analysis and Intelligence Unit; and to Superintendent Kenneth E. Lavallee for their commitment to quality improvement and their assistance in all aspects of the Shannon initiative.

CHAPTER 8—Jack McDevitt and Russell Wolff would like to thank James Stark and Keith O'Brien, currently and formerly of the Executive Office of Public Safety and Security (EOPSS), respectively, with whom they worked closely on the Shannon Community Safety Initiative (SCSI) during the period described in this chapter.

Disclaimer

These projects were supported by Grant #2005-DB-BX-0014, #2007-DJ-BX-0060, #2008-DJ-BX-0715, and 2009-DJ-BX-0104 awarded by the Bureau of Justice Assistance, Office of Justice Programs, U.S. Department of Justice, through the Massachusetts Executive Office of Public Safety and Security (EOPSS) Office of Grants and Research. Points of view in this document are those of the authors and do not necessarily represent the official position of the U.S. Department of Justice and EOPSS.

Contents

Chapter 1

Introduction to Gang Reduction Responses

Erika Gebo & Brenda J. Bond

Gangs are part of the social fabric of many modern U.S. cities. The headlines of their stories splash the covers of newspapers: "Five shot in attack police link to gangs" (Irons, 2010); "Gang dispute blamed for fatal shooting of girls, 14, in Lancaster" (Gold & Lopez, 2010); "NYPD arrest dozens after gangs run amok in Times Square, Herald Square" (Armaghan, Parascandola, & Kennedy, 2010). Gangs are viewed as a public enemy, and communities are responding with a multitude of activities, mostly consisting of suppression strategies. This chapter will discuss the various responses to gangs as well as definitional and etiological issues before focusing on one specific comprehensive strategy to address gangs.

Gang reduction responses are created by formal social control agents to reduce the incidence of gang violence, gang membership, and gangs themselves. Police have created gang units (Katz & Webb, 2006) and have initiated educational programs in schools (Esbensen, 2009), while service providers have developed specialized programs to address the risk factors of gang membership (Crime & Justice Institute, 2006) as well as crafted ways to conduct better outreach to gang involved youth (Braga, McDevitt, & Pierce, 2006). State legislatures have further recognized the detrimental nature of gangs in their state statutes by creating gang member and gang crime definitions (National Gang Center, 2009), civil injunction remedies for gangs (Maxson, Hennigan, & Sloane 2005) and in some cases, enhancement penalties for gang affiliation (Rios & Navarro, 2010).

Informal social control agents also have taken up the cause to respond to gangs. Religious leaders have always been torchbearers of peace, but have turned their attention to the gangs in very specific ways. The Ten Point Coalition in Boston, for example, is made up of clergy who work together to conduct their own outreach to gang members and those at risk for gang membership to reduce the harm and fear of gangs in their catchment areas (Fagan, 2002). Key members of the group have served as a bridge between young people and law enforcement, a role that some suggest was critical to Boston's violence reduction strategy (Winship & Berrien, 1999). Community members themselves also have taken matters into their own hands by crafting their own collaborations aimed at responding to gang violence. Howell and Curry (2009) discuss the Alliance for Concerned Men that came together in Washington, D.C., for example. Their approach was similar to more formalized street outreach by informally mentoring gang involved youth, helping them access appropriate services, and mediating gang conflict.

Meanwhile, federally-backed large-scale comprehensive initiatives to reduce crime, such as Weed & Seed, often have included a gang component in them. This edited collection focuses on the implementation of a specific, federally promulgated comprehensive gang reduction policy adopted by communities across the state of Massachusetts that included the collaboration of formal and informal social control agents. For those who study gangs, this book will add to the understanding of the interaction between gang policy and gang etiology. The book also assists those who practice by examining the diverse approaches to policy implementation given a variety of local contexts. Finally, for policymakers, this book will highlight the successes and challenges of implementing a comprehensive gang policy across communities.

GANG DEFINITIONAL PROBLEMS

What exactly is meant by gangs and how problematic are they? "Street gangs" refer to those gangs that claim some sort of territory in their cities. The term "youth gangs" is used interchangeably with street gangs, though some scholars believe that limits the scope of gangs, given that some active gang members are in their forties (Klein, 1995). There is no agreed upon definition of gangs by practitioners, policymakers, or scholars (Ball & Curry, 1995; Esbensen, Winfree, & Taylor, 2001). Consequently, this muddies the waters when discussing gangs and attempting to implement effective responses to gangs. Some states and some communities have created their own definitions for their purposes (Decker & Curry, 2002), but those definitions may not hold over time as the nature of gangs change, as gangs differ across communities, and as different entities come to the table to address gangs.

The number of gangs, gang members, and the level of gang violence can be documented in different ways. Ethnographic studies, in which researchers go into a given area to document gangs and their activities, may more accurately record the number of gangs and gang membership in a given location (Decker & Van Winkle, 1996). Though richly detailed, ethnographies are time consuming and do not necessarily address the nature of gangs in other areas outside of the location(s) being studied. Alternative methods are necessary. The National Youth Gang Survey provides a yearly estimate of gangs and gang members from a survey of law enforcement agencies. This is the standardized barometer in the United States A definition of gangs and gang members is provided so that law enforcement uses the same criteria to judge their gang problem. According to this survey, there were approximately 27,300 gangs and 788,000 gang members in this country in 2008 (National Gang Center, 2009).

Most gangs are located in impoverished, urban areas. Gang members tend to be young, generally ranging in age from 12–15 and tend to be male and single (Harrell, 2005). Estimates of female membership are around 10% of all members (Esbensen, et al., 2008), while female gangs estimates vary from approximately 9% to 22% (Moore & Hagedorn, 2001). Latinos are more likely to be involved in gangs than any other ethnic groups, though gang membership crosses all ethnic lines (Harrell, 2005). Relying on the subjective perceptions of officials does have its pitfalls, but it provides some measure of the national landscape of gangs.

Gang violence has also been difficult to quantify. Beyond the definitional problems of gang and gang members, the issue of what constitutes gang violence is debatable. Some law enforcement agencies characterize any violence committed by a gang member as gang violence, while other agencies limit the scope of gang violence to only those acts that were committed on behalf of the gang. Maxson (1998) describes these very different classification systems as gang-related and gang-motivated, respectively. For example, a gang member who gets into a fist fight over a girl with another, non-gang related youth, would be classified as gang violence under a gang-related definition. That same incident would not be recorded as gang violence under a gang-motivated definition because the youth was not acting on behalf of his gang when he got into the fight.

Definitional issues are important in any discussion of gangs and gang policy. Understanding that different definitions produce different information is fundamental when interpreting gang literature and when trying to understand what policies to invoke and the implications of any particular policy. That said, regardless of what gang definitions are used, research suggests that gangs tend to commit more crime and more serious crime than non-gang member groups (Miller, 1990), and that individual gang members commit more crime than individual non-gang members (Esbensen, et al., 2001). The gang milieu clearly ups the ante with regard to criminal behavior (Klein, 2007), and it is the issue of reducing gangs and gang violence which will be addressed in this edited volume.

GANG ETIOLOGY

To understand policies that best address gangs, it is important to understand gang etiology. There is no one explanation for the development and persistence of gangs, nor is there one explanation for why individuals join gangs. The lack of consistent findings in the theoretical literature presents problems for trying to address gang issues in the policy realm. If the reasons that lead to gangs and to individuals joining gangs are unclear, then policies to reduce gangs, gang violence, and the number of gang members will likely not be as successful because these policies are not necessarily targeting the specific mechanisms that produce gangs. There are, however, some things that are known about gangs that must be taken into account when crafting good policies. Successful policies are based on the incorporation of solid theoretical knowledge (Dye, 2007); our knowledge about gangs is examined below.

Gangs develop and persist in large part because of social environmental factors, including social and economic marginalization of certain groups (Vigil, 2003), lack of economic and social opportunities (McKay & Shaw, 1972), and the breakdown of social institutions, including families, schools, civic organizations, and neighborhood cohesion (Anderson, 1999; Bursik & Grasmick, 2001). Two ethnographic studies of urban areas bring home these points. Thrasher (1927) states:

> The failure of the normally directing and controlling customs and institutions to function efficiently in the boy's experience is indicated by disintegration of family life, inefficiency of schools, formalism and externality of religion, corruption, and indifference in local politics, low wages and monotony in occupational activities, unemployment, and lack of opportunity for wholesome recreation (p. 37).

Anderson (1999) uncovered similar themes in his study of northeast Philadelphia in the 1980s to 1990s:

> With widespread joblessness, many inner-city people become stressed and their communities become distressed. Poor people adapt to these circumstances in the ways they know, meeting the exigencies of their situation as

best they can. The kinds of problems that trigger moral outrage begin to emerge: teen pregnancy, welfare dependency, and the underground economy. Its cottage industries of drugs, prostitution, welfare scams, and other rackets are there to pick up the economic slack (p. 110).

It is apparent from such descriptions that policy that aims at reducing gangs must address the basic social and economic circumstances in which they arise: the social ecology of place. Gang policies aimed narrowly at one or two aspects may not be as effective as those which are more holistic, given that the social environment plays a critical role in gang development and persistence.

Individual adaptations to these social conditions also play a role in youths' decisions to join gangs (i.e., Thornberry, Huizinga, & Loeber, 1995). There are complex interactions between individual circumstances and outside social forces, but a useful way of categorizing those factors are into the ecological domains of youths' lives: individual, peer, family, school, and community (Howell & Egley, 2005). In general, youth who have more deviant attitudes, who are more delinquent, who have deviant friends, and who do poorly in school, are more likely to join gangs, though more research is needed to refine the casual pathways to gang membership (for a review of risk factors, see Howell & Egley, 2005).

COMPREHENSIVE GANG POLICIES

Arguably, more is known about why gangs develop and proliferate than about how to address gangs and gang violence. The two issues are intertwined, but there needs to be more study of the latter, taking into account what we know about gangs, if we are to start unraveling the gang fibers that are wound around many of our cities. Policy efforts to reduce gang violence that involve suppression alone, such as heavy enforcement and prosecution of gang members, are unsuccessful, though they are the most oft tried strategy (Decker, 2003). Given what we know about the development and persistence of gangs, and given what we know about why individuals join gangs, a holistic, comprehensive approach to gang policy is needed. The ecology of the community forms the basis upon which gangs are born and develop, while the ecological domains of individuals' lives provide windows of opportunity for prevention and intervention.

Large-scale crime initiatives are not new to the public policy arena. The Chicago Area Project, the longest running delinquency prevention and intervention initiative, was started in the 1930s to address delinquency and strengthen communities in some of Chicago's most distressed neighborhoods by utilizing a social ecology approach (Schlossman & Sedlak, 1983). Resurgence in tackling social problems in a multi-agency, multi-strategy framework has occurred in the last decade. Research from the public health arena has shown that comprehensive community-wide strategies are effective ways to reduce public health problems, such as teen pregnancy, and such strategies increase the likelihood of sustaining the intervention (Parcel, Perry, & Taylor, 1990). Clearly, some of the interest in tackling crime problems comprehensively has been driven by federal funding that mandates multi-agency partnerships, but it is just as clear that social problems are multi-faceted. As has been shown with gangs, effective policies are those that target the broad reasons for gangs and gang membership. Thus, it only makes sense that effective strategies would be comprehensive.

There are three comprehensive crime policies that will be offered below as illustrations of contemporary, comprehensive approaches: Boston's Operation Ceasefire, Project Safe Neighborhoods, and the Weed & Seed program. None of these began as exclusive gang reduction initiatives, but the strategies employed and the way in which they evolved address gangs as core issues of the problem. A discussion of these projects help set the stage for the Comprehensive Gang Initiative, the comprehensive community initiative that is the focus of this book.

Boston's Operation Ceasefire

The Boston Gun Project began as "a problem-oriented policing project aimed at preventing and controlling serious youth violence" in Boston in the mid to late-1990s (Braga & Winship, 2006, p. 173). At the time, Boston was experiencing intolerable levels of gang violence, alongside the growing problem of youth homicide. Law enforcement and community partners struggled to get a handle on the small percentage of gang offenders who lay "at the heart of the city's youth violence problem" (Braga & Hureau, Chapter 7; Kennedy, Piehl, & Braga, 1996). From the Gun Project, Operation Ceasefire was created to deal with Boston's growing violence problem and has become one of the most well-known violence reduction initiatives in the nation.

Employing the "pulling levers"-focused deterrence strategy, Operation Ceasefire represented a comprehensive, inter-agency strategy focused on preventing and reducing youth violence. Their multidimensional approach centered on a small group of chronic offenders; established an inter-agency working group representing a variety of criminal justice and social service organizations; and a thorough and localized assessment of the nature and characteristics of violent incidents, offenders and victims (Kennedy et al., 1996; Kennedy, Braga, & Piehl, 1997). A history of collaboration allowed police and criminal justice, social service, and faith-based actors and researchers to gather regularly to address incidents involving violent offenders or geographic areas of concern. At the core of the strategy was the communication of expectations to offenders about their criminal behaviors, coupled with an offer of support and resources via social service and other community agencies. Community partner agencies were the carrot used as leverage for individuals of interest to compile with conventional behavior. If individuals failed to comply, the stick was the use of the criminal justice system to gain compliance with expressed expectations (Braga & Winship, 2006; Kennedy, 1997; Kennedy, Piehl, & Braga, 1996).

Boston experienced a reduction in violence—specifically, homicides and gun-related violence—following the implementation of Ceasefire, and there is evidence that the strategy facilitated a larger reduction in violence in comparison to other cities (Braga, Kennedy, Piehl, & Waring, 2001; Wellford, Pepper, & Petrie, 2005). The work in Boston has been well documented and replicated elsewhere. There is now promising evidence that this type of crime prevention model works. As part of a systematic review for the Campbell Collaboration, Braga & Weisburd (2011) found 11 evaluations (10 quasi-experimental and one randomized control trial) of "pulling levers"-focused deterrence approaches. Nine out of 11 evaluations reported significant reductions in crime, with five of the evaluations focused specifically on gangs and representing direct replications of the Boston model.

Outside of the challenges of program replication and evaluation, this strategy is appealing because it brings together the various formal and informal controls of a community in a concerted effort. The Boston experience has contributed greatly to the field as it serves as a model for comprehensive, partnership-intensive approaches to community violence. It also reinforces the idea that a thorough analysis and understanding of local problems is a necessary first step in strategy development, implementation, and evaluation (Braga & Winship, 2006).

Project Safe Neighborhoods

Project Safe Neighborhoods (PSN), an ongoing comprehensive crime reduction initiative, developed out of lessons learned from other gun reduction initiatives—in particular, the Boston Gun Project, Richmond (VA) Project Exile, and the work from Strategic Approaches to Community Safety Initiative (Dalton, 2003). The goals of PSN are to reduce gun and gang violence through comprehensive suppression and intervention strategies coordinated across agencies in local communities. PSN seeks to better link local, state, and federal resources to address those problems. The federal government has been supporting PSN sites around the country since 2001 with funding, training, conferences, technical assistance, and research partners who help communities refine the problem and evaluate the outcomes. Reductions in gangs and gang violence were added to the goals of PSN in 2006 in response to the gangs-gun-drug nexus that existed in PSN sites. At the time of this writing, an impact evaluation of the Comprehensive Anti-Gang Initiative of PSN is currently being conducted.

There are three 'C' principles upon which PSN is based: comprehensive, coordinated, and community-based. The comprehensive aspect of the project refers to the need for prevention and intervention services along with traditional suppression strategies. Coordination among those who offer these services, such as local community-based organizations and faith-based leaders, is essential to success. Finally, community-based refers to the recognition that gun and gang crimes occur locally, and communities implementing PSN need flexibility in their approaches to appropriately address their problems. In other words, PSN is sensitive to the social ecology of place. While there are certain elements of the project that should be implemented in all areas for the initiative to be successful, there are often local dynamics or contextual factors, often uncovered through coordination of problem-solving efforts with research partners, that must be taken into account to accomplish those goals.

There has been a national evaluation of PSN as well as numerous local evaluations of PSN sites. The national evaluation has found that there have been modest yet statistically significant reductions in violence in PSN cities compared to other cities (McGarrell, et al., 2010). Key success factors were the collaboration of multiple agencies in a problem-solving approach as well as the flexibility of jurisdictions to incorporate their own strategies based on local knowledge of their communities (Roehl, et al., 2008).

Weed & Seed

In contrast to PSN, Weed & Seed is a federal initiative directed toward neighborhoods, rather than entire cities. The program started in 1991 with two goals: "Weed" out gang activity, violent crime, and drug abuse and "Seed" those areas with prevention and intervention programs along with the rebuilding of bricks and mortar neighborhood infrastructure (Dunworth, et al., 1999). The local U.S. Attorney's Office is responsible for the coordination of Weed & Seed, while local police and community-based agencies do most of the work of suppression, intervention, and prevention.

Similar to PSN, Weed & Seed places an emphasis on coordination between law enforcement and local agencies as well as neighborhood involvement. Community participation is viewed as essential to success and sustainability. Collaboration and coordination of services and programs among federal, state, local, and neighborhood entities, including neighborhood groups, must occur to achieve program goals. Finally, using the above partnerships to leverage other existing resources, such as funding, among others, are critical pieces of the puzzle. A federal evaluation found that Weed & Seed locations that were better able to target a specific population, had strong leadership, and had broad participation from local community organizations and associations were more successful in meeting their goals and reducing crime (Dunworth, et al., 1999).

COMPREHENSIVE GANG MODEL

A gang-specific comprehensive community initiative was developed by Spergel in the early 1990s. He believed there were five key target areas to effectively reduce gangs and gang crime. Not surprisingly, these are similar to the critical elements of PSN and Weed & Seed. They are: community mobilization, organizational change and development, social intervention (prevention), opportunity provision (intervention), and suppression (Spergel, 1995). This comprehensive initiative was first implemented in the Little Village Area of Chicago. Evaluation results showed a significant reduction in gang and gang violence, and subsequently, the federal Office of Juvenile Justice and Delinquency Prevention (OJJDP) funded five replication sites around the country: Bloomington-Normal, Indiana; Mesa, California; Riverside, California; San Antonio, Texas; and Tucson, Arizona. In separate evaluations of these programs, Spergel and his colleagues discussed numerous implementation problems throughout the sites (Spergel, Wa, & Sosa, 2005), though Riverside came the closest to true program implementation.

Although these replication sites were not as successful in reducing gangs as the Little Village Project, they did achieve some success in reducing overall violence. However, Klein and Maxson (2006) note that the goals of reducing gangs and gang violence were often displaced to smaller, more manageable goals. Nonetheless, successes have outweighed the challenges and OJJDP has adopted the CGM as a promising strategy to reduce gangs and gang violence. The initiative is often now termed the OJJDP Model (Howell, 2010).

The five strategy areas in the CGM are intended to work together to reduce gangs and gang violence (National Gang Center, 2010). Suppression strategies are most familiar to the field of criminal justice. These involve the exertion of formal control, especially law enforcement and prosecution, on gangs. Social intervention, more commonly known as prevention, involves a cross-section of community agencies and institutions providing prevention services to youth and their families at risk for gang involvement. These include school-based programs, community-based organizations' outreach services and recreation programs, and faith-based initiatives. Opportunities provision, akin to traditional intervention, refers to providing educational, training, and job programs to gang-involved youth that will encourage them to desist from gang life. Re-entry programs also fall under this heading (National Gang Center, 2010).

The last two strategies, community mobilization and organizational change and development, are often the most difficult to implement (Gebo, Boyes-Watson, & Pinto-Wilson, 2010). Community mobilization engages the wider community in the gang reduction efforts. Under this strategy, former gang members, residents, and community groups band together with community-based organizations and government agencies to reduce gangs and gang violence. Organizational change works across all the previously mentioned strategies, such that agencies change their policies and practices to adopt partnership approaches to better address the comprehensiveness of the gang problem, to better coordinate practices and service, and to share information in a way that leads to a reduction in gangs and gang violence that is sustainable over time.

The CGM as a promising strategy needs more study. Research on how and why communities implement the CGM in a certain way is needed, especially because there are no proscriptions about how best to implement the model to achieve positive outcomes. This edited volume will address those issues in order to significantly contribute to the knowledge on how various communities addressed gang problems, not just from the point of view of one or two agents of the justice system (e.g., police), but from a broader community perspective, which takes into account criminal justice agencies, social service providers, and community leaders who are implementing a collaborative gang reduction policy. Again, such community-wide efforts are becoming more common with federal and state emphasis on comprehensive initiatives as effective strategies to address social problems (Gray, et al., 1997). To date, over 20 communities around the country have been funded by the federal government to implement the CGM (National Gang Center, 2010), and it is important to examine what has occurred therein.

MASSACHUSETTS SHANNON COMMUNITY SAFETY INITIATIVE

The CGM is the framework under which communities across the state of Massachusetts have implemented gang reduction responses since 2005. The state has allocated over $40 million to communities plagued by gang problems. Similar to Project Safe Neighborhoods, research partners simultaneously have been funded over that same time period to support fidelity in the CGM application in those communities and to help document the efforts and outcomes of each community's activities. The editors and contributors have worked with funded communities for over five years to assist them in reducing their gang problems through an action research model in which there is real time information-gathering, collaboration between researchers and community partners, and feedback on community efforts.

This entire initiative represents the first time in U.S. history that a state has offered such an opportunity to communities in partnership with researchers to help the community assess their gang problems and their progress over time. This book showcases the collaboration, and advances current gang research by describing strategies communities have actually used to respond to gangs that are rooted in the rich community environment and how each community defined its gang problems; this is quite unlike many other scholarly works on gangs and anti-crime initiatives. The social ecology of a community contributes to the understanding of how gangs develop and persist, but it also is a critical piece to the understanding of how and why policy gets implemented the way it does. Responses to gangs and social problems more generally are intertwined in their own community environments. A better understanding of how local context shapes problem orientation and strategy selection in the implementation of national policy is important to scholars, practitioners, and policymakers alike. The stories within this book offer valuable lessons to the reader on those issues.

The chapters document the implementation of the CGM in multiple communities in one state at the same time. Instead of being a patchwork of stories about how different communities responded to gangs, the book focuses on one promising framework (CGM) from which all communities operated. Thus, the CGM provides the glue for the community strategies, creating a patterned mosaic. Each chapter addresses how a community has implemented the CGM, emphasizing a key, but tailored, element of that approach and then connects results and lessons to the larger literature on gang responses. The social landscape of place is described by the authors in order to better understand how the model was implemented in each site.

A unique feature of this book is that each community's gang initiatives involved the pairing of *both* scholars and practitioners at the outset. As a result, knowledge of gang initiatives and theoretical background (scholars) were merged with applied local knowledge (practitioners) in a conceptually coherent whole. Process issues inherent in implementing model programs are better documented and addressed within such collaborations. In this way, this book stands out from what exists in gang literature today. Readers benefit from the insights of contributors who have been involved with the comprehensive gang response from inception.

OUTLINE

The book is organized into three sections that address the CGM, implementation, and evaluation. Sections I and III introduce and conclude the discussions respectively. The chapters in Section II illustrate the strategies communities used as part of the CGM. Chapter contributors set the stage for a discussion of their community's strategy by describing the ecological context, including demographics and violence that led to the gang problem orientation. The majority of the chapters are devoted to the gang strategy that was emphasized in combating the specified problem. Finally, authors will discuss why their findings are of interest to the study of gangs and to other locations dealing with gang problems.

Boyes-Watson addresses foundational issues of the CGM, focusing on the community mobilization and organizational change strategies in Chapter 2. She demonstrates how non-white communities became actively involved in the CGM initiative through non-white leadership, and how shifts within organizations were a natural outgrowth of gang and youth violence reduction work. Ross and Foley (Chapter 3) follow up with a chapter that identifies low income and primarily non-white youth as neglected in the arena of prevention and intervention. They show that a careful analysis of services to at-risk youth in Worcester, the second largest city in Massachusetts, demonstrated that those most in need of programming—gang-involved and chronic offending youth—had no other options to receive help except through the criminal justice system. The CGM initiative in that city is used as a catalyst to change that.

Several other chapters illustrate the challenges of gang work. Gebo and Tobin (Chapter 4) describe the creation and implementation of an instrument used to identify youth on a continuum from at-risk for gang membership to hardcore gang members. This process in Springfield, Massachusetts, the state's third largest city, revealed the difficulty of shifting, long-standing organizational relationships between organizations as well as highlighted the problems with identifying 'gang members' in practice. Similarly, in Chapter 6, Bond, Rivers-Kustanovich, and McLaughlin describe the problems of tackling one of the key instigators of gang violence in Lowell, Massachusetts: retaliatory violence. They describe the nascent work in this area and suggest ways that understanding, measuring, and preventing retaliatory violence could be improved.

Varano and Wolff (Chapter 5) chronicle a story of gang outreach within a comprehensive context. Outreach is a critical strategy of any gang reduction initiative, but there is little research in this area. Their rich discussion of the outreach story in New Bedford, Massachusetts highlights the complexities, and the rewards, of working with gangs and with those who have been former gang members, both of which impact the larger comprehensive partnership functioning in a myriad of ways. They also illustrate the importance of local creativity involving non-traditional criminal justice entities that can have far reaching impacts on gang violence.

Braga and Hureau (Chapter 7) compare Boston's Operation Ceasefire, as discussed above, with the current strategies used today in the city, noting where the strategies converge based on solid problem analysis of gangs. They further draw parallels between the problem-oriented strategy and the CGM, demonstrating that they are compatible with each other in a comprehensive approach to gang violence.

McDevitt and Wolff (Chapter 8) provide a context in which to evaluate the CGM and comprehensive violence reduction strategies generally. They illustrate the difficulty with measuring statewide impacts of these large-scale initiatives as each location takes its own approach to gang reduction, depending on the ecology of place. Tailored approaches are part of best practice procedures, as discussed above, but they present problems when attempting to piece together what works and what doesn't in the amelioration of any social problem. A key point from their analyses is that creative relationship-building beyond the walls of traditional criminal justice structures are important elements in developing CGM strategies and engaging in true organizational change and community mobilization. Bond and Gebo offer conclusions to these contributions in Chapter 9, illustrating key themes across these chapters. This book offers valuable insights for the reader to engage with communities who are working to combat their present day gang struggles utilizing the CGM as a conceptual focal point. These insights are important for practitioners, scholars, and policymakers alike.

REFERENCES

Armaghan, S., Parascandola, R., & Kennedy, H. (2010, April 5). NYPD arrest dozens after gangs run amok in Times Square, Herald Square. *The New York Daily News*. Retrieved from http://www.nydailynews.com.

Anderson, E. (1999). *Code of the street: Decency, violence, and the moral life of the inner city*. New York: Norton & Company.

Ball, R. A., & Curry, G. D. (1995). The logic of definition in criminology: Purposes and methods for defining "gangs." *Criminology, 33*, 225–245.

Braga, A. A., Kennedy, D. M., Piehl, A. M., Waring, E. J. (2001). *Measuring the impact of Operation Ceasefire*. Washington, D.C.: National Institute of Justice.

Braga, A. A., McDevitt, J., & Pierce, G. L. (2006). Understanding and preventing gang violence: Problem analysis and response development in Lowell, Massachusetts. *Police Quarterly, 9*, 20–46.

Braga, A. A., & Weisburd, D. L. (2010). *The effects of pulling levers focused deterrence strategies on crime: A Campbell systematic review*. Unpublished manuscript, Campbell Collaboration's Crime and Justice Group.

Braga, A., & Winship, C. (2006). Partnership, accountability, and innovation: Clarifying Boston's experience with pulling levers. In D. Weisburd & A. Braga (Eds.), *Police Innovation: Contrasting Perspectives*. New York: Cambridge University Press.

Bursik, R. J., & Grasmick, H. G. (2001). *Neighborhoods and crime: The dimensions of effective community control*. New York: Lexington Books.

Crime & Justice Institute. (2006). *Interventions for high-risk youth: Applying evidence-based theory and practice to the work of Roca*. Boston, MA: Community Resources for Justice, Crime & Justice Institute.

Dalton, E. (2003). *Lessons in Preventing Homicide*. East Lansing, MI: School of Criminal Justice, Michigan State University. Retrieved from http://www.cj.msu.edu.

Decker, S. H. (2003). Policing gangs and youth violence: Where do we stand, where do we go from here? In S. H. Decker (Ed.), *Policing Gangs and Youth violence* (pp. 287–293). Belmont, CA: Wadsworth.

Decker, S. H., & Curry, G. D. (2002). "I'm down for my organization: The rationality of responses to delinquency, youth crime, and gangs." In A. R. Piquero & S. G. Tibbets (Eds.), *Rational Choice and Criminal Behavior: Recent Research and Future Challenges* (pp. 197–218). NY: Routledge.

Decker, S. H., & Van Winkle, B. (1996). *Life in a gang: Family, friends, and violence*. New York: Cambridge.

Dunworth, T., & Mills, G., Cordner, G., & Greene, J. (1999). *National evaluation of Weed and Seed*. Washington, D.C.: National Institute of Justice.

Dye, T. R. (2007). *Understanding public policy*. (12th Ed.). Alexandria, VA: Prentice Hall.

Esbensen, F. A., Brick, B., Melde, C., Tusinski, K., & Taylor, T. J. (2008). The role of race and ethnicity in gang membership. In F. van Gemert, D. Peterson, & E. Lien (Eds.), *Youth Gangs, Migration, and Ethnicity* (pp. 117–139). Uffculme, Devon, UK: Willan.

Esbensen, F. (2009). *Evaluation of the teens, crime and the community works program*. Washington, D.C.: Department of Justice, National Institute of Justice.

Esbensen, F., Winfree, T. L., & Taylor, T. J. (2001). Youth gangs and definitional issues: When is a gang a gang, and why does it matter? *Crime & Delinquency*, 47, 105–130.

Fagan, J. (2002). Policing, guns and youth violence. *Children, youth, and gun violence*, 12, 132–151.

Gebo, E., Boyes-Watson, C., & Pinto-Wilson, S. (2010). Reconceptualizing organizational change in the Comprehensive Gang Model. *Journal of Criminal Justice*, 38, 166–173.

Gold, S., & Lopez, R. J. (2010, September 6). Gang dispute blamed for fatal shootings of girls, 14, in Lancaster. *The Los Angeles Times*. Retrieved from http://www.latimes.com.

Gray, B., Duran, A., & Segal, A. (1997). *Revisiting the critical elements of comprehensive community initiatives*. Retrieved June 20, 2010, from http://aspe.hhs.gov/hsp/cci.htm.

Harrell, E. (2005). *Violence by gang members, 1993–2003*. Retrieved September 27, 2011, from http://bjs.ojp.usdoj.gov/index.cfm?ty=pbdetail&iid=695.

Howell, J. C., & Curry, G. D. (2009). *Mobilizing communities to address gang problems.* Tallahassee, FL: National Youth Gang Center.

Howell, J. C. (2010). *OJJDP Bulletin: Gang prevention: An overview of research and programs.* Retrieved from https://www.ncjrs.gov.

Howell, J. C., & Egley, A. (2005). Moving risk factors into developmental theories of gang membership. *Youth Violence and Juvenile Justice, 3,* 334–354.

Irons, M. E. (2010, August 16). Five shot in attack police link to gangs. *The Boston Globe.* Retrieved from http://www.bostonglobe.com.

Katz, C. M., & Webb, V. J. (2006). *Policing gangs in America.* New York: Cambridge.

Kennedy, D. (1997). Pulling levers: Chronic offenders, high-crime settings, and a theory of prevention. *Valparaiso University Law Review, 31,* 449–484.

Kennedy, D., Braga, A., & Piehl, A. (1997). The (un)known universe: Mapping gangs and gang violence in Boston. In D. Weisburd & J. T. McEwen (Eds.), *Crime mapping and crime prevention.* New York: Criminal Justice Press.

Kennedy, D., Piehl, A., and Braga, A. (1996). Youth violence in Boston: Gun markets, serious youth offenders, and a use-reduction strategy. *Law and Contemporary Problems, 59,* 147–196.

Klein, M. W. (2007). *Chasing after street gangs: A forty-year journey.* Upper Saddle River, NJ: Pearson.

Klein, M. W. (1995). *The American street gang: Its nature, prevalence, and control.* New York: Oxford University Press.

Klein, M. W., & Maxson, C. L. (2006). *Street gang patterns and policies.* New York: Oxford.

Maxson, C. (1998). *Gang members on the move.* Retrieved from http://www.ncjrs.gov.

Maxson, C. L., Hennigan, K. M. & Sloane, D. C. (2005). It's getting crazy out there: Can a civil gang injunction change a community. *Criminology & Public Policy, 4,* 577–605.

McGarrell, E. F., Corsaro, N., Hipple, N. K., & Bynum, T. S. (2010). Project Safe Neighborhoods and violent crime trends in U.S. cities: Assessing violent crime impact. *Journal of Quantitative Criminology, 26,* 165–190.

McKay, H. D., & Shaw, C. R. (1972 [1942]). *Juvenile delinquency and urban areas.* Chicago: University of Chicago Press.

Miller, W. B. (1990). Why the United States has failed to solve its youth gang problem. In C. R. Huff (Ed.), *Gangs in America* (pp. 263–287). Thousand Oaks, CA: Sage.

Moore, J. W., & Hagedorn, J. M. (2001). *Female gangs: A focus on research.* Washington, D.C.: U.S. Department of Justice, Office of Juvenile Justice and Delinquency Prevention.

National Gang Center. (2010). *Best practices to address community gang problems: OJJDP's Comprehensive Gang Model.* Tallahassee, FL: National Gang Center.

National Gang Center. (2009). *Brief review of federal and state definitions of the terms "gang," "gang crime," and "gang member."* Retrieved from http://www.national gangcenter.gov.

Parcel, G. S., Perry, C. L., & Taylor, W. C. (1990). Beyond demonstration: Diffusion of health promotion innovations. In N. Bracht (Ed.), *Health Promotions at the Community Level* (pp. 229–252). Newbury Park, CA: Sage.

Rios, V. M., & Navarro, K. (2010). Insider gang knowledge: The case for non-police gang experts in the courtroom. *Critical Criminology, 18,* 21–39.

Roehl, J., Rosenbaum, D. P., Costello, S. K., Coldren, J. R. Jr., Schuck, A. M., Kunard, L., & Ford, D. R. (2008). *Paving the way for Project Safe Neighborhoods: SACSI in 10 U.S. cities.*

Schlossman, S., & Sedlak, M. (1983). *The Chicago Area Project revisited.* Santa Monica, CA: Rand.

Spergel, I. (1995). *The youth gang problem: A community approach.* New York: Oxford University Press.

Spergel, I., Wa, K., & Sosa, R. (2005). *Evaluation of the Mesa Gang Intervention Program (MGIP).* Washington, D.C.: National Institute of Justice.

Thornberry, T. P., Huizinga, D., & Loeber, R. (1995). The prevention of serious delinquency and violence: Implications from the program of research on the causes and correlates of delinquency. In J. C. Howell, B. Krisberg J. D. Hawkins, & J. J. Wilson (Eds.), *A sourcebook: Serious, violent and chronic juvenile offenders* (pp. 213–237). Thousand Oaks, CA: Sage.

Thrasher, F. (1927). *The gang: A study of 1313 gangs in Chicago.* Chicago: University of Chicago.

Vigil, J. D. (2003). Urban violence and street gangs. *Annual Review of Anthropology, 32,* 225–242.

Wellford, C., Pepper, J., & Petrie, C. (2005). *Firearms and violence: A critical review.* Washington, D.C.: National Science Academies Press.

Winship, C., & Berrien, J. (1999). Boston cops and black churches. *Public Interest, 136*(52), 52–68.

Chapter 2

Process Matters: Mobilizing Non-White Communities to Respond to Gangs

Carolyn Boyes-Watson

Community mobilization is one of the five key strategies in the Comprehensive Gang Model (CGM), defined as, "involvement of local citizens, including former gang-involved youth, community groups, agencies, and coordination of programs and staff functions within and across agencies" [National Youth Gang Center (NYGC), 2008, p. 2]. Research from criminology, sociology, and community psychology suggests that effective and sustainable community improvements depend on mobilization of the community (Florin & Wandersman, 1990). Engaging the wider community and building community capacity to respond to violence are essential components of any comprehensive crime initiative (Sabol, Coulton, & Korbin, 2004).

There is ample evidence beyond criminology of the positive results of working together to accomplish shared goals (Alter & Hage, 1993; Benard, 1990; Bond & Keys, 1993; Lasker & Weiss, 2003; Provan & Milward, 2001). Unfortunately, minority communities are often left on the sidelines in public safety initiatives; yet they are an integral part of any initiative, particularly when much of the initiative effort is focused on issues within their communities and interventions directly target youth from their communities. Given a long-standing distrust between minority communities and agents of formal social control, it is important for them to be at the table as equal and contributing partners (Watson-Thompson, Fawcett, & Schultz, 2008).

Recent gang research identified several core elements that led to successful community mobilization efforts. They included: (a) local citizens

17

involved with local agencies; (b) coordination of services within and between agencies; (c) a steering committee consisting of diverse community leaders and organizational managers who guide the vision of the entire effort and who are available to assist in overcoming barriers to participation and action; and (d) support for initiative across justice systems, governmental organizations, and NGOs (NYGC, 2008). Yet pathways to successful implementation of the community mobilization strategy are unclear from the above description, and there are many challenges. The power imbalances from professionals engaging with community members to mobilize against a social problem leads to community members being relegated to 'client' status rather than partner status.

Minority citizens, especially those in immigrant communities, are often uncomfortable engaging with governmental agencies (Payne & Williams, 2008). Nor do minorities trust that they share a common set of interests with government. Although residents in gang-ridden neighborhoods tend to disown and disapprove of acts committed by gang members, they still see individual gang members as part of a network of relatives, neighbors and friends, and thus are reluctant to participate in initiatives which they perceive to be only suppression-driven (Comack & Silver, 2008).

Furthermore, deeply held cultural attitudes rooted in class, race, ethnicity and professional roles are fertile ground for miscommunications which continuously undermine collaboration between community residents and agents of formal social control (Spergel, et al., 2005). Community mobilization also demands coordinated action among different agencies and organizations within the community. Law enforcement and social service agencies, however, have distinctly different organizational missions and occupational subcultures. Deeply held but often unspoken norms, attitudes, and values often form yet another barrier to the sustained collaboration required for successful community mobilization (Waldeck, 1999).

This case study will highlight important elements of the strategy of community mobilization that contribute positively to tapping into and enhancing the "collective efficacy" of the community. Collective efficacy refers to the capacity of the community to come together and effectively address issues of common concern (Morenoff, Sampson, & Raudenbush, 2001). Successful mobilization of the community to address gangs relies on an existing capacity for collective efficacy within a community at the same time that it helps to strengthen that capacity for future initiatives. The key elements of this mobilization strategy in this analysis are: (1) deliberate investment in an inclusive process of relationship-building focused on creating a foundation of shared values, expectations, and understanding and (2) the development of joint leadership based on shared relationships between charismatic individuals from within the community and key leaders within formal agencies of social control.

Community mobilization is first defined below, followed by a description of the core mobilization concepts of social capital and collective efficacy. An examination of strategies to mobilize communities follows. The mobilization process in the Tri-City Initiative to reduce gang and youth violence is then analyzed, demonstrating the key process and relationship-building elements.

COMMUNITY MOBILIZATION, SOCIAL CAPITAL, AND COLLECTIVE EFFICACY

Community mobilization, by necessity, is a time-intensive, complex, and process-oriented approach which aims to address entrenched issues by shifting the focus from the individual to the social ecology of the community itself (Kim Ju, et al., 2008). A community's capacity for mobilization can also be thought of as a neighborhood characteristic. At its most basic level, community mobilization can be understood to mean the involvement of citizens and/or community based organizations (CBOs) in public issues through the political process (Skogan, 1989). But the centrality of the strategy of community mobilization within a comprehensive gang approach is connected to a more pivotal role for the community than mere political participation. The importance of community mobilization is tied to the idea of community empowerment based on the belief that activating community networks will not only enhance the effectiveness of any given immediate agenda (such as reducing youth gang involvement) but is itself a community building process that generates greater ties and trust among residents by fostering positive connections among individuals, groups, neighborhoods, institutions, and systems (Lawrence, et al., 2004). Because youth gang formation is rooted in community conditions, community building through a comprehensive gang strategy is actually a long-term investment in prevention.

A critical resource for community mobilization is the level of social capital within any given community. The concept of social capital refers to a broad array of resources which are generated as a by-product of certain kinds of social relationships and social processes prevalent within the community (Coleman, 1988; Leventhall & Brooks-Gunn, 2000; Putnam 2000). These resources include the flow of useful information, a variety of social supports, the reciprocal exchange of obligations and favors, and the articulation, transmission, and enforcement of social norms. The utility of the concept of social capital is that it shifts attention from the behavior and characteristic of individuals to the quality and pattern of relationships among individuals and groups (Schuller, et al., 2000).

By engaging individuals from local communities with leaders and actors from agencies and organizations within the wider community, the comprehensive gang model is attempting to strengthen the "bridging" form of social capital that extends across different sectors of the community. Bridging social capital refers to the resources which come from relationships between heterogeneous individuals and groups within the community (Putnam, 2000). This form of social capital is especially important given the economic, racial, and ethnic isolation and concentrated disadvantage associated with poor inner city neighborhoods and immigrant enclaves (Massey, 1996; Wilson, 1987). Community mobilization is, therefore, a long-term strategy for prevention and intervention that builds the foundation for ongoing social change by strengthening, shifting, and expanding cohesive social networks, both within the local neighborhood and beyond, to connect with wider ecological units such as the police, schools, and local government.

As noted above, the concept of collective efficacy refers to a neighborhood's capacity for collective action over shared concerns (Sampson, et al., 2002). Frequency and density of social interaction are not sufficient alone to generate collective efficacy. Gang formation and other criminal activities, for instance, can be fostered by dense social networks that draw individuals into the sphere of criminal activity, which in turn decreases the level of trust within the neighborhood and depresses social interaction beyond criminal networks (Pattillo-McCoy, 1999). Additional factors which shape a neighborhood's capacity for collective efficacy include a sense of mutual trust and shared expectations across residents which foster the likelihood that individuals will act to protect the safety and well-being of their community (Sampson, et al., 2002). These actions include the willingness to engage in informal social control—for example, to discipline unruly youth on the street or to call a parent if a neighbor's child is seen out of school. Research indicates that the level of collective efficacy within a neighborhood as indicated by the pattern of social ties, levels of trust, shared norms, and willingness to enforce norms has measurable impact on levels of crime (Bellair, 2000; Elliot, et al., 1996; Sampson, et al., 2002; Veysey & Messner, 1999; Warner & Rountree, 1997) as well as other aspects of community well-being (Elliott, 2000; Ross, 2000).

Community mobilization is meant to be an intentional strategy within the CGM to engage and extend the capacity for collective efficacy at the neighborhood-level and bring it into a partnership with formal agencies of social control. By increasing the amount of trusting relationships across different segments of the community, a CGM perspective increases the level of bridging social capital within the community by generating strong cohesive relationships between neighborhood residents, law enforcement, community organizations, and local government. These relationships in turn support collective efficacy, or the ability of the community to act effectively to reduce youth gang participation and violence (Morenoff, et al., 2001).

The combination of formal and informal social control is viewed as the most effective approach to reducing gang activity among youth (Bazemore, 2001). Ultimately, a community that is mobilized is better able to engage in collective action to address its issues and to more effectively articulate and enforce norms through mechanisms of informal social control (Bennett, 1995; Kim Ju, et al., 2008). The greater amount of social capital within a neighborhood—that is, the prevalence of strong and sustainable patterns of social interaction that generate trust and shared norms and expectations—the greater the level of collective efficacy at the neighborhood level. A community with higher levels of collective efficacy will more readily mobilize to address common concerns.

COMMUNITY MOBILIZATION STRATEGIES

There are numerous ways to mobilize a community. They can be grouped into top-down and bottom-up strategies (Foster-Fishman, et al., 2006). Top-down strategies consist of high-level institutions and/or agencies going into a community to help impose a structure for community participation in a pre-determined agenda. In contrast, bottom-up strategies involve grassroots activities where local leaders define and control the agenda and work to influence policies and programs that affect residents.

In poor communities, there is often a lack of capacity to generate activism via bottom-up grassroots organizing (Foster-Fishman, et al., 2006). Mobilizing communities who need it most is often difficult because of a lack of underlying capacity for collective efficacy. Stressed family units, particularly single, female-headed households, are socially isolated with few ties beyond the immediate family, and institutional resources such as churches and voluntary associations are limited. Further, high levels of crime, joblessness, incarceration, drug use and trafficking, and violence generate fear and mistrust, which undermines the willingness of residents to engage in informal sanctioning in public spaces, especially with regard to youth behavior in these spaces. Thus, bottom-up approaches to community mobilization may require input of resources from outside the community to generate the capacity, willingness, and participation of local residents. Local CBOs and practitioners often initiate and coordinate discussions over a particular shared concern (Arcidiacono, Sommantico, & Procentese, 2001), which is then taken over by local community leaders once buy-in, support, and participation has been achieved (Foster-Fishman, et al., 2006).

Community policing can be seen as a top-down approach to community mobilization that relies heavily on police recruiting citizens to act in concert with formal agents of social control. The philosophy itself is based on a proactive problem-solving approach that engages the police and citizens in solving community concerns. Jointly, it is theorized that a strong police-community partnership can reduce crime and disorder and create a better quality of life for residents (Zhao, Loverich, & Thurman, 1999). Practically speaking, police are charged with leading community involvement in a crime control agenda.

There have been mixed results about the effectiveness of community policing initiatives to mobilize the community. While community policing has been associated in some instances with increased citizen satisfaction with police and with a reduction in citizen fear of crime (Zhao, et al., 1999), there is little empirical evidence that police have been able to establish successful partnerships with citizenry in the way envisioned by the theory of community policing (Grinc, 1994). Reasons for this include the high levels of hostility towards law enforcement particularly in urban, minority neighborhoods; the unwillingness of citizens to be the "eyes and ears" of the police; skepticism that this is anything other than a short-lived intervention which will disappear when the money is used up; and a lack of training and information, on both sides, about the goals of community policing.

It is particularly difficult to get people to participate in anti-crime initiatives because the goals may be out of sync with residents' priorities (Lindenberg, et al., 2001). Residents of disadvantaged communities are concerned about crime, but believe it is a by-product of larger social problems, such as lack of economic opportunities, racism, and adequate education; in other words the social ecology of their communities (Bennett, 1995; Comack & Silver, 2008; Schnieder, 2000; Ward, 1997). Residents often find their priorities are not reflected in crime initiatives and, consequently, community mobilization strategies that stress community safety over social problems have been found not to be as effective (Schnieder, 2000).

There is a question as to whether top-down strategies are actually sustainable; some feel that communities need to take on problems as their own and feel empowered to do something about it (Lasker & Weiss, 2003). The issue of sustainability (what happens after the money runs out) is one reason for reluctance on the part of residents of poor neighborhoods to respond to some community mobilization efforts. Essentially, they have seen such projects, and the people and resources associated with them, come and then go.

RELATIONSHIP AND LEADERSHIP IMPORTANCE

Regardless of approach, relationships and leadership matter. Robinson and Hanna (1994) found a relational-focus approach to community mobilization based on shared values and emotional ties that had more lasting outcomes than top-down strategies. Pattavina and colleagues (2006) also found that citizens in more crime-ridden neighborhoods were more likely to participate in collective action if they felt they were part of the neighborhood. A sense of social cohesion—that is, a sense of shared norms and values—played a dominant role in predicting individual action in their study.

Similarly, in their review of educational reform in six communities in Ghana, Nkansa and Chapman (2006) found that the two key factors that led to large-scale community involvement and sustainability of programs were social cohesion among residents and trust in local committed leadership (also see, Donnelly & Majka, 1998; Schnieder, 2000). Communities that had charismatic leaders who invested time and their own resources beyond what was expected were more likely to see sustained engagement. Leaders were the ones who helped plan and secure commitments to tasks among individuals and leadership structure was more flat than hierarchical, with people working collaboratively toward shared goals. Other research also confirms that in communities of color, it is important that local leaders are active in crime initiatives (Foster-Fishman, et al., 2006).

The comprehensive gang model is a classic top-down approach in which outside agencies including law enforcement and local and state governments bring both resources and an agenda of reducing youth gang violence to a community. The track record of successful community mobilization under these conditions including applications of the comprehensive gang model has not been impressive for all the reasons discussed above (Spergel, et al., 2005). It is important to understand the mechanisms and the factors that facilitate community mobilization and citizen participation particularly those with top-down crime control agendas operating in disadvantaged communities.

COMMUNITY MOBILIZATION IN THE TRI-CITY AREA

This chapter discusses the work of three cities in central Massachusetts, termed the Tri-City area. The mobilization process began two years prior to the region's investment in a comprehensive anti-gang initiative when a community-based organization put together a city-wide partnership to address the poor educational outcomes for Latino youth within the region. Called the Partnership for Latino Success (hereafter partnership), this coalition applied for state funding to launch the Tri-City Anti-Gang Initiative (hereafter TCI) based on the comprehensive gang model. The TCI, along with an action research team from a local university, has been funded for five consecutive years. Thus, the period of community mobilization described below spans seven years and is still ongoing. The story of community mobilization begins before the start of the TCI and as I argue below, should be expected to continue even after the funds are no longer available.

Data collected for this study includes information about the mobilization process that took place during the formation of the Partnership for Latino Success. This involved a series of structured face to face interviews with thirty-five members of the partnership and observations at public events, meetings, and specialized dialogues organized by the CBO to engage the community. Once funding for the TCI was received, a university-based research team collected quarterly data from a variety of sources. These included focus groups of police, youth workers, community residents and court personnel; a multi-year series of interviews with steering committee members; participant observation at steering committee meetings; community circles and anti-racism and economic development workshops; and open-ended interviews with youth, parents, and school personnel. In addition, the research team analyzed local crime, school, and economic data and presented this data at public meetings and steering committee meetings. The author of this chapter served as evaluator for the CBO and was a member of the local action university research team for the first two years of the TCI.

Background

The Tri-City area of Fitchburg, Leominster, and Gardner combine to make up the urban centers of North Central Massachusetts, with a total population of 101,655. Factors such as high rates of unemployment, low median household incomes, and an average high school dropout rate for Hispanic students of 25% contribute to the gang and youth violence problem in this community (MA DOE, 2009). In the city of Fitchburg, the largest of the three cities, the per capita income is $22,311, and 19.2% of individuals live below the poverty line, including 28.8% of those under the age of 18 (U.S. Census, 2009).

Fitchburg and surrounding towns are former mill and industrial towns which have seen a steady decline in jobs over a fifty year period, most dramatically in the 1980s and 1990s with the closing of the last of the paper mills and plastics industries within the region. The knowledge economy has bypassed this region with little or no job growth associated with the technology of the information sector. Well before the current economic crisis during the first decade of the 21st century, the region experienced a net job loss of nearly 12% (Muro, et al., 2007).

As a gateway city, immigrants are drawn by inexpensive housing and the presence of ethnic enclaves. The most recent Census Bureau data indicates Latinos are the largest and fastest growing minority group in each of the three cities. Between 1990 and 2000, this population grew by 40.1% (United Way, 2007). The non-Latino population only grew by 1% during this same time (U.S. Census, 2009). Overall, Latinos in Massachusetts are much younger than non-Latinos, and a large portion of them are children. In 2000, more than one in three (36.2%) of Latinos were younger than 18 years old, compared with less than one in seven whites (15%). Thirty-nine percent of those who speak Spanish within their homes are living below poverty (U.S. Census, 2009). Geo-crime mapping reveals that crime is concentrated in neighborhoods where residents experience the most poverty, which also have the highest concentration of Latino residents (Gebo, 2007).

The Tri-City region has served as a hub for drug trafficking and distribution for decades. According to one state police informant and health data, for nearly fifty years this region has had some of the highest rates of substance abuse within the state (MA DHHS, 2011). The extent to which gangs are involved in drug trafficking and drug distribution is unclear. The state police gang unit leader estimates that about 25% of gang-involved youth are also involved in the drug trade but acknowledges there is little data to substantiate this estimation (Personal communication, 7/11/05). Several well-known leaders of drug involved gangs are currently serving long sentences for drug convictions leading to a perception among state law enforcement that the chronic gang activity within the region has been successfully suppressed by targeted prosecutions within the past ten years.

According to data collected by the university research team from law enforcement, street workers and community residents, the current gang problem within the region is best described as 'emerging' rather than 'chronic.' Under "emerging" conditions, gangs are more localized, with little connection to national or transnational entities, participation is less serious and more situational than conditions where the gang presence is more chronic or entrenched (Huff, 1990). Although Fitchburg, Leominster, and Gardner police do not have established gang units, law enforcement have identified twenty-one active gangs within the three communities (Personal communication, 3/18/11). While some gangs such as the Latin Kings have operated within the area for a very long time and are well established, street workers and residents believe most of the gangs are more accurately described as fluid crews or cliques with little formal organization beyond a

charismatic older youth leader or loose network of friends or kin. Observ-
ers note that gang-involved youth within the region rarely display colors
or participate in prominent activities such as tagging, and both law enforcement and street workers agree that this is a deliberate attempt on the part
of gang-involved youth to operate "below the radar" from law enforcement
(Gebo & Boyes-Watson, 2007).

A Citywide Partnership from the Ground Up

It is the premise of this chapter that it is necessary to pay attention to the
process by which a community is mobilized to address issues of common
concern. As noted above, the community mobilization process in the TCI
began with an earlier initiative to address the poor educational outcomes
for Latino youth in the region and then later shifted to crime-related issues. What accounts for the success of this community mobilization in the
TCI was the intentional on-going strategy of relationship-building across
diverse segments of the broader community described below.

The mobilization process focused on developing solid strategic relationships within Fitchburg, Leominster, and Gardner leadership in order to
begin to influence systemic change within the schools and in the broader
community. The strategy to develop relationships with area leaders entailed two objectives: (1) to develop a shared language, values, and vision
for change and (2) to develop relationships of trust. The implementation
of this strategy led to the organization of a series of lectures, board meetings, and events that would create reasons for leaders to come together
and interact with each other and with members of the Latino community.

The process of peacemaking circles was used as a form of structured
dialogue. The circle is an alternative method of communication which
fosters inclusion, equality, and respectful listening among groups (Ball,
et al., 2010). Shaped by indigenous values and teachings, the process of
the circle encourages people to share what is most important to them in a
way that builds mutual understanding. The unique structure of the circle
affords everyone an equal opportunity to be heard, and listening to each
other's stories across boundaries of race, class, and social position is an
experience that helps to develop a sense of personal trust and respect
(Pranis, et al., 1999).

Community mobilization as a form of community empowerment is
fundamentally about generating social capital. The periodic use of circles
helped to forge a deeper sense of trust among the partnership members
and facilitated the emergence of a shared vision based on an articulation
of shared values. Gradually a sense of "we" emerged among the group
that transcended the original agenda to address the educational needs of
Latino youth. The leadership from the largely white establishment joined

with the minority community members in articulating a vision and mission for the partnership which profoundly came to view Latino youth as "our" young people. The process also formed connections across different sectors of the agencies and organizations which were accustomed to working in isolation from one another and also across different segments of the minority community.

The work of community mobilization has often been described as invisible (Bennett, 1995) especially to funders, evaluators, and often the public at large. Building relationships between the police, the minority community, the street workers, and the school superintendent all may seem and can be insignificant especially if these relationships are only tied together by a short-term agenda to "split the pie" on a given source of funds. As Spergel and colleagues (2005) note, relationships based on "convenience" are not deep enough to sustain the long-term work required to address systemic issues like youth gangs. The element of social cohesion—a sense of common norms, trust, and shared fate—are all part of community building. Yet there is nothing easy or straightforward about this process. For every accomplishment, there are as many setbacks, failures, and obstacles which alter the course and composition of the partnership.

Crime Control Agenda: One Step Forward, Two Steps Back

The partnership turned its attention to the problem of crime, drugs, and gangs in 2005 in the wake of a crisis generated by an incendiary newspaper series on the problem of illegal drug trafficking in the region. The highly publicized series revealed underlying fault lines of race and class within the partnership. Members of the minority community felt the issue of drugs in the community was portrayed as an issue of "those people" who had brought the problem to the community. They perceived that recent immigrants were being blamed for the long standing problems of drugs within the region. They argued that the city should adopt an approach which addressed underlying causes of drug abuse and invest in long-term solutions. White members of the partnership, on the other hand, favored a heightened law enforcement response which they saw as "realistic" and "practical." The conflict touched a deep nerve for community participants, most of whom seriously considered walking away from the coalition.

It is a testament to the investment in relationship-building and shared leadership that the coalition survived through this difficult period. The shared leadership between a respected local Latina and the white police chief was a critical ingredient in the sustained mobilization of the community. Despite the intense conflict, the partnership continued the dialogue and it was during the course of these discussions that the partnership applied for and received funding to implement the TCI, a comprehensive, data-driven approach to youth gang violence and drugs within the region.

One Step Forward

Again process mattered. Two consistent features of the process were the use of data and analysis to put the region's problems within a larger context and the use of the circles for dialogues to discuss the data. A steering committee was formed within the partnership to plan and direct the use of funds for the anti-gang initiative. Although formally led by the police department, the locus of leadership was the highly cohesive but diverse steering committee chaired by the Latina leader. The data, now brought to the steering committee by the university research partners in the project, was widely shared throughout the community through workshops, systems thinking sessions, and other kinds of presentations that included large numbers of both the majority and minority community.

This collaborative community mobilization model created stronger connections between local residents and outside agencies while seeking to enlist the expertise of universities and professionals to share knowledge with community members so that they are able to make informed decisions about their own community. Sessions were organized at community colleges, local churches, and other venues so that presentations by experts were combined with opportunities for community members to discuss and respond to the information and help develop action plans based on this knowledge. Furthermore, the TCI continued to make use of the circles to engage the community in meaningful conversations in which every voice could be heard and values could be expressed. The dialogic structure of the circle ensured a level of equal participation for all members of the community and created a consistent opportunity for knowledge to flow bottom-up as well as top-down.

As a result of the diverse leadership within the steering committee with strong input from the Latino community, there was a clear priority to use the funds for prevention and intervention along with suppression. The TCI was the only CGM site within the state to use funds to strengthen youth connection to schools and prevent school dropouts by promoting a restorative approach to school discipline. The funds were also used to strengthen local community institutions, such as investing in a local church to create an after-school program for Latino youth that brought their parents in to the church at unprecedented levels and subsidizing several existing neighborhood-based youth programs. Efforts also began to create new community institutions to meet the needs of older youth who had little recreational outlets within the region.

A far more significant change that resulted from the newly-mobilized Latino community was the election of the city's first minority mayor. Facing a long-time city councilor as her opponent, a young Asian woman decided to run for election and won, with the support of the Latino community who turned out to vote in significant numbers. Although the TCI was not directly involved in voter registration drives or political organizing to support the candidate, the increase in connectivity, activism, and networks within traditionally marginalized communities increased their political participation and contributed to a long-term change in the governance structure in the city.

And Two Steps Back

The Fitchburg chief of police was a highly visible leader in the community mobilization process. At the same time, he was committed to a transition within his own department towards a data-driven community policing approach. As noted earlier, he had made it a priority to improve the largely negative relationship between the Latino community and the police. Yet there was a disconnect between the leadership within the police department, which included the chief, a captain, and a handful of officers involved with the community mobilization efforts, and the majority of officers who were not part of the dialogues forging a city-wide vision for addressing gangs and youth violence. Most members of the police department were uninvolved in the process and understood little about the CGM or the specific TCI. Many of them were skeptical of the community policing model itself and suspicious of the changes the chief brought to the police department, which is not unique to this department. Within certain segments of the city, and the department, the police chief was perceived as "soft on crime" and intense political pressure was brought to force his resignation after five years on the job.

This lack of understanding of the CGM among the rank and file of the police was apparent to researchers in a working group called the Youth Gang Intelligence Working Group (YGIWG) formed by the research team of the TCI. The purpose of the YGIWG was to provide the steering committee with on-the-ground understanding of youth gang dynamics within the city. Comprised of law enforcement, court personnel, youth workers, and community residents, these confidential meetings revealed a significant lack of understanding by the police of the CGM strategy adopted by the TCI.

The police assumed that community residents and youth workers were brought to these meetings to share information about individual youth participating in gang activity so the police could better engage in surveillance and suppression activities. The police felt considerable frustration at the unwillingness of the community to be the "eyes and ears" of the police. On the other side, the residents bristled at comments by law enforcement which they perceived as demonizing their youth and at the characterization of all youth gang activity as criminal in nature. In order to complete the research, specific confidentiality agreements needed to be crafted to accommodate the high levels of mistrust and miscommunication between officers and the community and ultimately, the two groups were separated in order to continue to collect data.

As noted above, the fault lines between law enforcement and minority communities run deep and are easily ruptured because of the lack of trust and social cohesion. Both sides come to the table with a significant level of mistrust and different perceptions of the purpose of the joint effort. Without social processes which intentionally work to build a sense of personal trust and allow for the development of shared values and expectations for a joint venture, the capacity to collaborate is very limited.

And Forward Again

Community mobilization is a long-term effort in any comprehensive crime strategy and as such needs to sustain changes in leadership if initiatives are to be successful. The resignation of the police chief coincided with the departure of the charismatic leader of the CBO, who were the two most committed and visible leaders of the TCI. But the mobilization of the Latino community had changed the dynamics of politics within the city and the commitment to sustain the efforts of the TCI continued under the leadership of the mayor's office. The mayor was in a position to hire a new police chief and was able to protect the anti-gang initiative from dropping off the agenda for the city. A decision was made to shift the leadership from the police department to the mayor's office itself under the direction of a highly active Latina with deep roots within the Latino community.

After five years, the TCI continues to sponsor restorative justice training in schools, youth-police dialogues within the schools, anti-racism dialogues within the community, the church after-school youth program, the development of a center for young adults who are out of school, and continues to invest time and energy in deepening the partnership with the police department and other agencies within the city. The TCI in this case study is more accurately understood as a product of an on-going and much broader community mobilization process. The legacy of genuine community mobilization is that new leaders emerge and the change process continues. The essence of a community that is genuinely mobilized is that it is not dependent upon any one individual nor is it under control of any one agency or program.

The mobilization also contributed to a change in the governance structure of the city itself. With the election of a minority woman mayor with strong connections to the Latino community, the minority community has become more engaged with the city government. The mayor recently launched an innovative neighborhood "mayors" program which recruited forty-nine recent immigrants to serve as "mayors" of their street, serving as connectors between residents and city hall (Sachetti, 2010). The schools have undergone changes in their awareness and attitude towards presence of the Latino student population and recent school data shows a significant increase in academic achievement and decrease in school dropout rates, especially among Latinos, and there has been a decrease in crime (Gebo & Rich-Shea, 2009). None of these achievements are the result of the TCI initiative alone, but the TCI clearly is part of and has contributed to a broad dynamic of community mobilization, which continues under the direction of the new police chief.

DISCUSSION AND LESSONS LEARNED

The most crucial lesson is that formal agents of social control are not effective as community organizers. The comprehensive nature of a systemic problem such as youth gangs requires that leadership originate within the community rather than from formal agents of social control, as was seen here. Mobilization of communities of color relies primarily on relationships of trust and a belief that crime will be addressed at the level of fundamental causes which are diverse and rooted in the social ecology of the community as well as at the level of public order. Community organizations with ties to the community like the partnership described herein are in a far better position to lead a comprehensive initiative and to recruit participation through the activation of social ties and networks. These ties have to include formal agencies and governmental organizations but must also extend into non-organizationally-based community networks, such as kinship network and neighborhood ties, in bridging social capital (Putnam, 2000).

A key factor is the presence of leaders who are able to create relationships of trust across different sectors of the community, as it occurred in this case. The leaders themselves must develop a level of trust and shared understandings in order to recruit more participants into the process. The shared leadership and deep friendship between the Latina leader and a white police chief provided a powerful model of collaboration that broke through barriers to trust. Mobilization of communities of color requires well-worn trusting and values-based relationships between key community leaders and systemic leaders (whether they are white or not).

Relationships of convenience simply do not generate the type of courage and investment required to bring change and to withstand a community's initial rejection of it.

Process matters. The work of community mobilization is the work of building relationships, creating opportunities for listening, articulating values, and talking about the things that really matter to people. The relentless and steady work of community mobilization is often invisible because it can seem as if there is no "product" or outcome which can also lead evaluators and others in the community to underestimate the nature of what is being achieved. Social cohesion within the community can be understood to be a product of community mobilization as well as a predictor of it, as evidenced here. The outcomes of community mobilization are not linear and should not be expected to be because once people are engaged, the energy of that mobilization will take directions that were unforeseen at the outset. If evaluators only focus on predetermined "outcomes" related solely to crime and violence, much of the value that is being created through intentional community mobilization efforts will be unrecognized and unacknowledged by the research community.

Process also matters because it is the quality of the relationship that produces social cohesion, not the quantity of interactions. The peacemaking circles process is an effective tool in order to forge values and vision-driven relationships between leaders and the diverse communities they serve. When professionals engage with communities there are significant asymmetries in power, status, and language that tend to relegate community members to the position of the "client" rather than partner. Circles bring participants to the table as human beings with equal voice in the dialogue. The process helps to diminish boundaries among all participants and helps to foster a sense of collective identity that is an element of social cohesion.

The final lesson concerns the need to anchor the mobilization process through institutional development within the community, without it being a top-down process. Churches, public schools, community organizations, and even governmental agencies can all serve as sites for community engagement and mobilization. The decision of the TCI to invest funds within the schools to make them more inclusive for Latino youth and their families is an outcome of community mobilization that may generate even greater levels of civic engagement as schools become institutional sites for social interaction. Parent groups have formed using the circle process and local schools have opened their doors to youth workers connected to the Latino community. The investment of CGM funds in the after-school program of a local church led to an influx of immigrant parents as congregants, thus revitalizing a local institution that had been in decline with an aging, dwindling white congregation.

Community mobilization may be the most difficult and yet most central element of the CGM if the goal is to generate a significant and long-term shift in the dynamics which contribute to the systemic problem of youth gangs. *Who* leads the process of community mobilization and *how* they lead are both critical factors to the success of a mobilization effort.

REFERENCES

Alter, C., & Hage, J. (1993). *Organizations working together: Coordination interorganizational networks*. Beverly Hills, CA: Sage.

Arcidiacono, C., Sommantico, M., & Procentese, F. (2001). Neopolitan youth's sense of community and the problem of unemployment. *Journal of Community and Applied Social Psychology, 11*, 465–473.

Ball, J., Caldwell, W., & Pranis, K. (2010). *Doing democracy with circle*. Minneapolis, MN: Living Justice Press.

Bazemore, G. (2001). Young people, trouble, and crime: Restorative justice as a normative theory of informal social control and social support. *Youth and Society, 33*(2), 199–226.

Benard, B. (1990). An overview of community-based prevention. In K.H. Rey, C.L. Faegre, & P. Lowery (Eds.), *Prevention Research Findings*. Washington, D.C.: Office of Substance Abuse Prevention.

Bennett, S.F. (1995). Community organizations and crime. *Annals AAPSS, 539*, 72–84.

Bellair, P.E. (2000). Informal surveillance and street crime: a complex relationship. *Criminology, 38*(1), 137–167.

Bond, M., & Keys, C. (1993). Empowerment, diversity, and collaboration: Promoting synergy on community boards. *American Journal of Community Psychology, 21*(1), 37–57.

Comack, E., & Silver, J. (2008). A Canadian exception to the punitive turn? Community responses to policing practices in Winnipeg's inner city. *Canadian Journal of Sociology, 33*, 815–844.

Coleman, J.S. (1988). Social capital in the creation of human capital. *American Journal of Sociology, 94*, 95–120.

Donnelly, P.G., & Majka, T.J. (1998). Residents' efforts at neighborhood stabilization: Facing the challenges of inner-city neighborhoods. *Sociological Forum, 13*, 189–213.

Elliot, M. (2000). The stress process in neighborhood context. *Health Place, 6*, 287–299.

Elliott, D.S., Wilson, W.J., Huizinga, D., Sampson, R.J., Elliott, A., & Rankin, B. (1996). The effects of neighborhood disadvantage on adolescent development. *Journal of Research on Crime and Delinquency, 33*, 389–426.

Florin, P., & Wandersman, A. (1990). An introduction to citizen participation, voluntary organizations, and community development: Insights for empowerment through research. *American Journal of Community Psychology, 18*, 41–54.

Foster-Fishman, P.G., Fitzgerald, K., Brandell, C., Nowell, B., Chavis, D., & Van Egeren, L.A. (2006). Mobilizing residents for action: The role of small wins and strategic supports. *American Journal of Community Psychology, 38*, 143–152.

Gebo, E. (2007). *Tri-City Anti-Gang Initiative Local Action Research Partnership.* Charles E. Shannon Community Safety Initiative. Boston, MA: Suffolk University.

Gebo, E., & Boyes-Watson, C. (2007) *Emerging Picture of Youth Gangs in Tri-City Region.* Research Presentation to TCI Steering Committee. Fitchburg, MA, June 20, 2007.

Gebo, E., & Rich-Shea, A. (2009). *Fourth Year Update on the Tri-City Anti-Gang Initiative.* Research Presentation to the TCI Partnership. Fitchburg, MA, October 24, 2009.

Grinc, R. (1994). Angels in marble: Problems in stimulating community involvement in community policing. *Crime and Delinquency, 40*, 437–468.

Huff, C.R. (1990). *Gangs in America.* Newbury, CA: Sage.

Kim Ju, G., Mark, G.Y., Cohen, R., Garcia-Santiago, O., & Nguyen, P. (2008). Community mobilization and its application to youth violence prevention. *American Journal of Preventative Medicine*, S5–S12.

Lasker, R.D., & Weiss, E.S. (2003). Broadening participation in community problem solving: A multidisciplinary model to support collaborative practice and research. *Journal of Urban Health, 80*, 14–47.

Lawrence, K., Sutton, S., Kubisch, A., Susi, G., & Fullbright-Anderson, K. (2004). *Structural racism and community building.* Washington, D.C.: Aspen Institute. Roundtable on Community Change.

Leventhal, T., & Brooks-Gunn, J. (2000). The neighborhoods they live in: The effects of neighborhood residence on child and adolescent outcomes. *Psychological Bulletin, 126*(2), 309–337.

Lindenberg, C.S., Solorzano, R.M., Vilaro, F.M., & Westbrook, L. (2001). Challenges and strategies for conducting intervention research with culturally diverse populations. *Journal of Transcultural Nursing, 12*, 132–139.

Massachusetts Department of Education (2009). 5 Year Graduation Rate. Retrieved from http://profiles.doe.mass.edu/grad/grad_report.aspx?orgcode=00970000&orgtypecode=5&

Massachusetts Department of Health & Human Services (2011). MA CHIP indicator data. Retrieved from http://www.mass.gov/.

Massey, D.S. (1996). The age of extremes: concentrated affluence and poverty in the twenty first century. *Demography 33*, 395–412.

Morenoff, J., Sampson, R., & Raudenbush, S. (2001). *Neighborhood inequality, collective efficacy, and the spatial dynamics of urban violence.* Ann Arbor, MI: University of Michigan Institute for Social Research, Population Studies Center.

Muro, M., Schneider, J., Warren, D., McLean-Shinaman, E., Sohmer, R., Forman, B., Ansel, D., & Leiserson, G. (2007). *Reconnecting Massachusetts Gateway Cities.* Boston, MA: Mass Inc. and Brookings Institute Metropolitan Policy Program.

National Youth Gang Center. (2008). *Best practices to address community gang problems: OJJDP's comprehensive gang model.* Washington, D.C.: OJJDP.

Nkansa, G.A., & Chapman, D.W. (2006). Sustaining community participation: What remains after the money ends? *Review of Education, 52*, 509–532.

Pattavina, A., Byrne, J.M., & Garcia, L. (2006). An examination of citizen involvement in crime prevention in high-risk versus low-to moderate-risk neighborhoods. *Crime & Delinquency, 52*, 203–231.

Pattillo-McCoy, M. (1999). *Black picket fences: Privilege and peril among the black middle class.* Chicago: University of Chicago Press.

Payne, P., & Williams, K. (2008). Building social capital through neighborhood mobilization: Challenges and lessons learned. *American Journal of Preventative Medicine, 34.*

Pranis, K., Stuart, B., & Wedge, M. (1999). *Peacemaking circles: From crime to community.* MN: Living Justice Press.

Provan, K., & Milward, B. (2001). Do networks really work? A framework for evaluating public-sector organizational networks. *Public Administration Review, 61*, 414–423.

Putnam, R. (2000). *Bowling alone: The collapse and revival of American communities.* NY: Simon and Schuster.

Robinson, G., & Hanna, L. (1994). *Bowling alone: The collapse and revival of American communities.* NY: Simon and Schuster.

Ross, C.E. (2000). Neighborhood disadvantage and adult depression. *Journal of Health and Social Behavior, 41*, 177–187.

Sabol, W., Coulton, C., & Korbin, J. (2004). Building community capacity for violence prevention. *Journal of Interpersonal Violence, 19*(3), 322–340.

Sachetti, M. (2010, October 4). Fitchburg aims to engage immigrants. *The Boston Globe.*

Sampson, R.J., Morenoff, J.D., & Gannon-Rowley, T. (2002). Assessing 'neighborhood effects': Social processes and new directions in research. *American Review of Sociology, 28*, 443–478.

Schnieder, S. (2000). Organizational obstacles to participation in community crime prevention programs. *International Criminal Justice Review, 10*, 32.

Schuller, T., Baron, S., & Field, J. (2000). Social capital: A review and critique. In S. Baron, J. Field, & T. Schuller (Eds.). *Social Capital: Critical Perspectives.* New York: Oxford University Press.

Spergel, I.A., Wa, K., & Sosa R. (2005). *Evaluation of the Riverside comprehensive community-wide approach to gang prevention, intervention, and suppression program.* Chicago: University of Chicago, School of Social Service Administration.

Skogan, W.G. (1989). Communities, crime and neighborhood organization. *Crime & Delinquency, 35*, 437–457.

United Way (2007). *United Way of North Central Massachusetts 2007 Community Assessment.* Cambridge, MA: Mt. Auburn Associates.

U.S. Census (2009). *City of Fitchburg, 2005–2009 American Community Survey, Five Year Estimates.* Washington, D.C.

Veysey, B., & Messner, S.F. (1999). Further testing of social disorganization theory: An elaboration of Sampson and Groves' community structure and crime. *Journal of Research in Crime and Delinquency, 36*, 156–174.

Waldeck, S. (1999). Cops, community policing and the social norms approach to crime control. *Georgia Law Review, 34*, 1253.

Ward, C.M. (1997). Community crime prevention: Addressing background and foreground causes of criminal behavior. *Journal of Criminal Justice, 25*, 1–18.

Warner, B., & Rountree, P.W. (1997). Local social ties in a community and crime model: Questioning the systemic nature of informal social control. *Social Problems, 44*(4), 520–536.

Watson-Thompson, J., Fawcett, S., & Schultz, J. (2008). A framework for community mobilization to promote healthy youth development. *American Journal of Preventative Medicine, 34*, 72–81.

Wilson, W.J. (1987). *The truly disadvantaged: The inner city, the underclass and public policy.* Chicago: University of Chicago Press.

Zhao, J., Loverich, N.P., & Thurman, Q.C. (1999). The status of community policing in American cities: Facilitators and impediments revisited. *Policing: An International Journal of Police Strategies & Management, 22*, 74–92.

Chapter 3

Using Action Research to Support Strategic Thinking and Data-Driven Decision-Making in Gang and Youth Violence Prevention, Intervention, and Suppression in Worcester

LAURIE ROSS & ELLEN FOLEY

Worcester, Massachusetts' rates of gun assaults and homicides defy expectation. With a population over 175,000 people, it is the second largest city in New England (Worcester Fact Sheet, 2010). Economic conditions are conducive to gang and youth violence, notably inner city neighborhoods with concentrated poverty, limited living wage jobs, and high rates of unemployment. As a former industrial city, much of Worcester's physical infrastructure is decayed and the majority of the housing stock dates back to the turn of the last century. Worcester has a reputation for being unsafe and is sometimes referred to as 'Wartown' and its residents as 'Woorats.' Yet, despite the statistics, physical conditions, and negative perceptions, Worcester is among the safest cities in the Commonwealth. It consistently has the lowest urban violent crime rates in New England, including non-fatal shooting incidents and homicides. For example, in 2005, other Massachusetts cities such as Boston, Brockton, Fall River, Lawrence, Lowell, and Lynn experienced increases in gun assaults (Worcester Police Department, 2007). In this same year, a year prior to the start of the Shannon initiative discussed in this book, Worcester not only had a decrease in such incidents, the city had the second lowest gun assault rate of all cities in the state. Worcester's homicide rate remains consistently in the single digits, while similarly sized cities across the region such as Providence, Hartford, Springfield, and Bridgeport have many times the number of murders.

Yet, the overall low numbers of gun incidents and homicides mask another reality in Worcester. When closely examining Worcester's small numbers of violent offenders and victims, we learn that young men of color between the ages of 19 and 30 with criminal backgrounds and histories of gang involvement are disproportionately on both sides of the gun. This particular demographic may be relatively small when considering that Worcester has a population over 175,000. Yet, for those who are part of the demographic and/or have loved ones who are, the numbers signify deeper community and societal problems. One is left with the sense that the story of violence in Worcester is actually a tale of two cities—one that is safe, collaborative and prevention-focused and the other that is dangerous, unsupportive, reactive, and punitive. Young men of color disproportionately live in the latter Worcester.

In 2006, the Comprehensive Gang Model (CGM) was introduced in Worcester through the Shannon Initiative to address the city's gang and youth violence problems. In this chapter, we briefly describe the CGM. We then discuss the ways in which the CGM complemented the youth development and policing approaches underway, and how it filled critical gaps in both of these systems. To this end, first we describe the prevention-orientation of Worcester's youth development sector. Strong youth development organizations are associated with violence prevention (Catalano, Berglund, Ryan, Lonczak, & Hawkins, 2004; Eccles & Gootman, 2002; Lerner, Taylor, & von Eye, 2002). These programs also offer young people alternative pathways and opportunities to belong to positive, supportive communities. Consistent local advocacy for youth has helped to direct resources to develop youth jobs, connect young people with educational opportunities, provide mental health support, and maintain recreational facilities for youth in all parts of the city. In spite of these positive efforts, a deeper analysis of this sector at the beginning of the Shannon Initiative revealed that there were service gaps and as a result some groups of young people fell through the holes of the prevention net. By directing resources to the highest risk and gang involved young people, the Shannon initiative sought to fill these holes.

In terms of complementarity with policing approaches, the promotion of Gary Gemme to position of Chief of Police in 2004 initiated significant organizational changes within the WPD. These organizational changes were characterized by community-oriented, problem-focused policing. The Department broke down silos and emphasized information sharing across units. The Department also formalized information-sharing protocols with external city, county, state, and federal law enforcement bodies. This information sharing led to more efficient police operations and the ability to target the most violent offenders even in a context of declining funds. In addition to internal change, Gemme forged strategic community partnerships to address the needs of the underserved youth through education, employment, life skills, and mental health programming.

This chapter concludes that the CGM allowed Worcester to build on successful practices that were keeping the overall gun crime and homicide rates low. Specifically, the CGM-informed Shannon Initiative provided resources to develop programs and systems aimed at serving the highest risk and gang involved young people in the city, which were primarily youth of color. While the evidence suggests that critical gaps were filled by Shannon, questions about the sustainability of these efforts remain in the context of unstable and declining funding.

THE COMPREHENSIVE GANG MODEL

Researchers and practitioners alike recognize that the act of joining a gang is shaped by multiple levels of often interrelated risk factors—from individual experiences, negative life events, personality traits and behaviors to family, school, peer, and community dynamics (Howell, 2010). While having or being exposed to the risk factors does not necessarily result in gang involvement, engagement in gang-related activities is highly correlated with young people growing up in low-income neighborhoods, single-headed households, association with gang-involved peers, and early use of drugs and alcohol (Hill, Lui, & Hawkins, 2001). Elliot (1994) explains how this constellation of risk factors increases youth's likelihood to engage in violence. He contends that in the context of limited future options, weak internal controls, and few external controls, youth's decisions to engage in violent behavior is rational, as the perceived rewards greatly outweigh the costs.

Given the complex drivers of youth gang involvement, there is a growing awareness that suppression alone is an inadequate response to gang activity. Research indicates that vulnerable young people are less likely to get involved with gangs if they have access to safe, healing, and developmentally appropriate spaces (Eccles & Gootman, 2002; Ginwright, 2009; Lerner, Taylor, & von Eye, 2002). For these reasons, more comprehensive approaches to assessing and then addressing a community's gang problems have been emerging over the past decade and a half. The strategies are comprehensive in that they go beyond suppression to also include prevention and intervention. Within this comprehensive framework, strategies segment the youth population according to levels of risk and then direct supports and interventions based on their particular risk factors and delinquency history. Figure 3.1 demonstrates this 'segmenting' of the youth population by risk factor and programmatic response. The relative size each segment occupies on the pyramid signifies the rough percentage of the youth/young adult population they represent (i.e. Category 1 youth represent the smallest

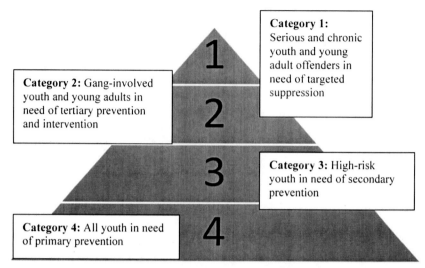

Category 1: Serious and chronic youth and young adult offenders in need of targeted suppression

Category 2: Gang-involved youth and young adults in need of tertiary prevention and intervention

Category 3: High-risk youth in need of secondary prevention

Category 4: All youth in need of primary prevention

Figure 3.1.   Gang Prevention and Intervention Strategies based on Wyrick (2006) and cited in Howell (2010)

number of young people in a community while Category 4 youth represent the largest number).

This approach to segmenting the youth and young adult population and then targeting different responses has been formalized into the OJJDP Comprehensive Gang Model (Howell, 2010; Spergel, 1995). In addition to multiple levels of prevention, social intervention, treatment, and suppression, the CGM also incorporates organizational change within community agencies, with a particular focus on police departments and community mobilization in an overall community change framework designed to reduce gang involvement and gang-related crimes (Howell, 2010).

YOUTH DEVELOPMENT SECTOR IN WORCESTER

The roughly 30,000 young people between the ages of 16 and 24 living in Worcester are exposed to a number of the risk factors associated with youth violence and gang involvement. For example, young people face higher poverty rates than the general population: almost one-third of all youth 16 to 24 live in poverty, and 44% of all Hispanic youth in Worcester live in poverty. Thirty-three percent of households in Worcester are headed by a female. The four-year graduation rate in the city is lower than the rate for the state of Massachusetts at 70% and is only 61% for Hispanic youth. Roughly 27% of the student population has limited English proficiency. Although young people ages 16 to 24 make up 16% of the total population of Worcester, they account for 39% of the people who are unemployed. Almost 7% of 16–19 year olds in the city were neither in school nor high school graduates (Worcester Fact Sheet, 2010). While gun violence levels are relatively low, there is a gang presence in the city. The Worcester Police Department has identified 24 gangs and tracks roughly 1,000 people in its gang database.

Given these risk factors, Worcester is fortunate to have a youth development sector rich with an array of school and community-based youth programs. There are organizations with national affiliations, such as the YMCA, YWCA, Boys and Girls Club and Girls, Inc., and 'home grown' youth organizations such as the Worcester Youth Center and the Mosaic Multicultural Complex. Many faith-based organizations also offer youth programs. There are environmentally-focused organizations that have developed youth components, such as Worcester Roots Project and Regional Environmental Council. There are also many multi-service organizations that serve youth, such as Friendly House and Worcester Community Action Council. Finally, there are numerous coalitions and collaborations that provide services directly as well as offer space for networking and advocacy, such as YouthNet, the HOPE Coalition, the Investing in Girls Alliance, and the Youth Violence Prevention Coalition.

There have been several recent assessments of the city's youth development sector. In 1999, Worcester's Promise (a local initiative modeled after Colin Powell's America's Promise) sponsored a study of 'Safe Spaces' for youth in the city, focusing on programs for children in kindergarten through eighth grade. This study analyzed over 200 different programs being offered by eighty-seven organizations (Coleman-Ross Consultants, 1999). In 2001, a group of high school-aged youth working as Peer Leaders in the HOPE Coalition conducted a citywide needs assessment of youth ages 12–20. Over 400 young people were surveyed about issues facing youth and their assessment of the youth programs in Worcester. Most recently in 2007, the newly formed city Youth Opportunities Office conducted an assessment of the youth development sector for young people ages 14–21. Fifty-six organizations offering 87 different programs were included in this assessment (Edwards & Ross, 2007).

These studies come to several similar conclusions regarding Worcester's youth development sector. First, both the 1999 and 2007 studies reveal that Worcester offers a diverse array of programming. The 2007 study, which focuses on programs for older youth found that the most common types of programming offered are leadership (52%), education (50%), employment readiness (45%), and recreation (39%) and the least common types of programming offered are gang violence reduction (15%), domestic violence (13%), emergency services (7%), truancy (6%), runaway/homelessness services (5%), and immigrant/refugee services

(1%). Health-related programs (including physical health, mental health, mediation, and substance use) are offered by roughly 20% of agencies. Both of the studies also found that the programming is spread throughout the city, much of it accessible by public transportation and at no or low cost.

Another similarity across studies is that these organizations serve large numbers of diverse youth. The 2007 study found that programs serve anywhere from 10 to 8,000 young people ages 14–21 with the median at 180 young people, and males and females are served at roughly equal rates. Most programs serve youth coming from low-income households. Both the 1999 and 2007 studies revealed that programs were serving large numbers of African American, Latino, and White youth. Asian youth had the lowest representation in these organizations. As a point of comparison, the racial/ethnic makeup of the Worcester Public Schools is 13.6% African American, 8.1% Asian, 38.3% Hispanic, and 36.5% White (Department of Early and Secondary Education, 2011). While males and females from most racial/ethnic groups participate in youth development programs, both of the 1999 and 2007 studies found the lowest levels of participation among the oldest youth. In the 2007 study, more than 90% of organizations surveyed reported serving 15–17 year olds; yet, 59% reported serving 20 year olds and 55% reported serving 21 year olds. The HOPE Coalition's needs assessment provides some explanation for rates of older youth—older teens felt that the staff did not have the skills or interest to work with them, that youth workers did not seem to understand their needs or youth culture, and when youth workers could not handle a young person's behavior, the tendency was to kick the youth out of the program.

This brief review shows that Worcester's youth development sector serves thousands of diverse young people with an array of programs and may be a factor that contributes to the city's relatively low levels of violent crime. In fact, the Chief of the Worcester Police Department, Gary Gemme, credits the role of community organizations in keeping Worcester's youth violence rates lower than many comparable cities in the Northeast. Yet, when comparing the results of these assessments of the youth development sector to the types of services and interventions required in a comprehensive approach to youth and gang violence reduction, we begin to see gaps. Primary prevention and secondary prevention programs for youth in Categories 3 and 4 as presented in Figure 3.1 above are present. Yet, youth and young adults who are in Category 2—gang-involved youth and young adults in need of tertiary prevention and intervention—do not appear to have many options. Indeed, older youth are not being served at high levels; nor are organizations offering many programs for gang violence reduction, emergency services, truancy, runaway/homeless services, and immigrant/refugee services—the types of supports gang-involved young people would need to be able to make immediate and substantive changes in their lives (De Rosa, Montgomery, Kipke, Iverson, Ma, & Unger, 1999; Thornberry, Krohn, Lizotte, Smith, & Tobin, 2003). These findings suggest that a significant group of gang-involved young men of color with criminal backgrounds were underserved by existing programs in Worcester.

VIOLENCE IN WORCESTER FROM 1997 TO PRESENT: AN EXAMINATION OF BOTH SIDES OF THE GUN

In order to substantiate Worcester's need for focused attention on Category 2 youth prior to the Shannon Initiative, this section presents trends in homicide rates and gun-related incidents. While Worcester's homicides and gun-related incidents have consistently been low, Figure 3.2 shows several spikes in gun-related violent crimes. The first occurred from late 1997 through 1999. During this time there were 21 homicides, 12 of which were gun-related. After a sharp decline in 2000, the number of shooting incidents increased 80% from 2000–2005. In 2004, 7 out of the 11 homicides in the city were by guns. Then, in 2005–2006 there was a 50% decrease in shootings, from 36 to 18; and an accompanying decline in gun-related homicides. After another sharp decline in 2006 that was sustained for several years, homicides and gun related incidents started to rise again in 2008. There were 29 shootings in Worcester in 2010, up from 18 in 2009 and 11 in 2008 (Croteau, 2011). Later, these trends will be examined in light of other events occurring in Worcester.

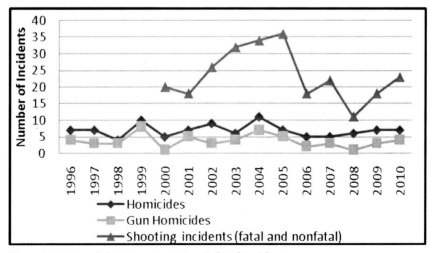

Figure 3.2. Trends in Worcester's Gun-Related Incidents

In 2006, a study of Worcester's gun-related incidents and homicides revealed that 43% of the homicides and almost 37% of non-fatal shootings during this time were gang-related (Braga, 2006). This study also showed that known offenders and victims shared many characteristics. For example:

- Most were African American or Latino males, with an average age of 26; 89% of offenders were 30 or younger; 82% of victims were 30 or younger.
- 96% of offenders and 76% of victims had at least one prior arraignment on their record and many were under active probation supervision at the time of the violent gun crime.
- 74% of the offenders and 70% of the victims had been committed to an adult and/or juvenile correctional facility for past criminal involvement.

These characteristics of victims and offenders provided glaring evidence for the need for more targeted programming for young people in Category 2, as presented in Figure 3.1 above.

Spatial analysis of the incidents revealed that most occurred in and near eight gang hot spots. This physical space represented only 1.8% of the city's landscape but generated 26.5% of shooting incidents and 46.4% of calls for police service due to shots fired. Temporal analysis showed that many of these incidents occurred from 2:00 to 3:00 AM on Saturdays and Sundays. Both the spatial and temporal trends pointed to bars and clubs as 'ground zeros' within the hot spots.

This report was an important step in defining Worcester's gang violence problem. It provided hard data behind anecdotal knowledge about who, where, when, why, and how serious violent incidents were being committed in the city. Homicide and serious gun violence was revealed to be a highly concentrated phenomenon, located in a few hot spots and generated by a small number of gang-involved, highly violent young adult offenders.

POLICE AND COMMUNITY RESPONSES

Gary Gemme became the Chief of Worcester's police department in 2004 during one of its most violent periods and immediately initiated a wave of organizational reforms to address gang-related homicides and gun violence. The major change was introducing the 'Split Force Model.' By splitting the police into two complementary divisions—a Community Impact Division and an Operations Division—WPD could overcome its prior hierarchical organizational structure that allowed specialized investigative units to operate in silos, with little communication or coordination. The Community Impact Division was responsible for developing and executing proactive and strategic problem-solving initiatives and projects. The Operations Division was responsible for the efficient response to day-to-day emergency and non-emergency calls for service. To facilitate sharing of information Chief Gemme instituted the Captain's Round Table to discuss patterns in violent crime across units and to generate creative ways to address these problems.

In late 2005, Chief Gemme introduced the Street Violence Prevention Group (SVPG), which brought WPD captains together with leadership from outside criminal justice agencies, such as neighboring police departments, the DA's Office, the Massachusetts State Police and Sheriff's Department, and federal law enforcement agencies. Described as a "working group" by Gemme, the SVPG met monthly to share intelligence on the relatively short list of very violent individuals in the city, including Category 1 youth, and on unsolved shootings, homicides, and drug activity. In addition to coordinating efforts and sharing information, the SVPG worked on overcoming shooting victims' unwillingness to cooperate with the investigations. This evolution in information-sharing and strategizing allowed the police to begin to focus attention on the small group of highly violent offenders and victims (Category 1 and Category 2 youth), and also begin to monitor those who appeared to be going down the same path. This new focus appeared to have an impact on violence. From 2004 to 2006, the rate of shooting incidents and homicides dropped significantly.

Yet, Figure 3.2 shows that the spring and summer of 2007 saw a renewed wave of violence. This served as a catalyst for the highest levels of leadership in Worcester, including Congressman McGovern, City Manager Michael O'Brien, and Gemme to convene a meeting of school officials and the youth development organizations in July 2007. Recognizing that the problem went beyond law enforcement, Gemme stated, "We don't want it to be simply a law enforcement solution." He suggested that a more comprehensive community response was required, including having a job training and substance abuse program in place for violent offenders during and after their incarceration. His remarks indicate that the WPD has a keen knowledge of the service and resource chasm that exists between the effective prevention programs that serve a majority of Worcester's vulnerable youth and the young men of color who live in Worcester's "second" more dangerous and violent city.

This meeting initiated a series of discussions about the WPD and the implications of Worcester's youth development approach that emphasized primary and secondary prevention approaches, but mostly overlooked tertiary prevention and intervention for the highest risk, gang-involved young people. Racial disparities not only in criminal justice involvement, but also in educational attainment, health, employment, and home ownership were raised in these conversations. Critical attention was focused on the fact that the city's leadership—public, private, and non-profit sectors—did not reflect the changing racial composition of the community. These very tense and at times painful conversations led to the formation of a new group, the Worcester Violence Prevention Coalition. The aim of this Coalition was to support the fledgling grassroots groups that focused specifically on the most vulnerable and struggling young people of color in the community. It was into this context—a new wave of violence and a renewed focus on the needs of Worcester's most disengaged young people—that the new Shannon Initiative was being launched.

WORCESTER'S SHANNON-FUNDED
COMPREHENSIVE GANG MODEL

In 2006, the year that Shannon was introduced, the WPD Crime Analysis Unit reported a total of 8,581 arrests—38% of these were young people between the ages of 17 and 24 for crimes such as assault and battery, disorderly conduct, distribution and sales of drugs, and firearms-related incidents. From 2004–2006, while there had only been 12 homicides in Worcester, four of them were youth murders where either the victims or the perpetrators were known to be involved in gangs. The WPD's Gang Unit estimated that there were at least 28 gangs in Worcester with approximately 700–900 members (Braga, 2006). WPD reported that only about 5% of gang members were to be considered seriously dangerous—among those would be the Category 1 youth.

Braga's research led to a tighter definition of the violence problem: 80% of the victims and 85% of the offenders from 2004 through 2006 were young men of color between the ages 21 and 26. Most of the victims and witnesses were uncooperative. Further, the evidence suggested that gang and group violence was usually retaliatory in nature and gun and knife violence appeared to be a self-sustaining cycle among a relatively small number of criminally active offenders. While the serious violence was being committed by young men in their early twenties, it is important to note that the average age of gang members in the WPD Gang Unit database was closer to 17. Given that the Gang Unit tracks roughly 1,000 people, this suggests that there was a large group of young people, Category 2 youth, in need of intervention to prevent them from becoming part of the small group of victims and serious offenders.

The analysis of Worcester's youth development sector showed that it provided little of this type of support, however. Thus, Shannon presented an opportunity to continue the organizational change efforts already underway within WPD as well as strengthen secondary and terfiary prevention efforts geared at the highest risk young men that many in the city were coming to recognize were essential but largely absent. By describing Worcester's Shannon strategy, we show how the Comprehensive Gang Model provided a guide to design systems that would fill gaps in Worcester's services and programs.

Worcester's Shannon Initiative has evolved since its introduction in 2006, but it has held four goals constant over the years, each involving collaborative approaches to reducing youth and gang violence:

1. Prevent vulnerable youth from becoming involved in gangs or adopting gang behavior,
2. Reduce current gun and gang violence,
3. Improve quality of life for high at-risk youth and young adults
4. Increase education, job skills, job opportunities, and life skills for youth and re-entry offenders

In order to accomplish these four goals, Worcester pursued best practice strategies that fell within each of the domains of the CGM: Prevention/Social Intervention, Provision of Opportunities, and Suppression. Worcester engaged in Community Mobilization through the creation of an Advisory Board consisting of WPD, local politicians, contracted partners, and other community leaders with a stake in the issue of youth violence. Additionally, Worcester included a Local Action Research Partner (LARP) into its overall gang and youth violence reduction strategy. These elements are described in greater depth below, with a particular focus on Provision of Opportunities programs, as these are the ones targeted to some of the Category 1, but mostly the Category 2 young men at the highest risk, many of whom have already had contact with the juvenile justice and/or criminal justice system but who could be diverted with tertiary prevention programming.

Prevention and Social Intervention Programs

Four main programs made up the Prevention and Social Intervention components of Shannon, several of which were based on evidence-based youth and gang violence prevention and reduction programs. The first, WPD's G.A.N.G. Summer Program, actually predated Shannon. Over the years, some Shannon resources were dedicated to the summer program and LARP analyzed intake data on participants in the program. The Summer Program immersed over 300 youth in a week-long summer camp experience. WPD records show that targeted participants are ages 8–15, many of whom have friends (over 35%) or relatives (20%) involved in gangs. Sports programming, guest speakers, field trips, and drug, alcohol, and violence resistance instruction formed a curriculum that develops strong decision-making skills. Made possible through a 1 to 3 participant-instructor ratio, the camp facilitates the development of positive relation-ships between program participants and WPD officers. Additionally, the summer program purposefully included participants from different neighborhoods. The effect was to blur geographic lines that can lead to gang violence, rather than exacerbate turf issues. Results of a 2005 survey of participants illustrated modest positive shifts in participant attitudes.

In addition to the G.A.N.G. Summer Program, Worcester's Shannon Initiative integrated Gang Awareness for the Next Generation (GANG) talks into the Worcester Public Schools. While other nationally evalu-ated programs, such as the GREAT model, were considered, Worcester decided to use this program, modified from a model developed by the Boston Public Health Commission. The Gang Unit felt it was more ap-propriate for local conditions than GREAT. The GANG Talks program involves visiting every 6th grade classroom three times over the year. Gang Unit officers deliver a curriculum that focuses on topics such as the myths of gang membership, conflict resolution, Gangs vs. Groups, cyber-bullying and cyber safety, and the consequences of dealing drugs. The curriculum focuses on strengthening decision-making skills and understanding consequences of actions taken. In a teacher survey, educators reported that GANG talks were relevant, that officers were approachable, and that 6th grade was a "perfect age" to dialogue about the risks of gang involvement. With the immediate goals of learning gang resistance and conflict mediation skills, the program's long-term goals seek to change the general perception of gang involvement and ultimately, to reduce youth gang membership. In 2010, close to 2,700 young people in 40 schools received the program.

The Police-Clergy Mentoring Program is a third component of the Shannon-funded Prevention/Social Intervention strategy area. This partnership is between the WPD, ten local churches, and the Southeast Asian Neighborhood Center. The objective is to provide a safe space for youth whose lives are affected by alcohol, drugs, crime, and violence and connect them with positive adults. In the program, youth engage with a police officer and church volunteers to engage in recreation, community service, sports, job skills, and homework help. In 2010, roughly 350 young people were served each week and 18 referrals were made to other Shan-non programs.

The final Prevention/Social Intervention program is the nationally eval-uated Boys and Girls Club of America Gang Prevention through Targeted

Outreach Case Management program. This program is endorsed by the National Gang Center and is a Promising Program according to the Office of Juvenile Justice and Delinquency Prevention. Informed by outcomes documented by national evaluations, this program aimed to improve school outcomes and reduce court and gang involvement by connecting youth to caring adults and to the community through jobs and volunteering. Located at three BGC sites, the program affected three of the 'gang hotspot' areas in the city. This program capitalized on existing programming at the Boys and Girls Club by utilizing case workers to reach the youth at highest risk for delinquency. Youth were identified and referred by the WPD, schools, community partners, and club professionals. Targeted youth were between the ages of 11–18 and had multiple risk factors that included: living in areas of gang activity, having problems in school, involvement in the juvenile justice system, displaying evidence of abuse or neglect, having family problems, and coming from a low-income household.

In 2010, 75 young people were enrolled in the Boys and Girls Club program. Almost 90% of the participants were male. Eighty-five percent were Latino or African American. The program served youth as a primary prevention tool (57% of 2009 participants had no prior involvement with the justice system or violence-related suspensions) as well as a secondary intervention (43% of 2009 participants had previous justice system involvement and/or violence-related school suspensions) (Ross, 2009). Using outreach strategies to engage hard-to-reach youth, the case workers connect youth to the most appropriate Club programs or refer them to programs at other agencies. Youth also have opportunities to volunteer, complete career prep programs, or seek employment. Data suggested program effectiveness. Of over 100 participants in 2009, only 6% became involved with juvenile justice during program enrollment, despite 50% involvement upon program enrollment (O'Brien, 2009). Further, 76% of the participants volunteered in the Club, 90% advanced in school, and many got summer jobs.

By providing support to the G.A.N.G. summer program, instituting GANG talks in the public schools, collaborating with clergy, and offering additional resources to Boys and Girls Club caseworkers, Worcester's Shannon program reinforced and expanded several primary and secondary prevention programs that were already in place that were geared largely to the Category 3 youth described in Figure 3.1. These programs successfully steered potentially vulnerable youth toward positive recreation and adult role models and away from school failure, gang involvement, and criminal activity. They capitalized on an existing strength in Worcester—a robust youth development sector that has served thousands of youth over the past several decades.

Suppression Programs

In addition to integrating the SVPG into Shannon, the Worcester Police Department included several new suppression strategies in the Shannon Initiative that were designed to fill the gap in programming for Category 1 youth. The Final Notice Program is based on one of the prongs of the Chicago Project Safe Neighborhoods Plan—offender notification meetings. Evaluators of the Chicago Project Safe Neighborhood Plan using a quasi-experimental design found that offender notification meetings were able to stress the importance of individual deterrence and in so doing were able to decrease positive attitudes toward offending behavior and increase offenders' positive views of procedural justice. These individual-level outcomes were part of an overall 35% decline of homicides in Chicago (Papachristos, Meares, & Fagan, 2006). In Worcester, Final Notice pairs the WPD with the Worcester County Sheriff's Department, the District Attorney, and the U.S. Attorney to meet with targeted inmates prior to release. Targeted inmates include violent and repeat offenders. Prior to release, a team representing the above agencies visits the offender, educates the offender about the penalties of re-offense, future monitoring, and community resources available to them upon release. In 2010, 26 inmates were referred to GED programs, 15 to jobs programs, and there were only 5 re-arrests. This one-year recidivism rate of Final Notice participants is roughly half that of a study conducted by the Massachusetts Executive Office of Public Safety and Security in 2004 of criminally sentenced inmates released from Massachusetts corrections institutions.

Project Night Light I, a program introduced with Shannon and modeled after Boston's Operation Nightlight, a component of the larger Operation Ceasefire program (Braga & Winship, 2006; Curry & Decker, 2003; Kennedy, 1997; Kennedy, Piehl, & Braga, 1996), aims to suppress recidivism rates, impact the attitudes of probationers, and make positive strides in community-based corrections by pairing WPD officers with Probation Officers from Worcester Central District Court to complete home visits. The goal of these visits is to use probation as a tool for prevention and suppression, by executing probation violation warrants, identifying and documenting at-risk or gang involved probationers, and providing referrals for employment. In 2010, 935 home visits were made and 14 new gang members were identified. Project Night Light II is modeled after Project Night Light I but is focused on juvenile probationers. This program was introduced after the second year of Shannon and provides referrals to other Shannon programs. In 2010, 355 home visits were made to juveniles with only one probation violation and 38 referrals were made to Shannon programs.

Opportunities Provision Programs

Each of Worcester's Opportunities Provision Programs was newly developed as a result of the Shannon grant. These programs began to fill the largest gap identified in Worcester's youth development and violence reduction programs—the dearth of initiatives targeting young people of color in their early twenties, many of whom already had criminal records and were known to be associated with or involved in gangs. This new tertiary prevention programming includes, for Category 2 youth, Worcester Community Action Council's Start Our Success (SOS) started in 2006 (Shannon's first year) and Worcester Youth Center's Lifeline to Opportunity Program, which was added in the third year.

The Worcester Community Action Council (WCAC), a long-standing anti-poverty organization, developed the SOS program to provide GED support, case management, life-skills workshops, paid job opportunities, work skills training, job placement, education referrals, and mental health counseling in order to equip young adults to sustain long-term employment. WPD's Gang Unit refers the young adults (aged 17–24) to an employment program designed specifically as a form of tertiary prevention, targeting young adults whose justice and law enforcement involvement creates challenges to employment. Participants have been placed at job sites that provide second chances for at-risk youth and youth with criminal backgrounds, such as a local contractor, the housing authority, a local community development corporation, and a homeless shelter. Ninety-two percent of participants in SOS were male and 72% have been Latino or African American. Eighty-one percent of 2009 participants had prior involvement with the justice system or violence-related school suspensions, but only 16% had court involvement since starting the program (Ross, 2009). It is important to note that while the program successfully placed many young people into work and seemed to prevent recidivism, in FY10, when the grant decreased, funding for this program was cut substantially to the point that Shannon participants only received case management, but no longer received a subsidized salary. Research demonstrates that quality wages and opportunities for advancement are critical components of an employment strategy for delinquency prevention when working with young adults (Staff & Uggen, 2003).

In 2007, Worcester's Shannon Advisory Group began to recognize the need for additional, more specifically targeted Provision of Opportunities programming for Category 2 youth, and recommended the development of the Lifeline to Opportunity Program. Through data and information-sharing meetings that LARP convened during the first year, the Advisory Group learned that many young people referred by the Gang Unit could not be successful in the SOS program due to their extremely low academic skills (many young people tested below the 7th grade level). SOS was not designed to do this level of GED work with these youth. Also, many young people were found to need more support before being ready for the workplace. In 2009, the Lifeline to Opportunity program was launched and included pre-GED classes, intensive workforce readiness, and wraparound services to ensure young people's success. Lifeline also included a street outreach component. The goals of the program include reducing court involvement, maintaining positive behaviors, completing work readiness training, and maintaining employment with the long-term goal of post-secondary jobs, higher education, or GED attainment. Findings from LARP's research indicate that since starting the program, over 60 young men have participated, 86% of whom were African American, Latino, or multi-racial (Ross, 2009). Only 5% of the participants were employed at the intake, but 41% were employed at follow-up interviews conducted 6 to 9 months after intake. Similarly, while 57% of the participants had prior criminal involvement, only 15% had a new violation at follow-up.

Information-Sharing Across Programs: The Role of the Local Action Research Partner (LARP)

One of the unique aspects of the Shannon program was its inclusion of Local Action Research Partners (LARP). LARP contributes to their local Shannon program by conducting action research to "work in close partnership as part of a team to provide strategic thinking, critical analysis, and continuous feedback to improve program operations" (Van Ness, Fallon, & Lawrence, 2006). The inclusion of action research partners in other violence prevention initiatives has been credited with youth gun use reduction in Boston (Braga, 2006; Dalton 2003).

A team of researchers based at Clark University, including the authors of this chapter, were asked by the Worcester Police Department to serve as Worcester's LARP. One of the researchers had previously worked with the police department as the evaluator on Worcester's Weed and Seed initiative. Since 2006, we have played three primary roles in the Shannon Initiative. During the first two years, we primarily used qualitative approaches to interview participants and observe programs. We provided project partners with data and insights into how Worcester's Shannon programs were operating in real time. While conversations about findings were tense at times, they led to refining the target population of programs, redesigning existing programs, and decisions to add new programs—such as the Lifeline Program as discussed above.

Towards the end of the second year and up through the present, we have played a more summative role in assisting Worcester in the development of an online information management system designed to capture the impacts of the array of Shannon programs. To this end, we operationalized Worcester's Shannon Logic Model into intake and follow-up forms to establish baseline conditions, monitor program involvement, and assess outcomes. The information management system allowed us to track progress at the individual level and aggregate up to the program level. We created standard reports that partners could run on their own programs. The outcome data presented throughout the discussion of the various Shannon programs was generated by the information management system we developed.

The final role was convening the partners to discuss particular youth, to share information across programs, and to discuss project successes and challenges. This role remained consistent over the years. We helped the Worcester partners to think about how well their selected strategies matched the collective understanding of Worcester's youth violence problems. Going further than that, we were able to use Logic Models and other types of diagrams and qualitative data to demonstrate how the individual programs related to one another as part of a larger system to intervene in the problem of youth violence and gang involvement. This "systems" approach helped each partner understand their role (and those of the other partners) in a larger, collaborative effort to tackle youth violence from many different angles. An example of this arose when the Lifeline project was introduced to the initiative. A new program meant a new community partner was at the table, the Worcester Youth Center. The immediate reaction among the original set of partners was to be concerned about turf—how would the introduction of Lifeline that seemed to have similar goals and objectives potentially direct youth (and therefore resources) away from their organizations? We assisted the group in drawing out the system of organizations in a way that made explicit that the age of the young person and the types of supports needed dictated where the Gang Unit would refer youth. As this system took root, it also facilitated the partners making referrals amongst themselves when they realized the needs of a young person would be better addressed by a different partner. Creating a visual representation of the system of programs circumvented potential misunderstandings and conflict over resources as each partner came to see how the disbursement of funding across the Shannon programs and partners was facilitating a holistic effort to improve the lives of Worcester's highest risk young people.

ANALYSIS OF SHANNON'S ROLE IN FILLING GAPS IN TERTIARY PREVENTION PROGRAMMING FOR CATEGORY 2 YOUNG PEOPLE IN WORCESTER

Before discussing the extent to which the CGM was effective in strengthening Worcester's efforts to address the particular needs of the highest risk Category 2 youth, it is important to recognize how Shannon programs evolved both as new needs were identified but also changes in the funding environment. In Worcester's first year, FY07, the city received $510,000 and received the same amount in FY08. In FY09, Worcester's award increased to $850,000. This increase was due to an overall increase in the funds designated for the statewide Shannon program. Then, as the economic downturn began to hit, Worcester's award decreased substantially in FY10 to $310,000. It is also important to note that at the time Shannon funds were declining, other state (and federal) funds for violence prevention and youth jobs also were cut drastically in Massachusetts. The component of the program that was cut the most—subsidized salaries for the young men in SOS—was the type of program that could potentially play the greatest role in addressing the needs of Category 2 youth (Lopez, McGrath, Ross, Foley, & Paskach, 2009; Posick et al., 2010). While the Shannon initiative provided the WPD and youth development agencies with important tools for building on their previous successful experiences with violence reduction, the long-term sustainability of these efforts is jeopardized by insecure funding streams.

Even in this funding environment, Shannon can be associated with improvements in participant outcomes. As of March 2010, LARP had collected data on 416 Shannon program participants. Intake data revealed that only 20% had a job history, 25% were high school drop-outs, and over 50% had been arrested prior to participation in Shannon. The follow-up data revealed that since participating in a program, 40% of participants were working, 33% of drop-outs started a GED program, and only 20% had a subsequent arrest. While it is often difficult to see the impact of individual programs on community-level indicators, Worcester has seen the number of juvenile arrests steadily decrease since Shannon funding began, with 647 arrests in 2007, 470 in 2008, and 451 in 2009.

Yet, at the same time violent crimes are rising in Worcester, and 2010 was a particularly violent year with 29 shootings overall, many involving youth victims and offenders. What do these two potentially conflicting stories say about the effectiveness of Shannon? Unfortunately, there are too many other variables to be able to make any direct statements about whether Shannon made a difference in Worcester. A significant factor that must be considered is the impact of the recent economic downturn. While the general population experienced a recession, communities of color endured an economic depression (Sum, McLaughlin, Khatiwada, & Palma, 2008). The elimination of jobs and the housing foreclosure crisis is decimating poor neighborhoods. The significant declines in Shannon funding and other state funding for youth employment and violence reduction is creating an incredibly bleak environment for young people, especially those of color who are trying to get ahead.

While it is difficult to state with certainty the specific effects of Shannon, there are several important points to be made about the extent to which the CGM not only complemented existing effective efforts in Worcester, but also filled critical gaps that most affected Category 2 youth. First, CGM, with its emphasis on organizational change fit well with the efforts underway in the WPD. Chief Gemme had started a process of organizational change when he took over the department and Shannon allowed him to continue that transformation, particularly by strengthening SVPG and continuing community partnerships. Second, Shannon supported the development of tertiary prevention programming for Category 2 youth—a critical need identified in Worcester. Further, this tertiary prevention programming was aligned with best practices and focused on jobs and wrap-around support for highest risk young men (Posick, et al., 2010). Third, by funding a LARP, Shannon facilitated the development of a community-based information-sharing system focused on prevention and provision of opportunity parallel to the role that SVPG played in suppression. Funded partners could share information and make referrals among a cohesive group, reducing the likelihood that youth would fall through the cracks. This form of system development based on enhanced collaboration is notable in that it is sustainable without programmatic funds. Fourth, by being data-driven, programming was developed in gang hot spots enhancing access to vulnerable, at-risk youth. In sum, the Shannon-funded CGM was aligned with ongoing strategies, fulfilled the need for tertiary prevention programming, moved away from isolated community-based programs towards a systems approach, and focused on gang hotspots. But, given funding decreases, we question the extent to which this application of CGM can affect youth of color most likely to be at the fringes of conventional society and more involved in gangs.

WHAT IS THE FUTURE FOR WORCESTER'S "TWO CITIES?"

Although it is difficult to measure the specific impact of Shannon initiatives, the long-standing efforts of the Worcester Police force and community agencies have produced admirable results in limiting youth violence. In spite of the 2010 data which appears to indicate a rise in violent crime, Worcester ranks 156 out of 400 cities in the United States for safety, and it is doing much better than similar urban centers in Massachusetts (Harris, 2010). Worcester's approach to the funding opportunity afforded by the Shannon Initiative was to consolidate existing strengths in prevention and suppression programs, and to address the most significant weakness identified to date: provision of opportunities for youth with criminal records and past gang involvement. In this way, Shannon served as a catalyst to help advance innovative approaches that had been in progress for several years as well as fill critical gaps that had been identified through comprehensive assessments of the city's youth development sector.

The opportunities afforded by programs like Shannon raise important issues about long-term sustainability. We believe that given an existing commitment to community partnerships and the encouraging outcomes to date, the WPD and its community partners would continue to institute a "systems" approach to youth violence even in the absence of Shannon funding. Nonetheless, there are dimensions of Worcester's Shannon program that would cease to continue without support. Most notably, helping youth with criminal backgrounds establish a stable employment record is next to impossible without subsidizing the employers who are willing to provide them with a job—at least over the short term. Given the extreme shortage of tertiary programs aimed at meeting this particular need among a very vulnerable population, Shannon funding was crucial to launching this provision of opportunities program.

There were several aspects of Worcester's use of the Shannon funding that distinguish its efforts from other communities in Massachusetts. First and foremost, Shannon came in at a time when the WPD was undergoing significant organizational change and therefore was very open to targeted and collaborative efforts to address the needs of Category 2 youth. Second, WPD led this effort with a small number of community partners. While some other cities had a dozen or more local partners, in Worcester the Shannon funding facilitated closer collaboration between three communities agencies: Worcester Public Schools, churches, and the WPD. Given the long-standing ties and history of trust among all of these partners, they were amenable to close collaboration under the direction of the WPD's central leadership. In terms of program content, the early focus on jobs for largely "unemployable" youth was a unique feature of Worcester's provision of opportunities focus. Yet our findings on the impact of SOS demonstrates that this approach must be used in conjunction with other kinds of support and opportunities for youth or there will be little ability to take advantage of employment options (Lopez, et al., 2009; Posick, et al., 2010).

While most Shannon recipients collaborated with a Local Action Research Partner, Worcester's sophisticated understanding of its crime patterns allowed us to focus our energies on relationship building and program implementation rather than crime data collection and analysis. One of LARP's significant achievements was helping the partners fine-tune Shannon programs to target the most vulnerable youth who were underserved by existing programs. Those deliberate efforts to build consensus on a shared logic model and to bring a systems focus to the group's work improved collaboration and helped institute an effective referral system among the Shannon partners.

People who work with vulnerable youth, from community agencies to police departments, would like to see structural transformations that would eradicate youth violence, yet many communities are limited to piece-meal programs and interventions dictated by the priorities of law-makers and the availability of public revenues to fund programs. In the presence of long-standing community initiatives to collaborate on youth violence reduction, periodic funding offers strategic opportunities to close gaps between existing services and youth needs. By employing the CGM, the Shannon initiative allowed the city of Worcester to enhance its efforts to close the gap between "safe" Worcester and "Wartown." The CGM was not able to address education, health, and housing dispari-ties—arguably comprehensive efforts that would lead to lower levels of gangs and youth violence. The deliberate allocation of resources toward the young men living on both sides of the gun, however, has undoubtedly opened new opportunities and pathways for them.

REFERENCES

Braga, A., & Winship, C. (2006). Partnership, accountability, and innovation: Clarifying Boston's experience with pulling levers. In D. Weisburd & A. Braga (Eds.), *Police Innovation: Contrasting Perspectives*. New York: Cambridge University Press.

Braga, A. (2006). *Homicide and serious gun violence in Worcester, Massachusetts*. Unpublished report, Worcester Police Department.

Catalano, R., Berglund, M., Ryan J., Lonczak H., & Hawkins J. (2004). Positive youth development in the United States: Research findings on evaluations of positive youth development programs. *The Annals of the American Academy of Political and Social Science, 591*(1), 98–124.

Coleman-Ross Consultants. (1999). *Discovering and Creating Safe Spaces for Youth*. Unpublished report, Promise/United Way of Central Massachusetts.

Croteau, S. (2011, January 10). Police respond to gang violence: Uptick in gang violence getting fast response. *Worcester Telegram and Gazette*.

Curry, G.D., & Decker, H. (2003). *Confronting gangs: Crime and community*. Los Angeles, CA: Roxbury Publishing Company.

Dalton, E. (2003). *Lessons in Preventing Homicide*. East Lansing, MI: School of Criminal Justice, Michigan State University. Retrieved from http://www.cj.msu.edu.

Department of Early and Secondary Education (DESE) (2011). Community Profiles. Retrieved from http://profiles.doe.mass.edu.

De Rosa, C., Montgomery, S., Kipke, M., Iverson, E., Ma, J., & Unger, J. (1999). Service utilization among homeless and runaway youth in Los Angeles, California: rates and reasons. *Journal of Adolescent Health* 24(6): 449–458.

Eccles, J., & Gootman, J. (Eds.). (2002). *Community Programs to Promote Youth Development*. Washington, D.C.: National Academy Press.

Edwards, J., & Ross, L. (2007). *Agenda for youth*. Unpublished report, City of Worcester.

Elliot, D. (1994). An overview of youth violence: Congressional program. *Children and Violence, 9*, 15–20.

Ginwright, S. (2009). *Black youth rising: Activism and radical healing in urban America*. New York: Teachers College Press.

Harris, C. (2010). Officials assert city is safe despite apparent crime wave. *Worcester Magazine*. Retrieved from http://www.worcestermag.com.

Hill, K.G., Lui, C., & Hawkins, J.D. (2001). *Early precursors of gang membership: A study of Seattle youth*. Washington, D.C.: U.S. Department of Justice, Office of Justice Programs, Office of Juvenile Justice and Delinquency Prevention.

Howell, J. (2010). *Gang prevention: An overview of research and programs*. Washington, D.C.: U.S. Department of Justice, Office of Justice Programs, Office of Juvenile Justice and Delinquency Prevention.

Kennedy, D. (1997). Pulling levers: Chronic offenders, high-crime settings, and a theory of prevention. *Valparaiso University Law Review, 31*, 449–484.

Kennedy, D., Piehl, A., & Braga, A. (1996). Youth violence in Boston: Gun markets, serious youth offenders, and a use-reduction strategy. *Law and Contemporary Problems, 59*, 147–196.

Lerner, R., Taylor, C., & von Eye, A. (2002). Positive youth development: Thriving as a basis of personhood and civil society. *New Directions for Youth Development: Theory, Practice, Research, 95*, 11–33.

Lopez, M., McGrath, D., Ross, L., Foley, E., Paskach, G. (2009). Work alone is not enough: Using action research to enhance employment programs for gang-involved and high risk young men in Worcester, Massachusetts. *International Journal of Prevention Practice and Research, 1*(1) 9–20.

O'Brien, A. (2009). *Application for Grant Funds Year 4—Project Sure STEPS*. Worcester, MA.

Ross, L. (2009). *Quarter Four Local Action Research Partner Intake Findings*. Worcester, MA.

Papachristos, A., Meares, T., & Fagan, J. (2006). *Attention Felons: Evaluating Project Safe Neighborhoods in Chicago*. Institute for Social and Economic Research and Policy.

Posick, C., Wolff, R., McDevitt, J., Germain, M., & Stark, J. (2010). *Preparing At-Risk and Gang-Involved Youth for the Workforce: An Analysis of Promising Programmatic Strategies from Local and National Youth Employment Programs: A Resource Guide For The Shannon Community Safety Initiative*. Northeastern University.

Spergel, I. (1995). *The youth gang problem: A community approach*. New York: Oxford University Press.

Staff, J. & Uggen, C. (2003). The fruits of good work: Early work experiences and adolescent deviance. *Journal of Research in Crime and Delinquency, 40*(3), 263–291.

Sum, A., McLaughlin, J., Khatiwada, I. & Palma, S. (2008). *The Continued Collapse of the Nation's Teen Job Market and the Dismal Outlook for the 2008 Summer Labor Market for Teens: Does Anybody Care?* Center for Labor Market Studies, Northeastern University.

Thornberry, T.P., Krohn, M.D., Lizotte, A.J., Smith, C.A., & Tobin, K. (2003). *Gangs and delinquency in developmental perspective.* New York: Cambridge.

Van Ness, Fallon, & Lawrence, (2006). *Resource Guide: A Systematic Approach to Improving Community Safety.* Massachusetts Executive Office of Public Safety.

Worcester Police Department (2007). *Countering an Influx of Gun Violence: A Comprehensive, Collaborative & Effective Approach.*

Worcester, MA Fact Sheet, 2005–2009. American Community Survey 5-Year Estimates. *American FactFinder.* U.S. Census Bureau.

Chapter 4

Creating and Implementing a Gang Assessment Instrument

Erika Gebo & Kim Tobin

There has been resurgence in risk assessment and classification tools in criminal justice that are used to identify special populations and manage correctional populations (Simon, 2005). Gang assessment instruments (GAIs) are part of a new development of criminal justice risk assessments for special populations. Other examples include assessments for sex offenders and first-time offenders (Hollin, 2004). This chapter explores the creation and implementation of a GAI in the city of Springfield, Massachusetts that was used as a service provider tool to gauge the level of risk for gang membership on a continuum from at-risk for gang membership to hardcore gang member.

This GAI differs from a gang database wherein 'confirmed' gang members and their associates are entered for the purpose of tracking and investigation. In Springfield, those on the continuum from at-risk for gang membership to gang members themselves were eligible for provider services. The purpose of this chapter is to illuminate the theoretical problems with the creation of GAIs in general and to explore the creation and implementation of the GAI in Springfield's anti-gang initiative, the Shannon Initiative, using an organizational framework to situate the discussion. The GAI was a key component of Springfield's multi-agency approach, and more generally, discussions of how that instrument was created and used are important as there is increasing demand from government and other funders for comprehensive community initiatives. In the age of the 'new penology' (Feeley & Simon, 1992), there is likely to be

continued development of instruments, such as the GAI, to gauge criminological risks for individuals. Springfield used the GAI as a mechanism
for an internal assessment, which tied into accountability and funding for
their multi-agency initiative.

Risk assessment implementation issues are just as important as creating a valid and reliable instrument. Research has shown that a variety of
factors, such as training, local context, and commitment to the procedure
have effects on the efficacy of risk assessment instruments. For example,
Miller and Lin (2007) found that a "homegrown" juvenile risk assessment
instrument (RAI) had better predictive capabilities than a generic model
RAI because of the importance of unique, local context variables. Several
researchers also have shown that proper training on RAIs is crucial to cor-
rect utilization and validation (Orlando, 1999). Further, Gebo and associates (2006) demonstrated that commitment to implementing a RAI was
essential to accuracy in its use. Thus, there is a crucial link between instrument creation and instrument utilization before appropriate reliability
and validity assessments can be completed. Discussion of creation and
implementation simultaneously, rather than as distinct, disaggregated
phenomena creates a more realistic picture of what drives the process and
can better be understood to help inform the future of such instruments.
The story of the GAI in Springfield will do so.

A background of the study and of the city is presented first. An overview of GAIs as distinct from gang databases and general risk assessment
instruments is then presented. A review of theoretical issues that compli-
cate the development of GAIs is presented next along with an 'ideal type'
of gang risk assessment instrument. Case study methodology and findings on GAI creation and implementation in Springfield are discussed using organizational literature as a context for understanding those issues.
Finally, implications for the continued development and refinement of
these instruments are explored, based on Springfield's experiences.

STUDY BACKGROUND

Springfield is a mid-size city with approximately 150,000 residents. The
majority of the residents are non-white (59%). The city has violent crime
and poverty rates which are almost triple that of the state averages. The
city has received much negative attention at state and national levels because of its poverty, unemployment, and education problems (Forman,
Lambert, Schneider, Ansel, & Silva, 2009). The development of the gang
assessment instrument in this city occurred within the larger Shannon
Initiative aimed at reducing gang violence. The GAI was designed to
serve as a tool to evaluate youth for secondary prevention and interven-

tion services. Youth who were at-risk for gang membership or involved as fringe and associate gang members were eligible for services. Hard core youth were typically subject to suppression efforts, and were not screened in the GAI process. As discussed in Chapter 1, communities had to utilize the Comprehensive Gang Model (CGM), considered an Office of Juvenile Justice and Delinquency Prevention best practice strategy (OJJDP, 2007). Under the grant conditions, communities applying for funding also had to partner with public, non-profit, and private organizations to ensure that prevention, intervention, and suppression strategies were being offered in a comprehensive approach to the problem. There were 22 agency partners initially funded in Springfield to address gang violence, including police, government agencies (such as the sheriff's office), and social service agencies, such as the Boys & Girls' Club and community centers. The funded partner agencies reflected the diversity in the city's population, with representatives from the sizeable Latino and Black communities. In theory, the Shannon Initiative was ideological, based in a conceptual framework of best practice in the CGM. The implementation of the program in this city, however, was political wherein the mayor's office retained control over who was funded, for how much, and under what circumstances grant funding would be removed, such as for noncompliance with funding mandates (Bond & Gebo, in press).

The authors were local action research partners (LARP) for the city and provided technical and research support in the implementation of the initiative. Researchers worked closely with community partners to identify and to define the local gang problems; to develop and implement best practices in gang prevention and intervention; to overcome implementation challenges; and to document the accomplishments of community partners. The authors have been part of the research team in Springfield for four out of the five years the grant has been in existence.

GANGS, DATABASES, AND RISK ASSESSMENTS

There is little published research on gang assessment instruments. Negola (1998) developed a lengthy self-report instrument to predict potential gang membership based on a factor analysis of personal, family, educational, behavioral, substance abuse, and peer factors. Known risk factors for delinquency, such as association with negative peers and lack of family supervision, were included in the instrument. The instrument was validated with committed youth, but there appears to be no other published research on its use in the general population. The instrument does not address the level of gang involvement, which is a crucial factor in determining risk status (Braining, et al., 1999). Alternatively, most available research on gangs and risk assessment instead tends to focus on criteria for entrance into a gang database for the purposes of suppression strategies.

Gang Databases

There has been academic and legal debate over the existence and content of gang databases. A gang database can be loosely defined as one wherein 'confirmed' gang members and their associates are entered for the purpose of tracking and investigation. Some scholars believe it is only natural to have a database of gang members and disaggregate them from other types of criminals for prosecution, investigation, and tracking (Barrows & Huff, 2009). The information is already kept by law enforcement officials, though usually unsystematically and with large validity problems (Klein, 2009). Other scholars question the need for such a system and point to possible reification problems should such attention be paid to the categories of 'gang' and 'gang member' rather than the violence that is caused by individuals and groups (Kennedy, 2009). Still others question the constitutionality of the criteria used for inclusion in a gang database (Zatz & Krecker, 2003).

Spergel (2009) contemplated whether a database can be modified to include social development spectra, such that this type of database would be useful to those who provide prevention and intervention services to young people. Short (2009) believed that social criteria should be included, and that law enforcement should not have exclusive purview over gang databases and definitional issues. The GAI in this study is more similar to what Spergel and Short suggest: one that addresses the needs of service providers. Regardless of academic or professional standpoint, there is little, if any, empirical evidence on the validity and reliability of gang databases. This may be due to legal liability issues (McKay, 2009), ever-changing gang dynamics, and/or local specific gang issues that law enforcement may feel compromises their intelligence by putting information in the public domain. Clearly more research is needed.

Risk Assessments

Risk assessment instruments, in contrast to gang databases, while used in criminal justice are not as readily used for gang intervention. Spergel (2009) and Short (2009), however, contemplated their development. Risk assessments in criminal justice have been used for general parole decisions (i.e. Hoffman, 1983), prison classification (i.e. Austin, 2003), pre-trial detention (i.e. Steinhart, 2006) and jail decisions (i.e. Van Nostrand & Keebler, 2009), and to determine risk for special populations, such as sex offenders and fire-setters (see Hollin, 2004).

Bonta and Andrews (2007) provided an overview of risk assessment, classifying them into four generations. First generation assessment used professional judgment to determine risk, while second generation began to use actuarial, or objective, risk assessments, based on key risk factors from the literature. The third generation of risk assessment focused more broadly on what information was needed to better target individual interventions. Such instruments were sensitive to dynamic factors that took into account the ever changing environment and behavior of the individual, such as employment and peer relations that affect criminality, not just static factors. The fourth generation has newly begun. This generation of risk assessment focuses on comprehensively viewing risk alongside needs, interventions, and monitoring in a case management approach.

Andrews and colleagues (2006) stated that the key principles of fourth generation risk assessments were "risk-need-responsivity." They documented that criminal behavior risk can be predicted well and, thus, interventions should focus on those who are most at risk. Providing intensive services to those at low risk can have a criminogenic effect (Bonta & Andrews, 2007). Interventions then must be crafted around individual needs that are dynamic and shifting. Finally, responsivity refers to matching the right offender with the right treatment and ensuring that cognitive behavioral treatment is included. Thus, the risk assessment instrument is used to identify the risk and needs of the individual over time as the individual changes and as the intervention(s) change. The risk assessment newly employed in Springfield does not yet include a services component, though a separate instrument addresses that, and can be best characterized as a third generation risk assessment instrument.

GAI THEORETICAL ISSUES

GAIs can borrow lessons from the general risk assessment literature, but GAIs are problematic because of the theoretical issues that surround the issue of 'gangs' themselves. Those can be broken down into three areas: definitional problems, risk factor distinction, and reification issues. Some level of precision is necessary for risk assessments to work properly. The lack of definitional clarity and mixed findings with regard to what distinguishes gang members from delinquents is problematic for proper GAI creation and utilization, and will be demonstrated in the case of Springfield.

Definitional Problems

Many states have added "gang" and "gang member" definitions to their statutes (See review by NYGC, 2008), but researchers and practitioners

Table 4.1.   GAI Typology

End User	Purpose	Methodological Ordering
Law Enforcement	Gang Database	Dependent Variable
Service Provider	Predictor for Needs Assessment	Independent Variable
State Statutes/Legal Inquirer	Prosecution Classification	Dependent Variable

alike disagree on gang definitions (Esbensen, et al., 2001). This is due, in part, to the function of the definition (e.g. legal, prevention, intervention, suppression). Table 4.1 illustrates this point.

A larger portion of the disagreement, however, is due to difficulty in developing a standard gang definition because of the variation that exists between groups (Maxson, 1998). Some gangs will be more organized, while others will be loosely structured. As a gang becomes more organized the level of sophistication in criminal behavior increases, and it requires a different criminal justice system approach to the problem. Similarly, some gang members will be well-connected to the group, while others will only be marginally involved. Hard-core gang members will be more deeply immersed in the gang and associated behaviors, whereas a fringe member is less invested in the group and related behavior. These different types of gangs and gang members differentially impact behavior and require different types of social and legal responses.

Concomitant to definitional problems are the acts that are committed by those in and associated with gangs. The fundamental nature of gangs is that delinquency takes place differently than traditional peer groups. Klein (1995) described gangs as peer groups that have reached a "tipping point," when the group becomes committed to a criminal orientation and self-recognizes their group status. As a result of this tipping point and associated characteristics, "street gangs are something special, something qualitatively different from other groups and from other categories of law breakers" (p. 197). This is supported by research that finds gang members engaged in more delinquency and drug involvement than non-gang youth with highly delinquent peer groups (Thornberry, et al., 2003), suggesting that the gang, by nature of its solidified group status, will exert more influence over an individual. Even with this understanding, there is no clear consensus on measurement of gang crime. As an example, Klein and Maxson (2006) described the difference between gang motivated and gang related crimes. The more conservative gang motivated crime requires that the motivation for the crime be based within a gang. This is compared to gang-related crime, which is a crime committed by a gang member, regardless of motivation.

While developing standard definitions may be a challenge, localized assessment of a gang problem is more easily navigated. This assessment is also imperative, as any effective response to gangs should be based on an understanding of the local problem (Fearn, Decker, & Curry, 2001). Gang assessment instruments may then reflect the nuances of definitional variation and behavioral differentiation, allowing for measurement of varying types of gangs and gang members within a localized environment.

Risk Factors and Reification

Research examining risk factors that distinguish non-gang members from gang members are inconsistent across studies (Howell & Egley, 2005); and researchers have not been able to rank the importance of any one risk factor for gang membership (Wyrick & Howell, 2004). Risk factors fall into the domains of community, school, peer, family, and individual (Wasserman, et al., 2003). Esbensen (2000) provided a solid and detailed discussion of common risk factors for gang membership, but noted that there is a wide variety of risk factors that may lead an individual to join a gang. Corroborating that sentiment, others have found that risk factors are age-graded, decreasing or becoming more important depending on the youth's age (Hill, et al., 1999). It appears that the only consistent finding is that multiple risk factors across multiple domains heighten the risk of gang membership (Hill, et al., 1999; Wyrick & Howell, 2004). Precision is needed for valid and reliable GAIs, but there is little direction from the practitioner or academic literature on how communities can create objective instruments.

Another criminological concern is the possibility of reification of youth violence. Sullivan (2005) used official data in New York City to illustrate the discrepancy between the sharp increase in youth gangs in the 1990s and the simultaneous decline in youth violence during the same period. He made a persuasive argument that youthful offending, which most often occurs in a group, can easily be relabeled as gang behavior, thus diverting attention from youth themselves to the nebulous category of gangs. This creates a moral panic about gangs, rather than a focus on the conditions and the issues that prompt youth violence. He pointed out that the obsession with gang violence obscured the real issue of youth violence in New York City. Kennedy (2009) in his response to the creation of gang databases echoed this point, stating that the focus should be on the violence, not the relatively subjective categories in which individuals and groups are placed.

Reification issues are important to keep in mind, yet distinguishing at-risk for gang membership and gang youth from other youth is useful, given that research shows that gang youth consistently report more delinquent activity than other delinquent youth (Esbensen, Huzinga, & Weiher, 1993; LeBlanc & Lanctôt, 1998; Thornberry, et al., 2003). If communities can identify the youth most at risk for gang membership or those who are gang involved, then they can target limited resources. Springfield attempted to do so. Given the above discussion, however, that was easier said than done.

GAI Ideal Type

Communities, who are interested in efficiently using limited resources and complying with funding mandates about specific populations to be served, have a series of challenges in creating a GAI. Notwithstanding the discussed problems, research does provide some guidance. Heuristically, it is useful to think of GAIs in terms of an "Ideal Type," where there are typical elements that all GAIs will have in common, but none will be perfectly aligned in reality. Gang definition and risk factors for gang membership should guide the process of GAI creation, though the problems with each of those have been discussed above. A youth who admits to gang membership, but who may not yet be a gang member, should automatically qualify for services, as one of the most robust findings in the literature on gangs is the ability of self-admission of gang membership to predict offending (i.e. Esbensen, et al., 2001).

Other elements that should be incorporated in GAIs include a continually updated assessment of the local gang culture, though who decides such things is another issue entirely as discussed below. City-specific gang idiosyncrasies should be assessed. For example, the wearing of certain sports team apparel or, in the case of Springfield, the association with local music labels, is associated with gang membership. In addition, gauging the level of gang involvement will provide information about entrenchment in gang life in order to better score risk status (Parker & Charleston, n.d.). Finally, a scoring scheme that accounts for the current level of violent activity in each gang in the city will help connect the group context of gang behavior to the individual (Miller, 1990).

A GAI that meets the needs of all members of a comprehensive community initiative, like the Shannon Initiative, would be ideal, such as the one theorized by Short (2009), but there are professional orientation problems with that. Law enforcement and state statutes typically view a GAI as a dependent variable that determines gang status or the purposes of entrance into a gang database and monitoring, such as the ones reviewed by Barrows & Huff (2009). Alternatively, service providers view a GAI as an independent variable, wherein gang status is considered along with other things, like mental health status and school/employment status, as a predictor of individual needs. Given the varying use of the GAI, there are inherent difficulties in creating a collaborative instrument, as previously illustrated in Table 4.1.

The question of whether law enforcement and service providers can truly collaborate to create a useable GAI that meets the needs of all partners and is methodologically sound, remains to be seen. Compatibility is possible, if the instrument is designed in such a way to meet the needs of service providers that use the instrument as a calculation in a larger assessment context and to meet the needs of law enforcement that use the instrument as an outcome for gang database entrance. The key is to distinguish individuals based on gang risk. For example, those who do not score as core gang members are not entered into the police database, but are used by service providers for a larger assessment piece, allowing youth at the highest risk or those already gang involved, but not core members, to be linked with needed services. Such a pairing is not a new idea. The identification of youth for services based on some sort of gang-involvement, but not shared with law enforcement, has been used in previous comprehensive community initiatives (Decker & Curry, 2002).

The larger risk assessment literature also should weigh in the creation and implementation of a GAI. Up to 10% of the total score may be discretionary points (Steinhart, 2006), as these are essential to make individualized assessments, but subjectivity should be limited (Gambrill & Shlonsky, 2001). Dedicated training on any risk assessment instrument is needed for proper utilization (Andrews, et al., 2006; Orlando, 1999). Trainings should address how to use the instrument and why the instrument is important to individual agencies (i.e. tracking, data-driven decisions, funding). Trainings also will assist with agency and individual buy-in to better insure fidelity in implementation (Andrew, 2006). As will be discussed below, Springfield incorporated many elements of an ideal type into their GAI, but law enforcement was never brought into the fold of utilizing the instrument, in part because their goal is suppression.

AN ORGANIZATIONAL PERSPECTIVE

Organizational literature helps to understand what organizational issues stand in the way of successful creation and implementation of multi-agency work products, such as a GAI. Further, this literature gives insight into how such joint projects may be beneficial or detrimental to such partnerships as a whole. While there are no definitive factors that always precede effective partnerships (Zackos & Edwards, 2006), four criteria stand out: shared vision of the problem, commitment to the process and the project, trust, and leadership (Googins & Rochlin, 2000; Senge, 2006; Zackos & Edwards, 2006). These same elements are necessary in any organizational enterprise.

Partnerships and organizations are most successful when they have a shared vision of the problem they seek to ameliorate (Senge, 2006). Research has found that a shared vision is difficult when there is diversity in the types of agencies represented in a partnership and when there is a lot of ethnic diversity (Gray, et al., 1997). Commitment refers to the level of investment partners have in the project (Gazely, 2010). Trust is essential to getting work done in partnership, but is often based on prior working relationships. Unfortunately, past problems may be difficult to overcome (Gazley, 2010). Finally, leadership involves taking charge of the direction of the partnership and its work products, being present to learn alongside others, and ensuring that accountability is part of the overall process (Senge, 2006). The work of the Springfield partnership is examined relative to these key elements. Often, risk assessments are examined solely based on their predictive capability without a thorough examination of the complexities of multi-agency partnerships in which they will be used. A comprehensive examination of the context of such partnerships relative to the use of the instrument is important if partnerships are to have useful work products and lasting outcomes.

METHODOLOGY

Case study methodology was utilized to examine the creation and implementation of the GAI, which cannot be divorced from the larger community crime reduction initiative in which it was produced. Case study methods are essential to best understand very complex, multi-agency, multidimensional phenomena (Rosenbaum, 1999), such as the creation and implementation of the GAI in Springfield. Case studies allow for the triangulation of data, or finding the convergence from multiple sources to better understand the how and the why of phenomena (Yin, 2003). Data sources for the case study included document review (n=28), observation at partner meetings (n=31), youth focus groups (n=3), formal interviews with project partners and stakeholders (n=37), and informal discussions with people connected to the project and community stakeholders. Data were collected over a four year period from the first discussions of the possibility of a GAI through one and half years post instrument implementation. Researchers used mixed method analysis to examine GAI creation and implementation. Basic descriptive measures from interviews and themes gathered from observation, and document analyses form the core of the evidence.

GAI Origins

During the first year of the Springfield Shannon partnership, there was discussion around which youth should be receiving services. At the beginning of the second year of funding, and the involvement of LARP, there was consensus among the community partners that there was a need to ensure appropriate youth were receiving the services. Time and again, the discussion arose informally of the distinction between youth that had high needs, such as mental health, family and school problems versus youth who were most at-risk for gang membership. The Shannon grant was meant to specifically target the latter population as well as those who were already gang-involved. Further, partners wanted to be able to track what they were doing as well as the successes of individual youth. Both of these issues were seen as central to what the partnership wanted to achieve and, more pragmatically, important for continued funding.

A law enforcement representative brought up the idea of a referral form that would help accomplish the goals of identifying appropriate youth (those at-risk for gang membership and gang involved) and track individuals and services provided to them. Observation at monthly meetings (n=5) and informal discussions with project partners revealed that there was unanimous agreement to create such a form as well as to create standard definitions of what is meant by "gang" and "gang membership." There was initial apprehension to this suggestion by a service provider's over concern that the information would be used by law enforcement to target referred youth. A central repository for such forms was to be kept by the coordinator of the initiative, but a formal written statement prevented law enforcement from accessing the database for any police purposes. After more informal reassurance from law enforcement that they would not have access to GAIs, a subgroup was formed to work on these pieces and report back to the larger group. All partners were invited to be part of that subgroup.

Unfortunately, subgroup meetings held to create the referral form were not well-attended by project partners who verbally professed their interest and commitment to be part of that group. There were only two people who attended the two subgroup meetings: the coordinator for the initiative and the member of law enforcement who first suggested the idea. This demonstrated a lack of commitment by the partners to the creation of that referral form, in which a GAI would be embedded. The researchers offered assistance to the subgroup and provided examples of risk/needs assessment instruments, but were not called upon to help in the first rendition.

Initial GAI

The two individuals who worked on creating the GAI and gang definitions examined research on factors influencing gang membership and gathered other available gang definitions to help them. They gathered the information from instruments provided by the research partners, web searches, and from discussion with various other law enforcement agencies at a national conference. Further, they used local information from a gang analysis report written by a LARP team member early on in their second year of funding to assist in the process (Tobin, 2008). One of the creators stated that he wanted to make sure they paid attention to what is known about gangs more broadly to connect that with what they knew about gangs in their own neighborhoods. The individuals drafted a GAI as well as gang definitions to bring back to the larger group for discussions and revisions. The initial GAI included general gang risk factors from the domains of youth, peer, family, and school, such as low attachment to prosocial peers and to school, and lack of supervision at home. The community domain that would assess risk of gang membership based on residence, however, was purposefully left out. The rationale was that youth from all communities in Springfield were at high risk of gang membership.

Following the subgroup meetings, the initial GAI and gang definitions were presented to all project partners at a monthly partner meeting. The meeting was acrimonious, with many service provider partners criticizing elements of the GAI and gang definitions. Some charged the creators with targeting specific youth; some questioned the purpose of the GAI, believing that it would not meet with the original intention of identifying and tracking appropriate youth. Several partners from non-white areas of the city brought up the fact that some communities were more at-risk than others, and that should be part of the assessment.

GAI Revision I

There was verbal acknowledgement during that meeting that the GAI referral tool was a cornerstone of their work and that it would help them hone in on their shared vision of ensuring appropriate youth were being served and to document their work. Subsequently, there was commitment by partnering agencies to be involved in the process. *All* partnering agencies sent representatives to subcommittee meetings to revise the GAI and to create gang definitions. The result of the subcommittee meeting soon after this event was a consensus around gang definitional issues—a feat unto itself, as many collaborations struggle to find common ground on this issue, and the Springfield partners pulled together to do so. The GAI was revised to reflect the diverse partner input. The desire to create a functional instrument based on shared definitions to meet the needs of the multi-agency partnership overrode longstanding mistrust among the partners in this particular instance.

The revised GAI was an amalgamation of both a risk and needs assessment, but one that paid little attention to research on gangs or to risk assessments. The community domain was added as a risk factor, as were questions about youth's anger issues, role models, and desire for money and status. This revised GAI was then implemented within four months of the initial version of the GAI. All funded social service partners were to use this form to track youth and to refer youth to other services. Police were noticeably left out. The subgroup that created the initial version, a police officer and the Shannon Initiative coordinator, stated that it was a social service tool, not meant to be used in police suppression. To date, there has been no further discussion at partner meetings or in interviews with project partners about the fact the GAI is only for service providers, though it could be used on a continuum for all partners, including police.

GAI Implementation

As agreed upon by all partners, service provider partners were required to submit GAI forms to the grant coordinator on a monthly basis. As part of a process evaluation, the LARP examined completed GAI forms and obtained formal interview feedback from partners one year after Revision I was implemented. There were 17 partners involved in the initiative at that time. Only 56% (n=10) of partners responded to a telephone survey, though at least three attempts were made to contact agency representatives via phone and/or email, and announcements were made in monthly partner meetings for two consecutive months. The partners who did respond tended to be those who were timely with their GAI form submissions. This is considered a low response rate (Fowler, 2009), and can in part be attributed to a lack of understanding of how such feedback can better assist the partnership as a whole. The responses are used here for illustrative purposes about the organizational issues in the partnership and not to make policy recommendations.

Results showed that slightly less than 75% (n=12) of all 17 partners used the form, even after announcements were sent out that the GAI was tied to funding. Those partners who did not use the GAI were not supposed to receive their money, based on entire partnership agreement. The appointed leader for the Shannon Initiative was the project coordinator who was supposed to report non-compliance to the mayor's office. This did not always happen, and no agency lost its funding as a result of non-GAI use, though some discussions occurred with agency executive directors and the project coordinator.

Survey results further showed that partners were less concerned over targeting individuals in the revised GAI than there was in the initial version. All interviewed partners still believed that the GAI would be helpful in their work, but there were many complaints about its current iteration. Three major complaints stood out, with the first two being contradictory. Some partners (n=5) felt that the form was too subjective, such that agency staff could fill out the form so that just about any person could qualify. In contrast, others (n=4), felt that the criteria were too strict, such that many youth who should qualify would not. Finally, some (n=6) felt that the form was too long, taking too much time away from other more important work.

The GAI was heralded as a tool to increase group cohesion and to promote the shared vision of the partnership. In reality, those sitting at the partner table were not necessarily the carriers of power in their organizations, and their views about what was important or not did not necessarily correspond to views of their agencies, which is essential to project success (Gray, et al., 1997). Lack of GAI use illustrates the concept of street level bureaucracy. Service provider staffs charged with completing GAIs for youth were not necessarily the same people at the partner table and used their own discretion in terms of utilization. This is not uncommon in loosely-coupled social service agencies where individualized decision-making is part of the work process (Lipsky, 1980). A strong commitment to the project would have meant that there would be GAI form oversight at each partnering organization, and there was not.

GAI Revision II

There was monthly meeting discussion about revising the GAI again with knowledge from the gang literature, and as a result of partner feedback discussed above. The LARP assisted in that process. As noted, there are no GAI models in the public domain and theoretical issues with gangs compound the task. Local context issues exacerbate the creation of an instrument that can accurately gauge level of gang membership as illustrated in focus group analyses.

The LARP conducted focus groups during the third year of the initiative with youth who were sentenced to a community court program. Their comments about gangs in the city illuminate the local context as well as the problems with GAIs in general. Youth discussed thinking about where they were going and who they were going with so as not to get jumped on a daily basis. One youth said, *"You need to be associated with a gang to back you up & need to put it on MySpace."* Gangs then were part of their security. This point was repeated by another youth who distinguished between gangs and crews. *"Gangs commit violence. Crews don't really, but you still claim a gang, even if you [are] just tight with your crew."* Participants also stated that beyond survival reasons, gangs gave them the opportunity *"to be known"* throughout the community while offering *"safety, respect, and support."* This is consistent with other research on gangs (i.e. Curry & Decker, 2003). These comments demonstrate the difficulty in deciphering gang membership at the local level where membership may be somewhat decoupled from risk.

Even with these problems, a GAI Revision II was created and has been in use for approximately nine months. The LARP will be conducting a reliability and validity assessment on that revised instrument with partnership consent. Elements of each version of the GAI are comparable against the previously discussed Ideal Type. Results of that comparison are shown in Table 4.2. There are two distinct differences. First, in the first revision of the GAI, service providers put in a host of needs assessment factors. In the current version (GAI Revision II), a separate needs assessment form was created to address those concerns, apart from the gang risk issues. Second, community risk factors were put in to Revision I, but removed in Revision II. While the LARP felt these were important, as did many of the service providers, the police officer who initially helped develop the form made an argument for its exclusion which was agreed upon by the partners. This issue will be interesting to examine in the context of a reliability and validity assessment as place matters in terms of gang risk (Tita, Cohen, & Engberg, 2005).

Table 4.2.   Ideal Type Comparison

Ideal Type Criteria	Initial GAI (Police & Coordinator Creation)	GAI Revision I (Partner Collaboration)	GAI Revision II (Action Researcher Assistance)
Self-Admission Automatic Qualifier			X
Individual Risk Factors	X	X	X
Family Risk Factors	X	X	X
Peer Risk Factors	X	X	X
School/Employment Risk Factors	X	X	X
Community Risk Factors		X	
Needs Assessment Factors		X	
Level of Current Gang Activity			X
Localized Risk Factors			X
Level of Membership			X

Multi-Agency Organizational Challenges

Overall, longitudinal action research analysis from observations, surveys, and documents show that a shared vision of what the GAI was (and continues to be) a key rallying point for the partnership. The commitment to GAI utilization vacillated over time. Trust was a major stumbling block for this partnership in terms of GAI creation and implementation and in terms of the overall functioning of the Shannon Initiative. Partner meeting observations and formal and informal interviews with project partners demonstrated the lack of trust. For example, police would ask for information from service providers, but not receive it; and police would not pass information on to service providers who would hear about police involvement in gang problems from local news sources.

Trust issues are not exclusive to Springfield. Issues of trust are common in ethnically diverse, multi-agency initiatives that seek to ameliorate social problems, especially in those that historically have had racial tensions (Gray, et al., 1997). The lack of trust around the creation of the GAI was illustrative of the larger lack of trust project partners had for each other in the initiative and in the city. Resources were always scarce and rationale for fund allocation was not always transparent. For example, one theme that continually arose in informal discussions as well as interviews with project partners was the city's mismanagement of prior grant funds that were to be targeted for the most impoverished, non-white neighborhoods. Both white and non-white partners mentioned that the city often received grant funding based on the data from these neighborhoods, but when funds arrived, they were diverted away from those neighborhoods that most needed them and put toward other projects that were only tangentially connected to those areas. As one non-white service provider partner put it, "*You can say or do all you want, but in the end it is still the good old white boy network.*"

Leadership and accountability in ensuring partners were engaging in the process also was somewhat missing from the GAI implementation piece. Problems with leadership were reflected in the lack of agency accountability for grant work. Though certain paperwork and actions were required for funding and continued funding, including use and submission of GAI forms, agencies historically did not have to produce or to document. These themes are illustrated at one partner meeting in May of 2009. The initiative coordinator told the partners that there needed to be representation from all funded agencies at initiative-sponsored events. Several partners spoke out about the need for such events to be located in the most distressed neighborhoods, which contained the most non-white residents. A discussion ensued about how community engagement met the goals of the grant and how to manage their time with the small amount of funding. The discussion was chaotic with many people talking at once. Two non-white partners, representatives of a service provider and a government agency, got up from the table and went outside to talk. Within a few minutes *all* non-white partners (n=7) were outside and only the white partners (n=4), the coordinator (white), and the researcher (white), remained at the table. One white partner stated, "*See, this is always how it is. The only people who actually do any work are those of us sitting around the table!*"

The coordinator did not attempt to reconvene the meeting, but partners did come back to the table the next month. Almost all agencies were represented in initiative-sponsored events almost all the time after that incident, though the incident was never further discussed in any partner meetings. The GAI has followed a similar path with challenges along the way. There was shared vision of the instrument, and after a rocky start, partners worked through some of their trust issues by committing to create a collaborative instrument. Some balked at first, but then there was total participation, and as of 2011, there has been some accountability in delayed or denied funding for non-submission of grant quarterly reports, though none yet for GAI non-submission. The creation of GAI was, and continues to be, a centerpiece of their partnership work in the comprehensive community initiative. They have documented that in their reports to the funder and discussions at statewide meetings.

Table 4.3 presents a summary of organizational elements that influenced the creation and implementation of the GAI. A shared vision of what a GAI could do for the partnership has been the most successful element, while trust issues have been the weakest. Commitment and leadership have vacillated over the course of the partnership. Trust has been a major barrier in the partnership, in part, based on historical city issues, but over time trust has improved as partners work together toward common goals. Leadership has been somewhat present throughout GAI creation, but has increased as partners are being held more accountable for their GAI use, and other initiative responsibilities.

Table 4.3.   Evaluation of GAI Creation and Implementation on Organizational Criteria

	Initial GAI	*GAI Revision I*	*GAI Revision II*
Shared Vision	2	2	2
Commitment	0	2	1
Trust	0	1	1
Leadership	1	1	2

0 = Lack of Presence, 1 = Somewhat Present, 2 = Clear Presence

MOVING FORWARD

There are many potential benefits to a GAI in a multi-agency collaborative. A validated GAI should identify appropriate youth for intervention, including those at the fringes and those in the core of gang membership. All agencies will not be able to do all things for all types of gang members; therefore, a GAI allows a community collaborative to direct gang-involved and youth at risk for gang involvement to the most appropriate services dependent on level of gang involvement. The instrument also ensures that proper youth are being targeted, thereby reducing any real or unfounded discrimination. Further, the instrument when analyzed in aggregate should be useful to make community-level decisions about prevention, intervention, and suppression, including the identification of aggregate classes of youth who need services, and areas where suppression tactics are needed. Finally, the tool should increase the organizational capacity to coordinate and to track work done toward the goals of the initiative, if used effectively. Such information would be useful to sustain funding efforts and to leverage other resources.

The question of whether there is a need for a gang risk assessment instrument as distinguished from a general risk assessment instrument, however, remains to be seen. If the main outcome of interest is offending and needs, then a general risk assessment may do. Fourth generation risk assessment instruments have good predictive capabilities and combine both risk and needs for better case management. Service providers and researchers are better off using instruments that have already been validated, leaving aside the gang label. This may obfuscate the point about the group context of gang behavior, though. If behavior is 'amped up' because of the group context, then that is an important feature of criminological behavior that should not be ignored and one that can be assessed through a GAI.

Initiatives that seek to alter gang membership and gang behavior, like Shannon, may need a GAI. An outstanding problem is that there are likely to be low base rates of gang involvement in any community. Prior research shows that approximately 25% of youth in any given high-risk neighborhood actually become gang members (Howell, 2000). Instruments are difficult to validate, particularly in terms of predictive criterion, when base rates are low (Andrews, et al., 2006). Yet, research also shows that if those highest risk offenders (i.e. most gang-involved) can be identified, these individuals benefit the most from services (Cottle, et al., 2001).

Comments like those from the youth focus groups illustrate the complexity of the gang problem in Springfield and the importance of gangs in the lives of these young people. Reification may only be a problem if the focus is on the category of gang, rather than assistance to the individual him or herself. The GAI in this study developed for the multi-agency purpose of identifying and delivering comprehensive services to the most at-risk youth for gang involvement and gang involved youth may be a useful vehicle to target the appropriate population and may not, as Sullivan (2005) fears, overshadow the issues of youth violence. Nor may it be seen as discriminatory toward youth of color, as some may argue (Zatz & Krecker, 2003), as it has been created as a social service tool by representatives from communities of color to help youth of color access needed and scarce services. The new penology focus on risk assessment and classification underscores the need to take the issue of GAI development seriously and to explore what a successful GAI may look like.

The practical reality is that there will continue to be grant funding that targets specific subpopulations, like gangs, and funders will require grantees to document that they are targeting the 'right' (i.e. at-risk for gang membership/gang member) population using empirically supported tools and strategies. Thus, GAIs are useful administratively. Further, GAIs may help refine the theoretical conundrums with gangs; how and if they are distinguished from other groups. In other words, GAIs can help test the hypothesis that gang members are different from delinquents and thus need specialized or more tailored services.

The GAI was a rallying point for the Shannon Initiative in this study, so while the jury is still out on the need for a gang assessment instrument, from an organizational perspective this tool has been beneficial to the Springfield partnership. The organizational problems with the GAI discussed above are interconnected to the problems in the partnership itself. The GAI is a focal point of the partnership that, if successful, can infuse the partnership to continue their growth and sustainability by focusing energies on specific youth and tracking individual youth and partnership progress.

The partnership has tackled the tough issues surrounding gang work. The inherent problems with gang definition and identification have compounded the organizational issues in partnership, but the benefits outweigh the costs. Forging ahead with the development and refinement of GAIs is important, as only then will what is possible be uncovered. Further, it may be that through application, theoretical problems that have been identified with GAIs may be able to be sorted out. As classification and assessment continues to become the norm in criminological practice, it is important to document the creation and implementation as well as assess the accuracy and reliability of such instruments as they evolve.

REFERENCES

Andrew, D. (2006) Enhancing adherence to risk-need responsivity: Making quality a matter of policy. *Criminology & Public Policy, 5*, 595–602.

Andrews, D., Bonta, J., & Wormith, J. S. (2006). The recent past and near future of risk and/or need assessment. *Crime & Delinquency, 52*, 7–27.

Argyris, C., & Schon, D. (1995). *Organizational learning II: Theory, method and* practice. 2nd Ed. Englewood Cliffs, NJ: Prentice Hall.

Austin, J. (2003). *Findings in prison classification risk assessment.* Washington, D.C.: US Department of Justice, Federal Bureau of Prisons.

Barrows, J. & Huff, C.R. (2009). Gangs and public policy: Constructing and deconstructing gang databases. *Criminology & Public Policy, 8,* 675–704.

Bond, B.J, & Gebo, E. (In Press). Comparing implementation policies of a best practices crime policy across cities. *Administration and Society.*

Bonta, J., & Andrews, D.A. (2007). *Risk-need-responsivity model for offender assessment and rehabilitation.* Toronto, ON: Public Safety Canada.

Braining, K., Thornberry, T., & Porter, P. (1999). *Highlights of findings from the Rochester Youth Development Study.* Washington, D.C.: Office of Juvenile Justice and Delinquency Prevention.

Cottle, C., Lee, R., & Heilbrun, K. (2001). The prediction of criminal recidivism in juveniles. *Criminal Justice and Behavior, 28,* 367–394.

Curry, G.D., & Decker, S.H. (2003). *Confronting gangs: Crime and community.* Los Angeles: Roxbury.

Decker, S.H., & Curry, G.D. (2002). "I'm down for my organization:" The rationality of responses to delinquency, youth crime, and gangs. In A. Piquero & S. Tibbets (Eds.), *Rational Choice & Criminal Behavior* (pp. 197–218). New York: Routledge.

Esbensen, F.A. (2000). *Preventing adolescent gang involvement.* Washington, D.C.: Office of Juvenile Justice and Delinquency Prevention.

Esbensen, F.A., Huizinga, D., & Weiher, A.W. (1993). Gang and non-gang youth: Differences in explanatory factors. *Journal of Contemporary Criminal Justice, 9,* 94–116.

Esbensen, F.A., Winfree Jr., T.L., He, N., & Taylor, T.J. (2001). Youth gangs and definitional issues: When is a gang a gang, and why does it matter? *Crime & Delinquency, 47,* 105–130.

Feeley, M.M., & Simon, J. (1992). The new penology: Notes on the emerging strategy of corrections and its implications. *Criminology, 30,* 449–474.

Fearn, N.E., Decker, S.H., & Curry, G.D. (2001). Public policy responses to gangs: Evaluating the outcomes. In J. Miller, C.L. Maxson, & M.W. Klein, (Eds.), *The Modern Gang Reader* (pp. 330–343). Los Angeles, CA: Roxbury.

Forman, B., Lambert, E., Schneider, J., Ansel, D., & Silva, J. (2009) *Building for a Future: Foundations for a Springfield Comprehensive Growth Strategy.* Retrieved from http://www.massinc.org.

Fowler, F.J., Jr. (2009). *Survey research methods.* 4th Ed. Thousand Oaks, CA: Sage.

Gambrill, E., & Shlonsky, A. (2001). The need for comprehensive risk management programs in child protective services. *Children and Youth Services Review, 23,* 79–107.

Gazely, B. (2010). Linking collaborative capacity to performance measurement in government-nonprofit partnerships. *Nonprofit and Voluntary Sector Quarterly, 39,* 653–673.

Gebo, E., Stracuzzi, N.F., & Hurst, V. (2006). Juvenile justice reform and the courtroom workgroup: Issues of perception and workload. *Journal of Criminal Justice, 34,* 425–433.

Googins, B., & Rochlin, S. (2000). Creating the partnership society: Understanding the rhetoric and reality of cross sectoral partnerships. *Business and Society Review, 105,* 127–144.

Gray, B., Duran, A., & Segal, A. (1997). *Revisiting the critical elements of comprehensive community initiatives.* Retrieved from http://aspe.hhs.gov/hsp/cci.htm.

Hill, K.G., Howell, J.C., Hawkins, J.D., & Battin-Pearson, S.R. (1999). Childhood risk factors for adolescent gang membership: Results from the Seattle Social Development Project. *Journal of Research in Crime and Delinquency, 36,* 300–322.

Hoffman, P.B. (1983). Screening for risk: A revised salient factor score (SFS 81). *Journal of Criminal Justice, 11,* 539–547.

Hollin, C.R. (2004). *The essential handbook of offender assessment and treatment.* Sussex: Wiley.

Howell, J.C. (2000). *Youth gang programs and strategies.* Washington, D.C.: National Youth Gang Center.

Howell, J.C., & Egley, A. (2005). Moving risk factors into developmental theories of gang membership. *Youth Violence and Juvenile Justice, 3,* 334–354.

Kennedy, D.M. (2009). Comment on "Gangs and public policy: Constructing and deconstructing gang databases." *Criminology & Public Policy, 8,* 711–716.

Klein, M.W. (2009). Street gang databases: A view from the gang capitol of the United States. *Criminology & Public Policy, 8,* 717–722.

Klein, M.W. (1995). *The American street gang.* New York: Oxford.

Klein, M.W., & Maxson, C.L. (2006). *Street gang patterns and policies.* New York: Oxford.

Le Blanc, M., & Lanctôt, N. (1998). Social and psychological characteristics of gang members according to the gang structure and its subcultural and ethnic make-up. *Journal of Gang Research, 5,* 15–28.

Lipsky, M. (1980). *Street-level bureaucracy: Dilemmas of the individual in public service.* New York, NY: Russell Sage Foundation.

Maxson, C.L. (1998). *Gang membership on the move.* Washington, D.C.: Office of Juvenile Justice and Delinquency Prevention.

McKay, J. (2009). *Law enforcement database tracks gang members statewide.* Retrieved from http://www.govtech.com.

Miller, J., & Lin, J. (2007). Applying a generic juvenile risk assessment instrument to a local context: Some practical and theoretical lessons. *Crime & Delinquency, 53,* 552–580.

Miller, W.B. (1990). Why the United States has failed to resolve its youth gang problem. In C.R. Huff, (Ed.), *Gangs in America,* (pp. 263–287). Thousand Oaks, CA: Sage.

National Youth Gang Center. (2008). *Best practices to address community gang problems: OJJDP's Comprehensive Gang Model.* Washington, D.C.: OJJDP.

Negola, T.D. (1998). Development of an instrument for predicting at-risk potential for adolescent street gang membership. *Journal of Gang Research, 5,* 1–14.

Office of Juvenile Justice and Delinquency Prevention. (2007). *Best Practices to Reduce Community Gang Problems: OJJDP's Comprehensive Gang Model.* Washington, D.C.

Orlando, F. (1999). Controlling the front gates: Effective admissions policies and practices. *Pathways to Juvenile Detention Reform.* 3. Baltimore, MD: Annie E. Casey Foundation.

Parker, D. M., & Charleston, D. (n.d.). *Understanding gangs: Beyond basic Identification.* Retrieved from http://www.ncjji.org.

Rosenbaum, D.P. (1999). Evaluating multi-agency anti-crime partnerships: Theory, design, and measurement issues. *Crime Prevention Studies, 14,* 171–225.

Senge, P.M. (2006). *The fifth discipline: The art and practice of the learning organization.* New York: Doubleday.

Short, J.F., Jr. (2009). Gangs, law enforcement, and the academy. *Criminology & Public Policy, 8,* 723–731.

Simon, J. (2005). Reversal of fortune: The resurgence of individual risk assessment in criminal justice. *Annual Review of Law and Social Science, 1,* 397–421.

Spergel, I. (2009). Gang databases: To be or not to be. *Criminology & Public Policy, 8,* 667–674.

Steinhart, D. (2006). *Juvenile detention risk assessment: A practical guide to juvenile detention reform.* Baltimore: Annie E. Casey Foundation.

Sullivan, M.L. (2005). Maybe we shouldn't study '"gangs": Does reification obscure youth violence? *Journal of Contemporary Criminal Justice, 21,* 170–190.

Tita, G.E., Cohen, J., & Engberg, J. (2005). An ecological study of the location of gang "set space." *Social Problems, 52,* 272–299.

Thornberry, T.P., Krohn, M.D., Lizotte, A.J., Smith, C.A., & Tobin, K. (2003). *Gangs and delinquency in developmental perspective.* New York: Cambridge.

Tobin, K. (2008). *Springfield Gangs: Shannon LARP Report.* Westfield, MA: Westfield State College.

VanNostrand, M., & Keebler, G. (2009). Pretrial risk assessment in the federal courts. *Federal Probation, 73,* 3–29.

Wasserman, G.A., Keenan, K., Tremblay, R.E., Coie, J.D., Herrenkohl, T.I., Loeber, R., et al. (2003). *Risk and protective factors of child delinquency.* Washington, D.C.: Office of Juvenile Justice and Delinquency Prevention.

Wyrick, P., & Howell, J. (2004). Strategic risk-based responses to youth gangs. *Juvenile Justice Journal, 9,* 20–29.

Yin, R.K. (2003). *Case study research: Design and methods.* 3rd Ed. Thousand Oaks, CA: Sage.

Zackos, R., & Edwards, E. (2006). What explains community coalition effectiveness: A review of the literature. *American Journal of Preventative Medicine, 30,* 351–361.

Zatz, M.S., & Krecker, R.P., Jr. (2003). *Anti-gang initiatives as racialized policy.* In D.F. Hawkins, S.L. Myers, Jr., & R.N. Stone, (Eds.), *Crime Control and Social Justice,* (pp. 173–196). Westport, CT: Greenwood Press.

Chapter 5

Street Outreach as an Intervention Modality for At-Risk and Gang-Involved Youth

SEAN P. VARANO & RUSSELL WOLFF

Street outreach is a direct service delivery model that is generally used to build connections to and relationships with at-risk populations. These strategies have been used for generations to work with at-risk youth, HIV/AIDS populations, and the homeless. Outreach worker programs have been identified as a key component of gang intervention strategies by the Office of Juvenile Justice and Delinquency Prevention's (OJJDP's) Comprehensive Gang Model (OJJDP, 2009). These programs are best used to connect with at-risk populations in their own environment and generally outside of the context of formal programs. Whether a stand-alone program or one coupled with more comprehensive prevention/intervention services, outreach programs represent mechanisms for providing prosocial role models and ensuring young people stay "connected" to other programmatic strategies. They seek to engage youth in a different environment, to learn more about clients, connect clients to services, to keep clients engaged in services, and to disrupt cycles of violence and retaliation when they occur.

Outreach strategies were used in large urban areas during the early-to-mid twentieth century to build relationships with gang members, but many ultimately fell out of political favor during the 1960s (Goldstein, 1993). Interest in these programs, however, has resurged in recent years. Although the motivations for implementing these strategies may vary across communities, a defining aspect is that traditional gang prevention and intervention programs often face challenges engaging the most at-risk populations and keeping them involved in services (Decker, By-num, McDevitt, Farrell, & Varano, 2008). While interest in these program models is growing, very little has been written about outreach worker programs in recent decades.

This chapter will provide an overview of a street outreach program that has been piloted in the City of New Bedford, Massachusetts since 2006. It will describe how the program has been organized and man-aged, the types and significance of collaboration with other community institutions, as well as identifying some of the most substantial chal-lenges in developing and sustaining New Bedford's outreach program. To contextualize the efforts in New Bedford, the chapter will provide an overview of the conceptual foundations of street-based outreach programs. Moreover, it will provide a historical account that traces the initial implementation of these programs in the early twentieth century and the eventual cycle of political antagonism and ultimate renewed support. Through the lens of outreach efforts in New Bedford, this study gives attention to the likely "pitfalls" (practical and political) in implementing a street outreach program and, in doing so, will provide recommendations about problems that should be anticipated by local communities attempting to implement similar efforts.

BACKGROUND

Conceptual Foundation of Outreach Programs

The approach used in street outreach programs resembles other forms of semi-formal or informal mentoring relationships where paraprofes-sionals work with clients usually outside of the parameters of formal "services" or "programs." These and similar forms of mentoring relation-ships have been identified as useful for engaging high-risk populations (Rhodes, 1994), particularly gangs (Decker et al., 2008; Howell, 2000; OJJDP, 2009; Spergel and Grossman, 1997). In a general sense, street-based mentoring is a process whereby older, often more experienced individuals provide a degree of "ongoing guidance, instruction, and encouragement aimed at developing the competence and character of the protégée" (Rhodes, 1994, p. 189). Street outreach represents a way to build a wider network of non-parental social relationships with young people, particularly among individuals who function as role models and create opportunities to model prosocial behavior and attitudes.

There is a strong theoretical foundation for the use of street outreach. Research shows that the nature and quality of *relationships to others and to community institutions* play extremely important roles in the lives of young people (Hawkins & Weis, 1985; Hirschi, 1969; Kornhauser, 1978;

Telleen, Maher, & Pesce, 2003). Control and attachment theories establish that one's prosocial *attachments* to families and conventional others functions as a resiliency factor against the onset of delinquency (Frattaroli, et al., 2010; Hawkins & Weis, 1985).

Street Outreach and Gangs

Early forms of outreach programs primarily focused on modifying aspects of group processes that defined success within the gang subculture (Delaney, 1954). These approaches were different from previous delinquency prevention/intervention strategies not only in terms of the "setting" (e.g., community-based versus institutional settings) but also in terms of the tones and strategies. As opposed to "preaching" to young people about the dangers of gangs, the focus of these early outreach programs was on the infusion of democratic decision-making whereby the group could take ownership of its own problems. Street workers were expected to interact with group members in a way that was focused less on dismantling the group itself but instead on altering intragroup socialization mechanisms and values. Street outreach programs focused on at-risk and gang-involved youth were operational in nearly every major urban center by the 1960s. Workers assumed a variety of roles in the day-to-day lives of the young people they encountered. Chief among their responsibilities was building relationships with school authorities, engaging young people in vocational and educational programs, and creating legitimate social and economic opportunities (Spergel, 1962).

Evaluations of these early efforts, while promising, were generally inconclusive in terms of their overall effectiveness. Gandy (1959) noted some modest decreases in delinquent behavior among program participants. Eisenberg and Feldstein (1959) also reported substantial reductions in problem behavior at the Jewish community center among young people who were previously very disruptive after street workers began interacting with the youth at the center. Miller's (1962) findings, however, were less positive and instead generally reflected little-to-no effect.

By the late 1960s there was a growing sense of dissatisfaction with street worker programs, particularly among many in the law enforcement community (Klein, 1965). The relationships between many street workers and public agents, police in particular, became strained over time in many communities. Some argued (see Klein, 1965) that street workers became too closely aligned with gang-involved youth. It was argued that street workers often lost their sense of objectivity and became a mechanism for enabling gang members instead of steering young people out of gangs and into conventional society. Some also questioned how effectively street workers identified the "right" groups and individuals to work with—that is, if street worker programs were actually able to engage high-risk groups and individuals. Assigning street workers to particular groups over others was also thought to provide a sense of "status" that actually *increased* the legitimacy of the gang and levels of cohesion within the groups. These criticisms, along with the lack of strong evidence of success, ultimately resulted in waning support for gang-oriented street worker programs by the late 1960s and into the 1970s. By the 1980s, the prevailing "get tough" orientation of U.S. criminal justice policy toward both juveniles and adults favored punitive approaches rather than those geared toward community-based opportunities provision.

Searching for Solutions to the Modern Day Gang Problem

Yet, by the 1990s a few communities across the United States began experimenting once again with the use of outreach workers to work with gang-involved young people. Boston's Operation Ceasefire was unique in that it used outreach workers to collaborate with police and probation to provide a web of support for gang-involved individuals (Kennedy, Braga, & Piehl, 2001). Chicago uses "violence interrupters" as part of their comprehensive effort to reduce the rising tide of firearm violence. Violence interrupters participate in a form of street outreach that is focused in a tactical way on breaking cycles of retaliatory violence. When violence erupts among known or suspected gang members, violence interrupters work with gang leadership to mediate these disputes before they escalate. Early evaluations suggest that the use of this form of street outreach has been successful in reducing retaliatory violence associated with gangs (Skogan, Hartnett, Bump, & DuBois, 2008).

STREET OUTREACH IN NEW BEDFORD

The City of New Bedford was one of the communities to receive grant awards to combat street gangs in 2006 under the Shannon CSI. The preliminary problem analysis conducted in the weeks leading up to development of New Bedford's community-wide effort was their ability to recruit and retain young people, particularly those at most risk for gangs, into prevention and intervention programs. Street outreach was viewed as an integral part of their comprehensive strategy. As the National Gang Center (2010) pointed out "[O]utreach . . . is critical to program success" (p. 20) of all comprehensive gang programs. The analysis below is a case study of New Bedford's experiences in designing, implementing, and managing a gang outreach program that was part of this larger community effort. Data were collected from a series of interviews and focus groups with law enforcement personnel and outreach staff. Before examining the outreach endeavor's characteristics and activities, a brief description is provided of the city and its background as it relates to the implementation of a street outreach component.

Study Location

The sixth largest city in the Commonwealth of Massachusetts with a 2010 population of over 95,000, New Bedford has a storied history and diverse population. A sizeable proportion of the city's population is of Portuguese ancestry (42.2%). New Bedford was once the richest city in the world per capita in the mid-nineteenth century as a result of the whaling trade (City of New Bedford, n.d.). Although cotton and other industry were profitable at various points in the first half of the twentieth century, New Bedford has since fallen on harder times. To provide a context in which to place the Shannon CSI, select statistics from the U.S. Census are illustrative (see Table 5.1). These data indicate that the City of New Bedford is distressed in many different ways. Compared to the United States and Massachusetts, a larger percentage of residents of New Bedford are immigrants, are linguistically isolated (does not speak English at all) to a much greater degree, earn substantially less in terms of household income, and are more likely to have serious educational barriers. These measures provide an important backdrop to the understanding of the challenges faced by local residents.

Table 5.1. Comparison on Key Census Measures*

Census Measure	City of New Bedford	Massachusetts	United States
Total Population	95,072	6,547,629	308,745,538
Median Household Income	$33,451	$50,502	$41,994
Percent Households Less Than $25k Income	42.9%	20.5%	24.7%
Percent Born in U.S.	74.9%	83.3%	86.1%
Population 25+ Less Than 9th Grade Education	18.4%	4.9%	6.3%
Does not speak English at all	16.8%	8.6%	8.6%

*Source: www.census.gov

The City of New Bedford has also faced challenges associated with crime. Between the years 1985 and 2009, New Bedford's homicide rate averaged approximately 5 per 100,000. While certainly lower than many comparably sized communities, New Bedford's homicide rate is nearly 60% higher than the statewide average of approximately 3 per 100,000 during the same timeframe. Homicide levels also increased dramatically in recent years. For example, the number of homicides increased from two in 1996 and one in 1997 to 11 in 2003 and eight in 2005.

The rise in crime was not limited to just homicide. New Bedford experienced a steady decline in its overall violent crime rate from a high in 1992 of nearly 1,400 per 100,000 to just over 700 per 100,000 in 2003. This more than decade long decrease quickly turned around in 2004 and ultimately increased just as steadily to approximately 1,300 per 100,000 in 2008. This "spike" in homicide and other forms of violence was a notable source of contention across the city. The local newspaper ran regular stories that documented that the city's crime rate had increased to a five-year high despite notable crime decreases after the 1990s (Fraga, 2010).

These crime trends are important because the increases in crime during the early 2000s provided an important catalyst that began to galvanize the public, law enforcement, and other governmental agencies to rethink crime control strategies. In addition to concern over the rising levels of crime, the targeted execution of the mother of a known gang member in May 2006 provided the foundation for the formation of expansion of an early working group that was eventually referred to as the H.O.P.E. Collaborative (Healthy Opportunities for Peaceful Engagement). The City of New Bedford developed a strong street outreach component as part of their efforts.

Operating a Street Outreach Program in New Bedford

The concept of street outreach was not new to the City of New Bedford but instead had been in place in different forms in the years leading up to the implementation of the H.O.P.E. Collaborative. Members of the faith community, for example, made some notable inroads into the world of street outreach by the early 2000s as violent crime began to rise. Modeled after Boston's Ten Point Coalition (see McDevitt, Braga, Nurge, & Buerger, 2003), members of an inter-denominational faith network called the Inter-Church Council (ICC), had been conducting regular ride-alongs with the New Bedford Police Department since 2003 that targeted young people identified as "at-risk" by schools. A drug treatment agency known locally as Treatment on Demand (TOD) had also been engaged in using outreach services to target risky-drug using populations in an effort to reduce HIV/AIDS.

These programs gave many involved in the planning stages of H.O.P.E. some familiarity with the role of street outreach in targeting difficult-to-reach populations. Although this early experience provided a baseline of working knowledge among key stakeholders about the utility of such a program, getting this program off the ground and making a transition to populations at-risk for gang involvement was a daunting challenge. In reality, there is no "playbook" to draw from when implementing a street outreach program. There has also been very little attention by the scholarly community to these types of intervention programs in recent decades, particularly as they apply to gangs and street violence (for notable exceptions, see Frattaroli, et al., 2010; NCCD, 2009).

New Bedford's gang-focused street outreach program was influenced heavily by the pioneering work done by the Institute for Study and Practice of Nonviolence (the Institute), in Providence, Rhode Island. The Executive Director of the Institute had a long history of street outreach work since the late 1980s when he became deeply embedded in Boston's efforts to address the exploding gang problem (Allen, 2009). The Institute is recognized as a national model and as a leader in the area of street outreach and has developed one of the most widely recognized outreach programs. In recognition of this established expertise, outreach managers and staff received training at the Institute during the first six months of the program in 2006 and 2007.

Program Design and Management

Since many across New Bedford had some familiarity with the use of street outreach services, it was a natural fit to integrate into the H.O.P.E. Collaborative. In making the transition to gang intervention work, TOD partnered with New Bedford's YMCA to strengthen the quality and types of the outreach services. The YMCA, for example, offered greater organizational capacity to manage a larger number of outreach workers, and it also offered staff and outreach clients access to a diversity of programming for referrals. The YMCA Executive Director co-directed the initiative along with the executive director of TOD during its early year. TOD assumed front-line management responsibilities of outreach workers while the YMCA was responsible for its overall management. Both individuals maintained joint responsibility for responding directly to the scene of critical incidents such as shootings, large fights, and murders to coordinate contacts and follow-ups with affected parties with the intent of reducing the likelihood of retaliation.

Much of that changed in 2008 when the Executive Director of the YMCA resigned from her position. Similar to what has been documented in the past when important champions leave programs for better prospects (see Decker & Curry, 2002), the future of the outreach program was unclear. While the YMCA expressed a willingness to keep the program, it was unclear if they appreciated the time and lifestyle requirements (e.g., responding to critical incidents during off hours) necessary for the individual appointed as the new program director. It also was unclear if the YMCA, particularly under the new leadership of the incoming executive director, was prepared to handle the challenges associated with employing outreach workers with limited employment experience and complicated life histories (to be discussed later). With these concerns in mind, the decision was made by the Executive Director of the H.O.P.E. Collaborative to move outreach to a different community-based program more capable of addressing these concerns and of maintaining the integrity of the initiative.

Finding the natural community-based partner proved more daunting than originally expected. There was no shortage of community agencies willing to absorb this programmatic component (and the resources associated with it), but the concern was in maintaining the design and focus of the program on street-based outreach targeted at high-risk areas and residents. The street outreach component was absorbed for one year by the Inter-Church Council (ICC), a well-known and respected inter-faith group of clergy dedicated to providing assistance to distressed neighborhoods and their residents through their own outreach services. After a relatively short time together, the decision was ultimately made that while ICC and street outreach shared a similar mission, their strategies and management practices were not compatible. Ultimately outreach evolved into a quasi-independent component of the H.O.P.E. Collaborative that would be financially accountable to the New Bedford Police Department.

There is an important story embedded in the transitions identified above. This transition should be understood as influenced by a combination of organizational capacities, internal willingness to absorb the potential political fallout with employing and managing employees with limited professional work experiences and their own life challenges, and simple differences in management philosophies. Yet under the surface are also the political struggles over programmatic resources. While struggles over resources were never the primary factors that explained these transitions, it certainly played a role in many different ways. These were meso-forces in operation, while general implementation issues of all outreach programs are discussed in more detail below.

KEY CONSIDERATIONS IN
STRUCTURING OUTREACH PROGRAMS

Selection and Hiring of Street Outreach Workers

When implementing an outreach program, it is important for program managers to consider the qualities and life experiences that will be required of employees (see Table 5.2). Outreach members in New Bedford are typically in their early-to-mid-twenties. Although some had past experience with gangs, all have grown up in the city and have had sustained

Table 5.2. Key Considerations in the Structure of Outreach Programs

Issues	Option	Tradeoff
Placement/ Location of Outreach Services	Within a human service agency (e.g., community-based treatment provider); Within other community-based organization (e.g., YMCA, Boys and Girls Club); Stand-alone entity.	Locating within Human Service Agencies: Pro-Creates synergy with service providers that make referral and follow-up easier. Con-May create tensions between other providers for control and resources. Stand-alone Entity: Pro-Maximizes internal control and direction. Con-Overhead costs associated with sustaining organization and related costs. Locating within other Community-Based Organization: Pro-May create stronger connections to high-risk neighborhoods and their residents. Con-May lose focus on most at-risk residents who tend to fall through the cracks of these programs.
Qualities of Outreach Workers	Employment requirements include professional clinical experience and formal training/ credentials; Employment requirements are minimal and preference given to individuals with past "street" experience.	Formally Trained Professionals: Pro-Staff with formal training/education in the areas of clinical treatment increases the quality of access to formal treatment services. Con-The ability to make personal connections to individuals in distressed life circumstances may be compromised. Workers with Past History with Street Life: Pro-Better ability to connect with individuals since they understand the challenging life circumstances of clients. Cons-Limited professional training reduces their ability to provide meaningful clinical treatment.
Linkage with Law Enforcement	Close working relationship; Working relationship, but at arm's length; Few, if any, relationships between outreach and law enforcement.	Close Working Relationship: Pro-May increase legitimacy within law enforcement circles; provides greater access to funding (e.g., grants); maximizes data sharing between both. Cons-May negatively impact legitimacy of outreach workers on the streets with the most at-risk populations; may create tensions if outreach does not share requested information. Arm's Length Relationship: Pro-Helps to foster sense of legitimacy within law enforcement circles and help gain some access to external funding. Cons-May negatively impact legitimacy of outreach workers on the streets with the most at-risk populations; may also create tensions if outreach does not share requested information. No Notable Relationship: Pro-May maximize legitimacy on streets with most at-risk population. Con-May create tensions between outreach and law enforcement, which may decrease the legitimacy of outreach in critical circles; greatly reduces access to external funding (e.g., grants).

exposure to problems such as drug use, drug selling, gang involvement, periods of incarceration, troubled family lives, and/or academic failure. Many of the outreach workers have children of their own, though few are married. Each comes from challenging circumstances that, in combination with their personal motivation to better their situation and various sources of support, provide them with the capacity to be taken seriously by at-risk and gang-involved youth. Most of those who apply for a spot on the team are recommended by current outreach workers.

Selecting individuals from troubled backgrounds is consistent with national examples from places like Providence and Chicago. Scrimshaw (2007) has noted that in places like Chicago, "street-smart" outreach workers can relate to those living troubled lives and offer young people living in similar situations models of success. Most importantly, they understand the lures and challenges of the streets in ways that others cannot, which is often seen as critical to young people who have witnessed levels of violence unknown to most. Individuals with "street experience" who demonstrate their ability to make measurable efforts to relinquish the negative aspects of that life are seen as crucial. Local experiences in particular may be particularly meaningful as these outreach workers "may be better able to gain access to the world of street gangs, particularly to individuals with influence in their gangs" (NCCD, 2009, p. 13). As one outreach worker from New Bedford noted:

> Javier [real name changed] has the street experience as far as, like, the gangs and the street life. So, he's more qualified just like we all are to associate with the kids and relate to the kids. 'Cause they'd rather talk to somebody like, no offense, than somebody with a college degree and say "Hey, don't do this" or "Don't do that." They're gonna look at you like, "Yeah, OK, who are you? You don't know anything about the street life." Basically all of us have come from some sort of screwed up background.

Selecting streetwise employees with histories of gangs and crime, although a strength in many ways, can also be a liability. While histories with street life may enable an outreach worker to connect with those in similar life circumstances, experience in New Bedford has also shown that these individuals sometimes lack the familiarity with legitimate work environments that facilitate the most basic management practices (e.g., dependability and maintaining a necessary distance from street culture). As one member of New Bedford's management team noted:

> It's a challenge. You want [the outreach workers] to be able to relate to people that they're dealing with, and they *certainly can!* Every struggle the kids on the street are going through, [the outreach workers are going through]. [Outreach workers are] living day-to-day, pay check-to-pay check. They

can't pay their rent half the time, they don't have enough food. I mean, we're [management team] trying to get [outreach workers] food half the time. The hope is that by them struggling through some of these life problems, they are better able to both understand and help others do the same.

Employing individuals with street experience also presents other more tangible management problems. Criminal histories, as the most tangible example, can preclude individuals from working in school or health care environments. This can represent a serious barrier to outreach programs and is an issue that must be proactively addressed by program managers and other community stakeholders. A newly appointed school official in New Bedford has recently hampered the ability of outreach workers to enter school because of concerns with criminal histories. Concerns about the past criminal histories of outreach workers and the extent to which they truly have relinquished the temptations of the streets remains a source of consternation among some in the broader community and the H.O.P.E. Collaborative alike.

Training of Outreach Staff and Structuring of Daily Activities

In many ways, outreach has traditionally been seen less as a profession and more as a "craft" to be learned informally on the job. Goldstein (1993), for example, identified lack of formal training and high staff turnover as among the most serious threats to sustaining an effective street outreach program (see also Frattaroli, et al., 2010). A lack of formal training often results in a lack of integrity to the outreach process and a lack of consistency to how street outreach is done among staff. Cheney and Merwin (1996) warn that "[s]ole reliance on . . . informal practical skills and life experiences of staff members may create interventions that are inappropriate . . ." (p. 83). While street knowledge developed from life experiences is valuable, this experience alone is not sufficient for outreach. Effective outreach workers are those who can effectively couple a well-developed working knowledge of street culture with professional skills such as conflict resolution, basic integration of counseling skills, and the ability to develop formal intervention plans from assessments (Cheney & Merwin, 1996; NCCD, 2009).

As noted above, New Bedford has drawn on the regional expertise of the Institute for the Study and Practice of Nonviolence in Providence, Rhode Island. Outreach workers from New Bedford have spent time shadowing outreach workers from the Institute as they perform their outreach activities in the City of Providence. The intent is to provide a training curriculum that is grounded both in theory and practice. This professional approach recognizes that the duties of outreach workers are best learned from a combination of classroom-based and field learning.

While the selection and training of outreach workers are critical tasks, developing a formal plan for structuring daily activities can also be daunting. When discussing the roles and activities of outreach workers, the literature regularly identifies core tasks such as "connecting with young people," "making contacts," and "building relationships" (see NCCD, 2009). In practice, however, the exact meaning of these concepts in terms of the day-to-day activities of outreach workers is unclear. Outreach work can be vague and nonspecific at times, often dealing with the most acute problems that have emerged in the relative recent past. Most important, outreach has a tendency to lack a strategic focus that clearly delineates daily activities in structured ways. Role uncertainty and confusion tend to plague these program models (Goldstein, 1993).

New Bedford's outreach program has a strong "place-based" component that focuses activities to gang hotspots and other high-intensity target areas such as schools, a local mall where youth hang out on Friday nights, local parks, and summertime street festivals. Outreach workers are expected to "patrol" these areas on a regular basis to engage youth they encounter. Workers are expected to spend time on the street, interacting with youth and their families, encouraging youth to take advantage of local service providers, and developing an understanding for emerging conflicts on the street. Spending time outside of the local high school at dismissal ("working the crowd" in particular) allows outreach workers to engage with young people in a non-confrontational setting and also hear about conflicts that may have emerged during school hours in an effort to diffuse these situations before they expand.

The Importance of Linkages with Key Community Institutions

For street outreach worker programs to be most effective, strategies must be focused on creating linkages both between at-risk youth and conventional institutions, but also between the *outreach program itself* and conventional institutions (OJJDP, 2010). Similar programs in the past have been criticized because they seemed to operate in isolation from— and in some cases were even antagonistic with—the goals of other key community institutions such as schools and the police (Spergel & Grossman, 1997). In the New Bedford model, the intention was not to *replace* anything but instead supplement what was already being done by other service providers. Street outreach is designed to be another avenue into the lives of at-risk young people, to make them aware of and connected to programs and service providers that already exist within the community. Local success continues to be dependent on creating linkages with schools, community groups, hospitals, and the police.

In New Bedford, the relationships between outreach and local institutions such as police and schools evolved in very organic ways, developing as the needs and opportunity for each developed. As will be described in more detail below, schools provide a relatively stable, pro-social environment in which the street outreach team may engage youth. Similarly, outreach workers' presence in hospitals when a victim of gang or youth violence has been brought in can serve to defuse emotionally volatile situations, and workers can serve as a liaison between family members and the medical staff when necessary.

Schools

Along with the street, schools represent one of the most important locations where outreach workers meet at-risk youth and build trust relationships. Young people spend much of their day in schools and the setting itself is important because it is a relatively stable environment in which to engage youth. Outreach workers describe their availability in the schools as one of the most effective ways of reaching youth, meeting their friends, and making new contacts. Until recently there was a daily presence in New Bedford High School by two members of the team and other members sought to provide coverage to the middle and alternative schools, although staffing limitations have prevented them from being there as often as in the high school. In this forum, engagement has primarily taken place at lunch periods, during which outreach workers have the opportunity to talk with existing contacts as well as make their way around the cafeteria to meet new youth. An associated benefit is their availability to become aware of rumors of violence/problems while in school and to develop responses before the incidents occur.

Street outreach was successful at gaining access to city middle schools and the high schools starting in 2008. School district leadership and individual principals were generally supportive of outreach efforts. Outreach workers, for example, were asked to provide some minor classroom instruction on conflict resolution in the middle schools. Outreach workers were also given latitude to spend time in the high school cafeteria during lunch periods in order to make contact with individuals they have identified as needing services, listen to the "rumor mill" about conflicts, and identify and resolve simmering conflicts. This was largely accomplished through the development of formal protocols agreed upon by all key parties (e.g., school administrators, school resource officers, and outreach workers) that governed processes for gaining access to schools (e.g., outreach workers were to first report to the main office to make their presence known), the use of technology while in school (outreach workers were not allowed to walk the halls using cell phones since students were prohibited from doing so), and rules for student engagement (outreach workers were only allowed to meet with students in pairs and in public spaces). Workers reported generally feeling welcomed in the schools and having good working relationships with most school staff.

Yet strategies like this that bring *gang* outreach workers, many of whom have criminal histories, into *schools* is not without risk. Key stakeholders must successfully and continually champion these efforts to offset the potential for problems. Strategies that are deemed to be risky, particularly in risk-adverse school environments, can be subject to the shifting political winds caused by changes in local leadership. The departure of the Superintendent of the New Bedford Schools in April 2010 had such an affect. Citing a variety of concerns, most notably the presence of outreach workers with criminal histories on school grounds, the newly appointed Superintendent was much more trepid about this effort and ultimately ceased all access to school buildings by outreach workers. Since this shift in policy, outreach workers are only permitted to access the *outside* of school grounds at dismissal. The policy change has been a source of frustration on the part of street outreach workers. Their ability to engage at-risk youth in a neutral location like schools was an important part of local efforts. Outreach workers have reported that many students have taken notice of and commented on their absence from the lunchrooms. One outreach worker stated:

> They're just wondering "Why are you not at lunch when I need you there?" So, that's pretty much what it is with them, because that's the time that they have to talk to us. We're not allowed to pull them out of class. We can't pull them out of any classroom, so their time with us is lunch time. It's tough for them. 'Cause now they all wind up with no one to talk to. So, if they're upset about something then they're just gonna be upset for the whole day. When we would be there to calm them down and send them back to their next class a little bit easier than they were feeling before they went to lunch. But now, they'll just be mad all day. And they'll call me when they get home from school and they'll just be in the worst mood ever because this kid's been dealing with this one problem all day in school and he had no one to talk to and he couldn't get it off his chest. So, he ended up with detention, and getting suspended, because he had no way to control his anger.

Fortunately, according to the outreach team, this did not seem to result in the students having less trust in the workers once they explained the reason for the change to the students. Given the importance of consistency of contact that the outreach team has noted, this reaction is a positive result. However, even if trust remains largely unaffected, this loss of time in the schools may be detrimental in several ways: the outreach workers may be unable to interact with as many youth, spend as much time with regular contacts as was done previously, meet as much of a student's social network or identify a student's antagonists, or engage students within the school environment, which provides a level of safety and stability that may not exist to the same degree outside of the school facility.

Hospitals

Emerging research shows that hospital emergency rooms are one of the most effective venues for intervening in the lives of people touched by violence and gangs (Cooper, Eslinger, & Stolley, 2006). The periods following events in which serious violence occurs are important opportunities for outreach workers to help prevent further violence resulting from attempts at retaliation. Crisis, in many ways, creates opportunities for outreach workers (Frattaroli, et al., 2010). A primary venue for the application of these efforts is the hospital where the victim has been taken, particularly the emergency room and the waiting areas, including the parking lot. After a shooting or other serious assault, a host of individuals representing different constituencies (family, friends, members of the victim's gang, members of rival gangs, police, onlookers, etc.) often will gather in and outside of the hospital. These situations can be quite volatile, while people wait for news of the victim's condition and prognosis. A major source of anxiety is an absence of information, and many people will additionally be frustrated by the lack of transparency around how and when information will be forthcoming.

One senior New Bedford law enforcement official reported that, prior to street outreach workers' being a regular presence, arrests not only frequently occurred at the hospital in the aftermath of gang violence but multiple arrests *were expected* as they became so commonplace. Family members or friends would frequently become enraged if information was not readily available or if competing factions showed up at the hospital at the same time. Both law enforcement and outreach staff indicated hospital staff (security and emergency department personnel) would have a tendency to become "on edge" during these events, not always sure what to expect. Family members or friends would be seen as "symbolic assailants" by emergency room staff and security, that is, as likely to be capable of violence because of their association with the victim. In the event of gang-related violence, the primary trauma center in the city had a typical response of completely shutting down the emergency department. Security personnel would be stationed at doors and all communication would be cut off from the crowd. This ultimately fueled levels of discontent, and violence was commonplace.

Although it took time some time to iron out the specifics of the protocols, outreach workers are now generally given carte blanche access to the emergency department when gang-related violence occurs. In fact, outreach workers have formal identification tags that grant them access to secured areas of the hospitals. In this role, outreach workers serve as liaisons between the hospitals and the family and friends of victims. Outreach workers commented that they really feel accepted by security, many of whom were initially distrustful. They have a unique ability to function as liaisons as they are better able to relate to the general sense of confusion that many family members and friends felt about the entire medical system. For example, one outreach worker noted that when victims are transported into Boston most family members have no idea how to get to Boston. Although only forty-five minutes away, it is uncommon for low-income residents to travel outside of New Bedford. Traveling to Boston is akin to taking a long journey for them and can be a big source of confusion and anxiety. Practically, transportation itself, particularly at off hours, is difficult for many. Sensitivity to this, often not fully understood by medical or security personnel, is very important to these families. The positive effects of outreach efforts in the emergency department are noteworthy. The Police Chief indicated that since the time outreach workers were initially brought into the emergency department he could not remember a single arrest taking place there during the treatment of a victim involved in a suspected gang-related incident.

Police

Effectively interfacing with the police has been one of the most important yet challenging aspects of the outreach program. NCCD (2009) notes that while some outreach programs attempt to distance themselves from the police, close personal relationships can be beneficial. Police can provide timely information about crime trends, hot spots, and other important features of crime, all of which can be important to conflict mediation strategies. Important issues that are central to this relationship include (1) garnering sufficient trust initially so that the police do not interfere with outreach workers; (2) establishing a relationship with the police through which information about gangs and violence flows from the police to the outreach workers and not the other way around; and (3) avoiding public perception of having too close a relationship with the police and thus being viewed as "snitches."

Senior law enforcement officials have made their support for outreach clear across all layers of the police department and within the broader city government. The now retired Chief of Police, for example, had outreach workers attend departmental roll calls where he introduced individual outreach workers, explained their roll within the H.O.P.E. Collaborative, and made his support for their efforts clear. The current Chief of Police and former Deputy Chief of Police have also been important champions of the strategy and have been willing to defend the strategy when criticisms have been raised. The level of support has, at times, been difficult to ingrain throughout the entire department. Prior life experiences that make individuals viable outreach workers, for example, are the same experiences that likely made them familiar figures to at least some police officers. Although difficult at first, outreach workers generally reported their presence in the periphery of crime scenes and broader community is generally accepted by most officers most of the time. Yet at the same time, outreach managers have been firm about holding true to "zero tolerance" policies prohibiting involvement with drug use or other criminal contacts. The early firing of a well-liked outreach worker for weapons charges provided an opportunity to demonstrate to skeptics the good faith nature of this promise. The lures of street life and the continued personal challenges many outreach workers face during their own life journeys make the threat of failure a perennial concern.

Questions about *information sharing* between police and outreach staff represent one of the most challenging aspects of this relationship and an issue that must be proactively addressed during the early stages of any outreach program (NCCD, 2009). The unidirectional flow of information from *police* to *outreach* is critical because any sense of inappropriate information sharing by outreach not only brings into question their capacity to perform their jobs but can result in harm. Police officials are encouraged to understand that outreach workers are in a position to share only a very limited amount of information, generally restricted to general patterns and trends observed in neighborhoods. Sharing information about specific people or specific incidents has the potential to violate promises of confidentiality or develop a sense on the street that outreach workers are "snitches," a reputation that both eliminates their credibility and raises serious safety concerns.

Although challenging at times, particularly when law enforcement personnel believe that outreach workers might be privy to information about parties involved in crimes (which they often know), commitment to this principle has been emphasized since its inception. Recognition of and commitment to this by the New Bedford Police Department suggests a significant level of trust. Despite earnest efforts at reputation maintenance, however, the workers continually feel the need to ward against accusations that they are police informants. This is a pressure they perceive even with youth they know and with whom they have built relationships. Thus, maintenance of this relationship, while important, is incredibly challenging.

The primary responsibility of outreach workers is to build relationships with at-risk and gang-involved young people, many of whom are reluctant to divulge much about themselves and to open up to others outside of their immediate social circles. Where legally permissible, these relationships should be handled with a high degree of confidentiality. That being said, outreach workers are strongly encouraged to set boundaries with individual clients about the type of information that is shared with them. For example, outreach workers are encouraged to limit discussions with individuals about their involvement in specific crimes to reduce any complications with mandatory reporting requirements (NCCD, 2009). There may also be instances where outreach workers are legally *compelled* to share information, particularly in the situations of an impending attack. What is most important is that outreach workers and police, particularly in programs where there are formal partnerships, must generate shared agreement about expectations around information sharing (Decker, et al., 2008).

LESSONS LEARNED

While street outreach programs may seem attractive to communities struggling with gang violence, they can be difficult to establish and sustain. Outreach worker programs, particularly those that employ "streetwise" individuals, often run political risks. It can often be difficult for a community-based organization to justify employing individuals with criminal records, maybe just recently returning from jail or prison, in programs targeted toward helping at-risk populations. In fact, the research team has often heard these very criticisms from a wide variety of constituencies across New Bedford, particularly some police officers and human service providers. In New Bedford, this issue was taken head-on and at least partially helped by the vocal and sustained support by law enforcement.

In addition, constrained funding may present real and continued challenges to communities, particularly to street outreach components of community-wide models. In New Bedford, for example, outreach workers until recently were employed for thirty-two hours a week and received no employment benefits. Grant funding, while continued for five years, has also been reduced considerably in recent years. As a consequence, outreach workers hours were reduced to sixteen per week. This has presented challenges for outreach workers to remain on call when critical incidents occur or youth call outreach workers to just talk about a problem at any time, yet there are insufficient funds to cover all required hours. Consistency in communication and commitment to relationships are essential qualities of outreach workers, which means "I'm off the clock" is often not considered a viable response. Outreach workers stated that as much effort as they put into making themselves available, they inevitably "fail someone every day." Recognizing that many outreach workers themselves are not in particularly good financial shape, reduced funding and time commitments that far exceed that which is remunerated can cause problems.

Communities are also strongly encouraged to recognize that when employing individuals with criminal histories as outreach workers, personal struggles/failure on the part of outreach workers themselves is an unfortunate possibility. In New Bedford, there have been instances where a few workers have "caught cases" (arrested or otherwise identified as engaging in illegal behaviors by formal authorities) while being employed as outreach workers. One outreach worker tested positive on a drug test and another was stopped while off duty by the police carrying a firearm. The legitimacy of the program as a whole requires that such transgressions be addressed swiftly and with zero-tolerance. Executive leadership has made it clear from the beginning that failed drug tests and illegal behaviors are one-strike offenses that will result in termination of employment. Firing staff that have violated these expectations has been critical to the reputation of the outreach program in the eyes of institutional partners and in maintaining the political viability of outreach in the city. Thus, other communities considering implementing similar programs are encouraged to develop policies and procedures that establish clear guidelines for how these violations will be addressed.

Communities are also strongly encouraged to recognize that outreach workers need to be closely supervised to ensure they are doing meaningful work on a day-to-day basis, that their efforts are focused in the right places and on the right problems, and that they are keeping out of trouble. Street outreach can be very fluid and reactive to specific incidents. While tactical agility is an important quality, outreach workers must be managed in a way that keeps them focused on larger strategic goals, such as prolonged engagement of specific high-risk individuals. These are two equally important roles that must be managed appropriately and deliberately.

The most important lesson to be learned is that a successful outreach program must be effective at gaining and maintaining access to key institutions. Outreach, simply speaking, cannot operate in isolation of other key community institutions such as schools, hospitals, and social service agencies. Yet even when established, these relationships can be fragile and tenuous at best. Changes in executive management, for example, can stop an otherwise productive relationship dead in its tracks. Developing and maintaining these relationships, particularly when problems emerge, requires leadership and political fortitude.

Linkages with important institutions and individual stakeholders may also help programs weather political and fiscal challenges that may emerge. Police who have served during the tenure of this effort have been strong, vocal supporters, which has been critical in securing support across a wide array of other key community stakeholders. There is no doubt that access to the hospitals and schools has been due in large part to this support. Decker et al. (2008) make it clear that this level of support, particularly within the law enforcement community, is among the most critical factors affecting the long term success of street outreach. Ritter (2009) cautions that these relationships are not natural but something to be cultivated. In the end, the success or failures of street outreach can be influenced heavily by the level of buy-in from the law enforcement community (see Klein, 1965).

While New Bedford has experienced many successes during the early years of their street outreach efforts, particular dimensions of the programmatic efforts continue to fall short of their full potential. One of the primary shortcomings of the street outreach program is that its role in the more comprehensive H.O.P.E. Collaborative was never fully clear. There has been a tendency for street outreach to be run somewhat independently of the larger comprehensive gang initiative being implemented across the city. The larger program has never fully devised a strategy that makes effective use of outreach workers in making referrals to social service agencies or the use of outreach workers to keep contact with specific high-risk clients. The use of street outreach is maximized when such resources are effectively leveraged with those provided by other partnering agencies (Frattaroli, et al., 2010). Communities considering similar programs are strongly encouraged to implement a well-developed understanding of how these partnerships function in practice.

REFERENCES

Allen, J. (2009, April 12). People making a difference: Teny Gross. *Christian Science Monitor*. Retrieved from http://www.csmonitor.com.

Cheney, R., & Merwin, A. (1996). *Integrating a theoretical framework with street outreach services: issues for successful training*. Public Health Reports, *111*(Suppl. 1), 83.

City of New Bedford (n.d.). Retrieved January 19, 2011, from http://www.newbedford-ma.gov/Tourism/OurHistory/Historyofnb.html.

Cooper, C., Eslinger, D. M., & Stolley, P. D. (2006). Hospital-based violence prevention programs work. *The Journal of Trauma, Injury, Infection, and Critical Care*, *61*(3), 534–540.

Decker, S. H., Bynum, T. S., McDevitt, J., Farrell, A., & Varano, S. P. (2008). *Street Outreach Workers: Best Practices and Lessons Learned*. Boston: Northeastern University.

Decker, S. H., & Curry, G. D. (2002). "'I'm down for my organization:' The rationality of responses to delinquency, youth crime, and gangs." In A. Piquero & S. G. Tibbets (Eds.), *Rational choice and criminal behavior* (pp. 197–218). New York & London: Routledge.

Delany, L. T. (1954). Establishing relations with anti-social groups and analysis of their structure. *British Journal of Delinquency, 5*, 35–45.

Eisenberg, A., & Feldstein, D. (1959). The detached worker in a new setting. *Berman Jewish Policy Archive, 36*(2), 201–209.

Fraga, B. (2010). *New Bedford violent crime increased in 2009 to highest level in five years.* Standard and Times. Retrieved from http://www.southcoasttoday.com.

Frattaroli, S., Pollack, K., Jonsberg, K., Croteau, G., Rivera, J., & Mendel, J. (2010). Streetworkers, youth violence prevention, and peacemaking in Lowell, Massachusetts: Lessons and voices from the community. *Progress in Community Health Partnerships: Research, Education, and Action, 4*(3), 171–179.

Gandy, J. M. (1959). Preventive Work With Street-Corner Groups: Hyde Park Youth Project, Chicago. *The ANNALS of the American Academy of Political and Social Science, 322*, 107–116.

Goldstein, A. P. (1993). Gang intervention: A historical review. In A. P. Goldstein & C. R. Huff (Eds.), *The gang intervention handbook* (pp. 21–51). Champaign, IL: Research Press.

Hawkins, J. D., & Weis, J. G. (1985). The social development model: An integrated approach to delinquency prevention. *The Journal of Primary Prevention, 6*(2), 73–97.

Hirschi, T. (1969). *Causes of delinquency.* Berkeley: University of California Press.

Howell, J. C. (2000). *Youth gang programs and strategies.* Washington, D.C.: Department of Justice, Office of Juvenile Justice and Delinquency Prevention.

Kennedy, D. M., Braga, A. A., & Piehl, A. M. (2001). *Reducing gun violence: the Boston Gun Project's Operation Ceasefire.* Washington: National Institute of Justice.

Klein, M. W. (1965). Juvenile gangs, police, and detached workers: Controversies about intervention. *The Social Service Review, 39*(2), 183–190.

Kornhauser, R. (1978). *Social sources of delinquency.* Chicago: University of Chicago Press.

McDevitt, J., Braga, A. A., Nurge, D., & Buerger, M. (2003). Boston's youth violence prevention program: a comprehensive community-wide approach. In S. H. Decker (Ed.), *Policing gangs and youth violence* (pp. 53–76). Belmont, CA: Wadsworth.

Miller, W. B. (1962). The impact of a 'total-community' delinquency control project. *Social Problems, 10*(2), 168–191.

National Council on Crime and Delinquency (2009). *Developing a successful street outreach program: Recommendations and lessons learned.* Oakland, CA: National Council on Crime and Delinquency.

National Gang Center (2010). *Best practices to address community gang problems: OJJDP's comprehensive gang model,* 2nd Ed. Rockville, MD: Juvenile Justice Clearinghouse.

Office of Juvenile Justice and Delinquency Prevention (2009). *OJJDP comprehensive gang model: planning for implementation.* Washington, D.C.: Office of Justice Programs.

Rhodes, J. E. (1994). Older and wiser: Mentoring relationships in childhood and adolescence. *The Journal of Primary Prevention, 14*(3), 187–196.

Ritter, N. (2009). CeaseFire: A public health approach to reduce shootings and killings. *National Institute of Justice Journal, 264,* 20–25.

Scrimshaw, S. C. (2007). *The violence virus.* Boston Globe. Retrieved April 22, 2007, from http://www.boston.com.

Skogan, W. G., Hartnett, S. M., Bump, N., & DuBois, J. (2008). *Evaluation of Cease-Fire-Chicago.* Washington, D.C.: National Institute of Justice.

Spergel, I. (1962). A Multidimensional Model for Social Work Practice: The Youth Worker Example. *The Social Service Review, 36*(1), 62–71.

Spergel, I. A., & Grossman, S. F. (1997). The Little Village Project: a community approach to the gang problem. *Social Work, 42*(5), 456–470.

Telleen, S., Maher, S., & Pesce, R. C. (2003). Building community connections for youth to reduce violence. *Psychology in the Schools, 40*(5), 549–563.

Chapter 6

The Fundamental Challenges of Defining and Measuring Retaliatory Gang Violence

BRENDA J. BOND, NICOLE RIVERS-KUSTANOVITZ,
& ERIN MCLAUGHLIN

In recent years, those interested in community safety have come to two very important conclusions. The first is that modern community safety challenges are complex and solutions require cross-agency collaboration (Bond & Gittell, 2010). Secondly, developing an effective strategy means starting with an accurate understanding of the nature and characteristics of these community safety challenges (Goldstein, 1979; Weisburd & Eck, 2004). In turn, these practical and analytical insights have informed policy and practice at local, state, and national levels.

One safety issue of concern is the proliferation of gangs and the violence associated with some gang activity. A standard definition of what constitutes a gang has not materialized, as gangs present themselves in different ways, for different reasons across different contexts (Curry, Ball, & Fox, 1994). Research points to a range of individual, social, and institutional factors that may influence an individual to join a gang, but there is not one single explanation for why an individual joins a gang (Decker & Van Winkle, 1996). Research also suggests that violence between gangs may account for the majority of violence perpetrated by gangs and gang members, yet there is a significant need to capture and make use of data to explain the driving forces behind gang violence (Curry & Decker, 2003). Additional insights into what fosters gang violence, especially retaliation between gangs, would influence practitioner strategies directed at gang violence.

In spite of the developing, but still tentative understanding of the motivations behind gang violence, community safety stakeholders have attempted to implement cross-agency strategies designed to prevent, intervene in, and suppress gang violence. The Comprehensive Gang Model (CGM) is one of the most recognized approaches and is viewed by the U.S. Department of Justice as a "best practice" for preventing, intervening in, and suppressing gang violence. The adoption of the CGM as the strategy of choice has given community stakeholders a roadmap from which they can work, but implementing the CGM via a thorough understanding of the community's specific gang violence problem remains a challenge.

In 2006, the City of Lowell, Massachusetts adopted the CGM. Indeed, the City of Lowell and the LPD have long recognized the value and impact of utilizing evidence-based strategies to prevent and reduce crime and disorder (Braga, Pierce, McDevitt, Bond, & Cronin, 2008; Braga & Bond, 2008). In that vein, the LPD and a number of community partners secured funding from the Massachusetts Executive Office of Public Safety and Security (EOPSS) to implement the Comprehensive Gang Model (CGM). A strategic plan created in the previous year formed the basis for their CGM application, which showcased the well thought-out, comprehensive strategy to affect gang violence. The primary desired outcome from the planning process was a comprehensive plan for preventing, intervening in, and suppressing gang violence.

A local action research partner (LARP) complemented the CGM efforts by working hand-in-hand with community partners to understand the gang problem and the community's response. Because city partners' understanding of what prompted gang violence was primarily based on anecdotal information rather than systematically defined and collected data, the police and community partners believed that a more thorough understanding of the gang violence would inform their CGM partnership. At the time, their discussions centered on how to define and measure retaliatory violence, which they believed represented the majority of Lowell's gang violence problem. They knew that an analytically-based strategy was aligned with research on problem-oriented policing whereby community safety problems are best addressed after a detailed understanding and analysis of the local problems (Braga & Weisburd, 2010; Goldstein, 1979). Yet, they also recognized that the absence of fundamental elements such as mutually agreed upon gang and gang violence definitions as well as the existence of multiple data sources were impediments to their analytical process.

This chapter describes the Lowell partnership's attempt to improve the implementation of the CGM by better understanding the nature and characteristics of gang violence in their own backyard, with a particular focus on defining and measuring retaliation as a driving motivator for Lowell's inter-gang violence problem. Taking the lead, the Lowell Police Depart-

ment (LPD) consulted with community partners about their collective desire to better understand the retaliatory nature of gang violence, offering
to start with a review of their own internal police data. In the process of
trying to uncover the motivations behind Lowell's gang violence problems, a number of critical lessons about data collection and utilization
were revealed. What resulted from this review was a set of lessons about
data collection and analysis systems that will inform the definition and
measurement of retaliation in Lowell. While the review involves a limited
data source (i.e. the police department), lessons about the existence and
utilization of data from community partners have arisen from this work
and have broad implications for other jurisdictions that want to address
retaliatory violence between gangs.

This chapter first discusses existing knowledge surrounding gangs
and retaliation between gangs. It then describes the Lowell review and
the valuable lessons learned from this review. The chapter concludes by
presenting suggested steps to ensure quality data collection, analysis,
and utilization by police organizations and their community partners.
This review and the lessons offer important insights for practitioners,
policymakers, and researchers interested in gang violence, the motivations behind inter-gang violence, and the most appropriate prevention,
intervention, and suppression strategies.

BACKGROUND

Gang Crime and Violence

Evidence reveals that gang crime varies across contexts (Curry & Decker,
2003) and is not always concentrated and/or focused on one specific crime
type (see also Klein & Maxson, 2006). Research shows that membership
in a gang is positively associated with delinquency (Melde & Esbensen,
2011) and that more generally, young people who engage in increasingly
violent activities increase the likelihood of engaging in violent behavior
later in life (Herrenkohl & Herrenkohl, 2007). Further, gangs tend to be
involved in more crime and violence than other youth engaged in delinquent deeds (Curry & Decker, 2003; Thornberry, 1998). Indeed, scholars
suggest that "there is something unique about gang membership itself
that increases youths' participation in serious and violent crime" (Egley,
Maxson, Miller, & Klein, 2006, p. 224).

In addition to increased violence, research suggests additional connections between gangs and criminal activity. At the group level, gang
violence is strengthened over time as a result of discord with others
(Thrasher, 1927). Research tells us that gang crimes and violence typically result from attempts to uphold gang norms and beliefs (Curry &

Decker, 2003), and that loyalty and commitment to gangs often includes confronting threatening gang adversaries (Felson, 1996; Klein, 1971; Miller & Decker, 2001).

There is a belief that intervention and disengagement away from gang membership can influence future offending (Melde & Esbensen, 2011; Sampson & Laub, 2005). If we know that escalating violent behavior by a young person can increase future violent offending, then intervening early in their violence trajectory seems paramount to their future and to public safety. Intervention requires accurate knowledge about the nature and characteristics of gang violence. Police documentation of gang-related crimes and the characteristics of these crimes are severely lacking (Curry & Decker, 2003) yet it is likely one of the most critical sources for understanding the criminal behaviors of gang members and gangs. Outside of our knowledge of gang-related homicide, the characteristics of gang crime and violence are not well known (Curry & Decker, 2003). Indeed, without an adequate understanding of the characteristics of gang violence and the factors associated with gang violence, prevention, intervention, and suppression, efforts may be misdirected or fall short of desired outcomes.

Retaliation as a Motivator for Inter-Gang Violence

As suggested in existing research, gang violence is strengthened over time via discord with others to deal with the real or perceived threats facing gangs or their members (Thrasher, 1927; Yablonsky, 1959). Those who engage in criminal behavior do not look to law enforcement as a legitimate or trustworthy mechanism to help protect them against violations by others. In truth, relying on law enforcement as a form of protection diminishes status on the street.

A good deal of gang research is focused on understanding the cyclical nature of gang violence. Loftin (1984) suggests that gang violence often intensifies via what's called "contagion." Contagion refers to continual acts of violence triggered by a primary offense spreading into episodes of unpredictable retaliation. Retaliation may be immediate or delayed, and does not always involve the individual or group of individuals who committed the preceding affront. Assessment of access to offenders, risk, and benefits are all part of the gang's or gang member's decision to retaliate (Jacobs, 2004).

Jacobs (2004) states that retaliation is a mutually reinforcing concept and that "retaliation is a potent regulator of offender conduct, arguably the most potent form of social control. . . . Retaliation is powerful testament to the norm of reciprocity—a norm that holds that every action should yield an equal and opposite reaction" (p. 295) (see also Gouldner, 1960). Retaliation is a way to preserve order between groups of individuals where violence is considered an acceptable means for resolving conflict (Goode, 1997).

Jacobs and Wright (2008) purport that retaliation also helps to reinforce one's reputation within a specific context or to even the score from a previous offense. "At the core of the code is respect—getting it, maintaining it, and enhancing it" (Jacobs, 2004, p. 295). This respect applies to both individual gang members and the gang as a whole. Not responding to a rival gang or gang member violation would put one's reputation into question (Jacobs, 2004). This idea is aligned with Anderson's (1999) code of the street, which asserts that individuals behave relative to the structural characteristics and influences that discriminate against some versus others—meaning people behave towards others as they have been treated.

Research reveals three primary motivators or triggers of retaliatory violence. Table 6.1 provides a definition and empirical sources for these triggers.

Table 6.1.   Retaliatory Violence Motivators

Motivation for Retaliatory Violence	Definition of Motivation
Conflict Resolution	Being disrespected or challenged; real or perceived (Jacobs 2004; Jacobs & Wright 2008). Includes disrespect toward gang or gang member and toward members' families, boyfriends, or girlfriends (Mullins, et al., 2004; Jacobs & Wright 2008). May be in response to issues of revenge, justice, or vengeance (Decker 1996; Jacobs 2004)
	For example, was the retaliatory incident in response to a prior act on the offender by the victim? Was the victim doing business in the offender's neighborhood? Was the incident over a girlfriend/boyfriend?
Upholding a Reputation	Action taken in response to having one's competence or honor being threatened or "perceived to be" threatened (Jacobs & Wright 2008; Mullins et al., 2004). For example, as the incident related to the offender's role or status in the gang?
Enforcing Street Code	Involves protecting the current norms and street culture of a given group (Anderson 1999). For example, did the offender feel his/her honor was being threatened?

The accurate specification of retaliation motivators or triggers is a complicated but critical task to informing an appropriate intervention. For example, conflicts arising from public displays of disrespect toward a gang or gang member may require one type of intervention, whereas a conflict surfacing from a dispute between gang member siblings may require another type of intervention. It is this specificity that remains obscure.

The Challenges of Measuring Gang Violence and Retaliation

The elusiveness of specificity and gang-related characterizations creates significant measurement challenges. Not only are there substantial variations in how gangs and members are understood across communities, but even within the same community there are divergent understandings and beliefs about the scope and scale of gangs and gang membership, as revealed by Decker and Leonard (1991). Also, the type of conflict is an important variable in the study of gang activity (Esbensen, Winfree, He, & Taylor, 2001). Failure to use a standard definition and measure (of gangs, membership, gang crime, and retaliation) affects policy and practice in several ways. The absence of a common definition and understanding affects the ability to accurately describe and understand the problem. Agencies or communities may over or underestimate the problem, the participants, and/or the services needed. This in turn leads to an inaccurate focus, and the targeting of prevention, intervention, and suppression resources (Esbensen, et al., 2001).

In addition to these definitional challenges, there exists no central data system on gang activity, but rather an assortment of surveys, program data, and local databases that hold these data, which are used to interpret the scale and scope of gangs and gang activity, patterns, and trends. And while law enforcement possesses a fair amount of data, their data have limitations (Curry & Decker, 2003). Even more challenging is when national data are used to inform local actions and decisions; the differences across definitions and measurement make this all but impossible and inappropriate (Curry & Decker, 2003).

The Fundamental Step of Specifying the Gang Problem

Research provides some insight into the characteristics of gangs and gang violence, while also pointing to the significant gaps in knowledge relative to definitions, data collection, and problem specification. Indeed, a fundamental first step in implementing cross-agency policies such as the CGM is the identification and characterization of a community's specific gang violence problem (Spergel, 1995). This focus on specifying the indigenous problem is aligned with what we know from the research on effective community safety policy, as this problem definition step requires that a local crime problem be broken down and understood in a more detailed and analytical way. This problem-focused paradigm can be traced back to Herman Goldstein (1979) who believed that to effectively deal with community challenges, police and others needed "a more systematic process into inquiring into these problems" (p. 243). By focusing in on specified problems, there is an attempt to understand *why* certain incidents are occurring in a specific location and to develop strategies that are most appropriate and effective given the nature and characteristics of the problem (Eck & Spelman, 1987; Goldstein, 1979). Armed with a better understanding of crime problems, police and communities are better equipped to identify the best possible solution to the problems they face. A problem-oriented approach and resulting use of systematic problem-solving techniques has gained empirical and practical support in recent years (Braga, 2002; Eck & Spelman, 1987; Kennedy, Braga, Piehl, & Waring, 2001; Weisburd & Braga, 2007). Thus, a thorough review and understanding of a specified community problem (i.e. gang violence) is necessary to inform individual and cross-agency action. Further, having a clear and consistent definition of a gang, a gang member, and what constitutes a gang incident is critical to delivering fair and legitimate community safety.

Researchers have been investigating the absence of a clear, concise, and standard definition of a gang, and then a way to measure gang-related violence (Klein & Maxson, 2006). Indeed, the notions of defining and measuring gang violence are complicated and interconnected. First, it is important that all partners in a community understand the importance of a shared definition, and agree to work towards a shared definition. This ensures consistency in characterization and validity of collected data. The absence of such an agreement results in extreme subjectivity in the characterization process, influenced by what a police officer or police agency representative knows about an individual or the individual's behavior in the context of the gang and the community. This characterization then drives how a crime-related incident is classified, meaning if it is labeled "gang-related or gang-motivated." Klein and Maxson (2006) describe the difference between gang motivated and gang related crimes. The more traditionalist gang motivated crime requires that the motivation for the crime be based within a gang. This is compared to gang related crime, which is a crime committed by a gang member, regardless of motivation. Conversely, crimes that are not directly related to the gang yet are committed by individual members are typically not connected to larger group goals or in defense of gang norms and gang reputation on the street (Curry & Decker, 2003).

The implications of these various perceptions create many challenges for practitioners. Practitioners may try to tackle the gang violence problem without a standard understanding, or individual agencies within a community may generate their own, rather than a collective definition. These approaches may impede the development and implementation of appropriate prevention, intervention, and suppression activities. Conversely, practitioners may embrace the fact that gangs and gang violence are idiosyncratic to the local community and attempt to define what they see as the gang violence problem within their community. This approach supports a localized and tailored prevention, intervention, and suppression strategy. This latter challenge was recognized by Lowell practitioners as they faced a concerning gang violence problem.

THE CITY OF LOWELL, MASSACHUSETTS

The City of Lowell, Massachusetts is an ethnically and economically diverse, mid-size city located 30 miles to the north of Boston and occupying just over 14 square miles. Lowell's population is 103,077 residents, with 74.5% of the residents characterized as white; 4.4% are Asian; 12.4% are black; and 7.8% were characterized as mixed or other race. Just over 15% of residents considered themselves Hispanic (U.S. Census, 2009).

Following the adoption of community policing in the 1990s, Lowell enjoyed a relatively low per capita crime rate. However, over time it began to change. As an urban community, Lowell faces a myriad of crime issues, including gang activity, drug-related crime, and gun crime. Gangs have historically contributed to violent crime in Lowell, particularly gun crime, and recently, Lowell has seen a more significant overlap between gang violence and guns. Firearm use and availability has become a major concern. From 2007–2008 there was a 5% increase in crimes involving a firearm. In 2008, nearly 25% of all gun incidents were attributed to gangs. In 2009, Lowell experienced an increase in non-fatal shootings with low-caliber weapons and police intelligence suggests that gang members utilize these types of weapons because they are easier to conceal (Personal communication).

Given the urban nature of the city of Lowell, there are other challenges that require the attention of many community stakeholders that could impact gang membership and violence. Lowell experienced a high unemployment rate (10.8%) in 2009 with 370 homes foreclosed upon in the past year, nearly twenty times more than 2005 (MA DOR, 2010; Middlesex North Registry of Deeds, 2005 & 2009). A dire economic situation forced many residents to relocate, resulting in an increased number of abandoned homes, making many areas in the city increasingly susceptible to crime and disorder (Wilson & Kelling, 1982). Research shows that crime hot spot areas are plagued by abandoned homes, unkempt property, and other disorder issues that send a message to criminals that no one cares this place in the community (Braga & Bond, 2008; Wilson & Kelling, 1982).

The Lowell Experience: A Model Process for Defining and Measuring Retaliatory Violence

A partnership between the City of Lowell and their Police Department and local action research partners (i.e. LARP) from Suffolk University was established in 2007. In October of that year, Lowell partners began meeting on a monthly basis to discuss pressing or emerging gang and youth violence issues. The LARP worked closely with Lowell on the development, monitoring, and assessment of CGM outcomes. The partnership also included technical assistance in a number of ways, including facilitation and agenda setting for a policymaking board overseeing the implementation of the CGM, and in working with public and non-profit partners in identifying and collecting useful program data to support improvements and strategic decision-making. The partner conversations were often hampered by limited information and data. Lowell partners would often turn to their LARP for assistance in understanding the challenges at hand, particularly data limitations, which were a common agenda item at partnership meetings. The desire to uncover the local dynamics associated with gang violence and retaliation naturally evolved via partner discussions at these monthly meetings.

Foremost, the partners acknowledged the lack of standardized definition of gang and gang membership in Lowell. Their experience mirrored the research which suggests that there are different definitions across time and context (Ball & Curry, 1995; Curry & Decker, 2003; Esbensen, et al., 2001; Klein, 1972; Thrasher, 1927). There have been numerous attempts by Commonwealth of Massachusetts policymakers to establish a standard definition and to create a centralized database of gang-related information, but efforts have been unsuccessful. Lowell Police crime analysts used some of the state's criteria, but their practice was not part of department policy, nor is it in harmony with the beliefs of various community stakeholders (e.g. community agencies, parents, schools).

Lowell's focus on retaliation was prompted by a number of interconnecting factors: a growing gang violence problem; the increased use of weapons in gang violence incidents; anecdotal accounts from police and non-profit service providers that retaliation was driving most of Lowell's gang violence problem; evidence from existing research that emphasized the need to thoroughly understand the nature and characteristics of a specified problem; and declining financial and human resources available to affect gang violence. This latter piece meant that Lowell had to be smarter about how they used their individual and collective resources, directing it at the most worrisome problems. In order to allocate resources according to the most pressing problems, the partnership would need to invest in this initial data collection and measurement phase and then direct their individual and collective resources to data driven problems.

To begin their quest to understand retaliation in Lowell, partners began with the most systematically collected and available data on gang activity: official police records. Like other partners, the police believed that retaliation was a significant motivation for gang violence, and that they may have data to support this. They knew from research that retaliation entailed a number of specific precipitating events, some of which could be targeted early for intervention with the idea of minimizing the escalation of violence between gangs. Although other agencies would likely have information, partner discussions revealed that the non-police data was less systematically collected, thus it would require a more intensive review and analysis process. By focusing specifically on retaliatory violence data within Lowell Police reports, Lowell partners would initiate a thorough and methodical assessment of existing research, combined with an internal review of current measurement activities to inform future policy and practice.

The LARP conducted a review of the LPD's existing data and identified steps needed to create a definition of retaliatory violence and then began to measure it. Researchers worked closely with LDP partners to understand the real data challenges and opportunities, but also to support the development of capacity so the LPD and the partners could improve their data collection and problem analysis practices in the future. This review would be an important first step in directing the resources of the CGM partnership. The partners agreed that once the LPD data review was completed, it would be important to conduct similar reviews of CGM partner data systems. As a partnership dedicated to the prevention, intervention, and suppression of gang violence, the availability of this information would help to prevent retaliation before it occurs, intervene in the immediate time before a retaliatory act occurs, or react after an incident with the appropriate response.

The Review Process

The goal of the review process was to identify and analyze the type and quality of gang data being collected by LPD representatives in order to assess its utility for defining and measuring retaliatory violence between gangs. While the review focuses on Lowell's data and data systems, the same process can be replicated in other individual organizations or amongst a collection of agencies that might be interested in assessing the quality of their data, and the collection and utilization of that data.

The review process entailed a number of steps. These included scanning the research for the motivations and factors related to retaliatory violence, talking with local officials and practitioners about their perceptions of retaliatory violence in Lowell, assessing the current process for collecting, identifying, and sharing gang-related data, and assessing the opportunities for systematically collecting and collating the data in the future. The ultimate long term goal of the partnership was to adopt and utilize a common definition of retaliatory violence and direct criminal justice and social service resources towards the prevention of future retaliation. Table 6.2 describes the review, with each step then further described in the sections that follow.

Table 6.2. Steps in the Review Process

	Articulate Review Goals: Define and Measure Retaliatory Violence
Step 1	Identify critical variables through empirically-based literature review
Step 2	Interview key informants
Step 3	Pull official LPD incident reports from the Records Management System (RMS) to assess quality and validity
Step 4	Compare incident report data (RMS) to empirically-based literature review variables
Step 5	Select sample from reports and conduct a qualitative review of narratives
Step 6	Pull LPD's Safety First presentations to assess data included within
Step 7	Compare Safety First data to empirically-based literature review variables
Step 8	Compare the data collection and utilization processes of the LPD's RMS system with Safety First to identify strengths, weaknesses, and recommendations to improve data collection, analysis, and utilization

Identifying Critical Variables

A literature review conducted at the onset uncovered very little to help clearly define retaliation. However, the evidence did highlight a number of motivation factors associated with inter-gang violence. Because Lowell was looking to define terms in their local context, variables were pulled from the literature to be used as a baseline for comparing the dynamics and nature of interaction and retaliation in Lowell to existing research. These variables are detailed in Table 6.3.

Table 6.3. Key Variables

Key Variable	*Key Variable Characteristics*
Means of Confrontation	Face to face versus not face to face (Braga, 2006; Decker, 1996; Jacobs, 2004, Jacobs & Wright, 2008; Mullins, et al., 2004)
Severity of Crime	Homicide, Assault, Gun, Property Crime, Sex-related, Burglary (Braga, 2006; Decker, 1996; Jacobs, 2004; Jacobs & Wright, 2008; Mullins, et al., 2004)
	Severity of Victimization (Jacobs, 2004)
Offender/Victim Relationship	Original Victim, Sibling, Peer, Witness (Braga, 2006; Decker, 1995 & 1996)
	Male/male, male/female, female/male, female/female (Mullins, et al., 2004)
	Previous use of either party of resolution within the criminal justice system to address original incident (Anderson, 1999; Jacobs & Wright, 2008)
	Gang affiliation (Curry, et al., 1994)

Key Informant Perceptions

The next step was to gauge the connections between retaliation motivators from the literature and the perceptions of those directly involved in community safety prevention and response in Lowell. The LARP interviewed a group of "key informants," or representatives from agencies that work with gangs and gang members or are in some formal way associated with community safety strategies in Lowell. Key informants (N=16) were crime analysts as well as detectives from the gang unit and the family services bureau, all from the LPD. The group also included criminal justice partners from Lowell's Safety First group, an interagency task force (e.g. staff from county, adult, and youth corrections; a staff member from the district attorney's office; a member of the federal U.S. Attorney's staff; various local police officials) and staff from United Teen Equality Center (UTEC), a non-profit organization providing gang intervention and street worker services in the city.

The LARP interviewed members of this group to learn about their perceptions of retaliation in Lowell. A brief survey accompanied these interviews to capture the extent to which these individuals and their agencies collect the data necessary to better understand retaliatory violence. Figure 6.1 presents informant perspectives on what motivates violence between Lowell gangs or gang members. When asked, "On a scale from 1 to 5, with 1 being the least frequent explanation and 5 being the most frequent explanation, please rate the following motivations in relation to gang violence in Lowell," respondents provided a number of explanations.

Figure 6.1 shows that key informants believe the most frequent explanation for gang-related violence is gang members being disrespected or challenged with revenge/vengeance following closely behind. These perceptions can be used as a starting point to then gauge perceptions from a broader audience of informants and community stakeholders (e.g. residents, service providers, or policymakers) relative to retaliation motivations. Secondly, the data can also be used to employ research-based strategies intended to affect these specific types of motivations.

Additional information was collected from key informants in the form of a brief survey designed to capture each agency's data collection practices. Informants were provided with the following instructions: "The following table lists variables associated with retaliatory violence. Please tell us which you currently collect, do not collect but can collect, and cannot collect. If you cannot collect the data, please tell us why." Table 6.4 shows informant responses (based on 16 respondents) with respondents allowed to check all that apply.

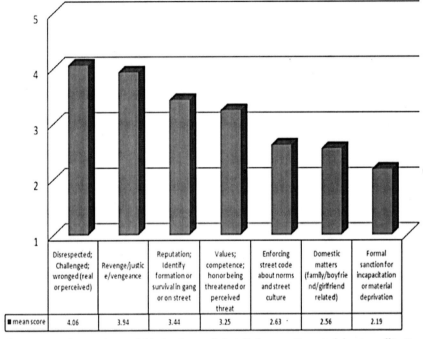

Gang Related Violence in The City of Lowell
Frequency of Motivations
N=16/ (1=least frequent explanation, 5=most frequent explanation)

mean score	Disrespected; Challenged; wronged (real or perceived)	Revenge/justice/vengeance	Reputation; Identify formation or survival in gang or on street	Values; competence; honor being threatened or perceived threat	Enforcing street code about norms and street culture	Domestic matters (family/boyfriend/girlfriend related)	Formal sanction for incapacitation or material deprivation
	4.06	3.94	3.44	3.25	2.63	2.56	2.19

Figure 6.1. Perceptions of Motivations of Retaliation as Reported by Lowell's Key Informants

Table 6.4. Data Collection Practices

Factors	Currently Collect	Do Not Collect But Could	Impossible to Collect
Type of Confrontation (Face to face?)	6	6	1
Severity of the Incident (Part I or II Crime?)	6	7	0
Specific Offense (e.g. homicide, assaults)	6	7	0
Offender and Victim			
Gender	6	7	0
Age	5	8	0
Relationship (Current & past)	6	5	2
Gang affiliation	4	8	1
Prior Criminal activities	4	8	1
Prior Involvement with CJ system	5	7	0

Positively, the majority of survey respondents indicated that all of the key variables noted in the research are being or could be collected. Police-related agencies (crime analysts, gang unit) indicated that they are systematically collecting almost all of the variables, while more than two-thirds of the other stakeholders reported that they are not regularly collecting (but could) collect the data. Only one of the respondents reported that it would be impossible to collect information on whether or not the victim and the offender had previous interactions prior to the incident. In very few instances did the informants suggest that collecting the data would be impossible. This insight adds promise to the development of a systematic data collection process in Lowell.

The informants' perceptions highlight two aspects of Lowell's challenge. From this review, we learned that respondents represented multiple organizations with varied data collection practices. These variations reflected financial, human, and technological differences across the agencies. However, informants believe they have a good sense of what drives inter-gang violence in Lowell, and that they have the ability to collect data to better account for retaliation between gangs. Their perceptions are aligned with accounts in the literature regarding retaliation motivators and can be used to create a collective and localized definition in Lowell.

A Review of Official Police Department Records

The key informant review helped to direct the next step—a comparison of the variable list to official police data. Armed with the list of variables from the research and insights from the key informants, researchers took a sample of police incident reports (N=207) from all 2007 cases (adult and juvenile) to compare the research and informant-based list to what was being collected in official police reports. We wanted to know if the motivation factors (i.e. disrespect, conflict resolution, and revenge) were being captured in police reports.

The LPD's record management system (RMS) stores crime incident data collected by officers on street patrol. The RMS captures demographic information (e.g. age, race, and gender) about the victim and the offender and provides details about the incident. Importantly, there is a "check-box" on the incident report form for the officer to note whether the incident was "gang-related." LPD analysts call this "flagging" of the incident as gang-related. The review was designed to look at the extent to which officers completed the required fields on the reports and to gain a sense of the extent to which the research-based variables were being collected within the narrative portion of the incident report. This comparison helped to point to the positive collection practices across the department as well as gaps in gang-related data collection.

Our review of LPD incident reports revealed critical weaknesses in the quality of the data. First, given that no standard definition existed in Lowell, officers capture only those data that seem relevant to the incident, based on their own knowledge and experience. There was tremendous variation in the scope of information included in the police reports. This was most evident in the review of the gang-related "check box." Through inquiry with analysts and officers, we confirmed that there was no standard criteria for "flagging" gang-related incidents in the RMS and that officers use their own discretion. Officers would check the box if they thought the incident was gang-related or even if the crime type (e.g. graffiti, trespassing, or disturbing the peace) may reflect what they believed was gang-like behaviors. This review revealed inconsistencies in how officers completed this critical data point of the report.

In addition to the assessment offered by officers, reports can be modified and "flagged" by crime analysts based on the understanding of gang locations and offenders. Other than individual knowledge of the analyst, there are no other criteria by which these modifications are made. This revelation shows that officers on the street and analysts within the police station can have very different understandings of what is and is not a gang-related incident and that their characterization can have an impact (positively or negatively) on how police resources are directed. This reveals additional sources of subjectivity in how Lowell data are categorized.

As a result of the divergent "flagging" practices, the LARP conducted a validity assessment of the report data. This assessment included selecting a small number of reports (N=21) from the original 207 incident reports to assess whether the qualitative data within the officer's narrative corresponded correctly with the report being "flagged" as gang-related. In some cases researchers found that reports were not "flagged" as a gang incident, when in fact officer notes included in the narrative suggested that the incident was in fact gang-related. Additionally, violent crimes were less likely to be "flagged" as gang-related, which conflicts with the perceptions of CGM partners who believed that gang retaliation was driving most of the gang violence in the community.

Researchers also found that a motive was identified in only 83% of the incident report narratives reviewed. In the remaining reports there is no mention of motive. It may be that officers on the street do not have enough or adequate knowledge of gangs needed to capture the most accurate data; therefore, different data are collected across reporting officers. Consequently, there are innumerable practices of data collection by hundreds of officers on the street, resulting in divergent data collection practices within this one organization. Addressing these discrepancies via standard definitions and collection practices would decrease, if not eliminate, subjectivity and improve the validity and integrity of the data collected. Defining and measuring retaliatory violence could only come after some corrective action.

A Review of Safety First Data

A supplemental source of LPD data was to be found within the Safety First task force, a group of criminal justice agency representatives who gathered monthly to discuss specific gang members responsible for violent incidents in the city. Given that Safety First was created to focus on violent gang offenders with multiple criminal justice partners participating, Safety First seemed like an additional source of information relative to data collection and analysis. Safety First focuses primarily on the "targeted offender" rather than a single incident as described in police reports. This "targeted offender" model was created during the notable "Operation Ceasefire" initiative in Boston in the 1990s and has been touted as an effective interagency approach to dealing with violent offenders (Kennedy, et al., 2001). The monthly meetings included a discussion of violent gang offenders and the exchange of information across relevant agencies to make sure criminal justice efforts were directed at preventing or minimizing the level of violence committed by these offenders.

The Safety First group utilized police incident reports as a baseline for their conversations. The LPD's Crime Analysis and Intelligence Unit would review reports on a daily basis and select those incidents involving gang members of interest. These individuals may be known to the police already, or may be persons of interest because of their violent behavior. It was, in fact, at the analyst's discretion to choose which offenders would be identified for discussion at Safety First meetings. In addition to the report data, Safety First participants would come prepared to offer information about probation or parole conditions, employment status, living situation, relationships with family, peers or co-conspirators, as well as intelligence about an individual's potential behavior in the future.

The LARP found the Safety First data to be of interest because it supplemented police officer reports with qualitative and anecdotal data from criminal justice partners. Combined, these data had the potential to be a powerful source of information about retaliation in Lowell. The LARP reviewed 260 targeted offender cases discussed over 23 Safety First meetings in 2007. Given the potential for information, the LARP wanted to determine the type and level of retaliatory-related data included in the presentations and within the case information. Like the report reviews, the LARP compared the data in these Safety First discussions to the research-based variable list to assess the scope of data being collected and used.

In an attempt to further assess the validity of Safety First data, the LARP compared the selected police officer reports (i.e. RMS) to the Safety

First case data included in the presentations. Aligned with the experience with incident reports, the LARP found inconsistencies in the data. Given that most of the case reports came from LPD incident reports, we were surprised to find that 56% of the cases that appeared in the 2007 Safety First presentations were *not* flagged as gang-related by officers in the RMS reports. What this means is that officers were not "flagging" the cases on reports, but analysts were subsequently selecting these same reports as gang-related.

We found a plethora of information within the Safety First case presentations that are not captured in official police department records. As we noted, the baseline of data reported at the meeting originates with incident reports, but the majority of police and other criminal justice partner data came from intelligence gathered as part of their work. It makes sense that since Safety First focused primarily on targeted offenders rather than incidents that there was very little data revealed on the motivation behind incidents. We selected a small number of cases from Safety First (N=26) to review in-depth, and we found less than half of those (N=10) included any data on motivations behind the individuals' violent behavior.

We confirmed through our Safety First reviews that there are several repositories of gang-related information within and outside the LPD (e.g. LPD's Gang Unit, Family Services, School Resource Officers). But nowhere did we find these data being systematically documented, communicated, and/or coordinated with pertinent individuals, groups, or criminal justice partners. More specifically, we learned that the LPD's Gang Unit was another source of data as they are assigned to street patrol, interacting with gang members, and responding to gang activity. Through their efforts they collect a tremendous amount of intelligence about past and future conflicts. Gang Unit detectives occasionally attend Safety First meetings to gather or communicate gang-related information. Further, the LPD's Family Services Unit, including School Resource Officers, conduct home visits and other special activities where they are able to collect information about gang members and activities. The dissemination of this information is also limited and not part of a systematic data collection and analysis strategy.

Additional Sources of Data and Information

As noted at the outset of this chapter, the review process focused on LPD data. However, there are many sources of information in the community that could inform Lowell's efforts. For example, the United Teen Equality Center (UTEC), the street worker and gang intervention agency has countless points of data from their outreach program (e.g. youth perceptions of conflict, concerns about future violence) that could inform a definition and measure of retaliation. A particularly unconventional example is the case regarding UTEC's work. According to UTEC staff, street workers keep a daily log to capture information about hot spots, peace work, and general gang happenings (e.g. rumors, interactions, conflicts) on the street. These notes are distributed among UTEC staff to ensure effective communication and coordination of resources. Importantly, at the end of every night, workers and staff meet to discuss what happens on their shift. UTEC believes that by documenting as many incidents and conflicts as possible, they will be better equipped to track motivations and actions of revenge over time. This data would offer a very different perspective of youth and gang members, as compared to the data provided by street officers or criminal justice partners.

Additionally, parents, the School Department and the Boys and Girls Club all interact with young people who are either at-risk of or currently involved with gangs, thus their insights would be of great importance to truly understanding gangs and gang violence motivations in the community. Most partners and key informants recognized the value to sharing and collating their data, but also acknowledge the legal constraints (i.e. confidentiality) as well as the importance of trust and relationships as influencing factors in sharing these data across agencies. Even so, because no such system exists for collecting and utilizing these varied sources of information and data, there is a scattered and limited view of gang violence in the City of Lowell.

CONCLUDING OBSERVATIONS FROM THE REVIEW

For Lowell to reach their goals of defining and measuring gang retaliation, there are several changes needed in their data collection practices. Their current practices offer a strong foundation, yet there are three different aspects of their practices that are barriers to reaching these goals. The first, in line with existing research, was having a clear and well understood definition of gang member, gang-related activity, and gang retaliation. The second observation focuses on improving the quality of data collected and analyzed, and the last observation centers on the multiple sources of data that exist relative to gang membership and activity. Without a doubt, the Lowell observations offer important insights and provide a solid foundation for measuring retaliation in the future.

Observation 1: Clarify the Meaning of Gang, Gang Membership, and Gang Retaliation

The review process in Lowell revealed that subjectivity is embedded within the gang-related data systems of the LPD. What seems to exist is an informal system whereby certain "experts" or key informants from the field help direct the community's understanding of gangs. These key informants might be police agency representatives from the Gang Unit or the Crime Analysis and Intelligence Unit. They may also be law enforcement partners from corrections or the prosecutor's offices, or they might be street workers from gang intervention programs. Because there exists no mutually agreed upon and utilized definitions related to gangs, gang membership, and gang retaliation, their perceptions are used to characterize what is happening in Lowell and ultimately how resources are directed. More positively, the perceptions of motivating factors described by key informants seems to be aligned with existing research, providing a foundation by which Lowell can build a standardized understanding across agencies.

Observation 2: Improve the Quality of Data

The second observation from the review focuses on the quality of the data collected. Divergent understandings result in divergent characterizations of individuals, incidents, and interactions. Absence of a standard definition results in flawed, erroneous, or deficient data which will surely produce similarly flawed, erroneous, or deficient information. Here, researchers found a need to develop standardized data collection processes across community safety partners which will improve the quality of data collected, and increase the validity and reliability of the data. These standards should be disseminated via training and professional development for those who are collecting gang violence data. In this sense, the ability to collect data is only as useful as the quality and completeness of the data being collected.

Observation 3: Bring Together the Multiple Sources of Information

In this review, it became clear that Lowell has no standardized method for collating research-based variables directly related to retaliatory violence (i.e. conflict-resolution, reputation, enforcement of street code). The review revealed multiple sources of data in existence that could help Lowell better understand and cope with gang activity, retaliation, and violence. Many people within and outside the police agency (e.g. Gang Unit, Family Services Unit, UTEC) have data that could be useful but because there is no agreed upon definition, or collection and collation process or system, it seems that this valuable information is lost.

Safety First participating officials were another source of gang data. Key data from these outside stakeholders gathered during Safety First meetings were not systematically recorded or utilized. These data are shared across Task Force partners but not systematically collated with other data (e.g. Gang Unit, officer reports). This has been seen in the broader policing field where information-sharing and problem-solving within and across agencies is weak (Boba, 2003). Combined with information from social service and education stakeholders, Lowell has the potential to create a powerful understanding of their local gang problem. To start, Lowell community safety stakeholders need to come together to discuss what data and information they have and identify a strategy to collate and disseminate the information in a way that is valuable to all interested parties. This may be a challenge, given individual agency goals as well as confidentiality issues, but, Lowell will not achieve its goal of preventing, intervening in, and suppressing gang violence without a step in this direction.

The above steps are certainly no panacea for addressing gang violence and retaliation in every community under varying circumstances. However, given the experiences of Lowell, it is possible that by attending to the above deficiencies, a community will be better prepared to collectively address their gang violence problem.

CRITICAL NEXT STEPS FOR LOWELL AND BEYOND

The Comprehensive Gang Model suggests that once a community recognizes that there is a gang problem in their community, they must conduct a detailed assessment of the nature and scope of the problem, the specific population involved, and the nature of their activities. It is not until this step is completed that a community can identify and integrate the necessary strategies to address the specified gang problem. This chapter described how one urban community attempted to focus on and better understand the motivations behind gang violence in their community. For the most part, Lowell is not unlike communities across the nation that are struggling with an elusive gang definition, challenges of collecting and analyzing data, and then bringing together multiple sources of data to inform their prevention, intervention, and suppression efforts. The desire to fully understand the gang and retaliation problem in their community is notable, yet the process revealed the challenges of thoroughly and adequately engaging in community problem analysis (Boba, 2003; Bynum 2001).

Given that definitional issues remain a problem relative to gang violence (Klein & Maxson, 2010) and that retaliation is a believed to be a critical factor in gang violence (Howell, 2003), then it behooves communities to use research on gang violence and the factors that influence gang violence as a baseline for understanding their own community's violence problem. Armed with a solid foundation of standardized data and a system for analyzing and utilizing these data, community safety practitioners and their community partners can more effectively direct their prevention, intervention, and suppression efforts.

REFERENCES

Anderson, E. (1999). *Code of the street.* New York, NY: Norton.

Ball, R.A., & Curry, D.G. (1995). The logic of definition in criminology: Purposes and methods for defining gangs. *Criminology, 33*(2), 225–245.

Boba, R. (2003). *Problem analysis in policing.* Washington, D.C.: The Police Foundation.

Bond, B.J., & Gittell, J.H. (2010). Cross-agency coordination of offender reentry: Testing collaboration outcomes. *Journal of Criminal Justice, 38*(2), 118–129.

Braga, A.A. (2002). *Problem-oriented policing and crime prevention.* Monsey, NY: Criminal Justice Press.

Braga, A.A. (2006). The crime prevention value of hot spots policing. *Psicothema, 18*(3), 630–637.

Braga, A.A., & Bond, B.J. (2008). Policing crime and disorder hot spots: A randomized controlled trial. *Criminology, 46*(3), 577–607.

Braga, A.A., & Weisburd, D.L. (2010). Editor's introduction: Empirical evidence on the relevance of place in criminology. *Journal of Quantitative Criminology, 26*(1), 1–6.

Braga, A.A., Pierce, G.L., McDevitt, J., Bond, B.J., & Cronin, S. (2008). The strategic prevention of gun violence among gang-involved offenders. *Justice Quarterly, 25*(1), 132–162.

Bynum, T.S. (2001). *Using analysis for problem solving: A guidebook for law enforcement.* Washington, D.C.: Office of Community Oriented Policing Services, U.S. Department of Justice.

Curry, D.G., Ball, R.A., & Fox, R. J. (1994). Criminal justice reaction and gang violence. In M. Costanzos & S. Oskamp (Eds.), *Violence and the law.* Newbury Park, CA: Sage Publications.

Curry, D.G., & Decker S.H. (2003). Suppression without prevention, prevention without suppression: Gang intervention in St. Louis. In S.H. Decker (Ed.), *Policing gangs and youth violence.* Belmont, CA: Thompson-Wadsworth.

Decker, S.H. (1995). Reconstructing homicide events: The role of witnesses in fatal encounters. *Journal of Criminal Justice, 23*(5), 439–450.

Decker, S.H. (1996). Collective and normative features of gang violence. *Justice Quarterly, 13*(2), 243–264.

Decker, S.H., & Leonard, K.L. (1991). Constructing gangs: The social definition of youth activities. *Criminal Justice Policy Review, 5*(4), 271–291.

Decker, S.H., & Van Winkle, B. (1996). *Life in the gang: Family, friends, and violence.* Cambridge: Cambridge University Press.

Eck, J.E., & Spelman, W. (1987). *Problem solving: Problem-oriented policing in Newport News.* Washington, D.C.: Police Executive Research Forum.

Egley, A., Jr., Maxson, C.L., Miller, J., & Malcolm, W.K. (2006). *The modern gang reader.* 3rd Ed. Los Angeles, CA: Roxbury Press.

Esbensen F.A., Winfree, L.T., Jr., He, N., & Taylor, T.J. (2001). Youth gangs and definitional issues: When is a gang a gang and why does it matter? *Crime & Delinquency, 47*(1), 105–130.

Felson, R.B. (1996). Big people hit little people: Sex differences in physical power and interpersonal violence. *Criminology 34*(3), 433–452.

Goldstein, H. (1979). Improving policing: A problem-oriented approach. *Crime & Delinquency, 25*(2), 236–258.

Goode, E. (1997). *Deviant behavior.* 5th Ed. Upper Saddle River, NJ: Prentice-Hall.

Gouldner, A.W. (1960). The norm of reciprocity: A preliminary statement. *American Sociological Review, 25*(2), 161–178.

Herrenkohl, T.I., & Herrenkohl, R.C. (2007). Examining the overlap and prediction of multiple forms of child maltreatment, stressors, and socioeconomic status: A longitudinal analysis of youth outcomes. *Journal of Family Violence, 22*(7), 553–562.

Howell, J.C. (2003). *Preventing and reducing juvenile delinquency: A comprehensive framework.* Thousand Oaks, CA: Sage Publications.

Jacobs, B.A. (2004). A typology of street criminal retaliation. *Journal of Research in Crime & Delinquency, 41*(3), 295–323.

Jacobs, B.A., & Wright, R. (2008). Researching drug robbery. *Crime & Delinquency, 54*(4), 511–531.

Kennedy, D., Braga, A.A., Piehl A., & Waring, E. (2001). *Reducing gun violence: The Boston gun project's operation ceasefire.* Washington, D.C.: National Institute of Justice.

Klein, M.W. (1971). *Street gangs and street workers.* Englewood Cliffs, NJ: Prentice Hall.

Klein, M.W., & Maxson, C. L. (2006). *Street gang patterns and policies.* Oxford: Oxford University Press.

Klein, M.W., & Maxson, C.L. (2010). *Street gang patterns and policies.* Oxford: Oxford University Press.

Loftin, C. (1984). Assaultive violence as a contagious social process. *Bulletin of the New York Academy of Medicine, 62*, 550–555.

Massachusetts Department of Revenue. (2010). *At a glance community reports: Lowell.* Retrieved from: http://www.mass.gov.

Melde, C., & Esbensen, F.A. (2011). Gang membership as a turning point in the life course. *Criminology, 49*(2), 513–552.

Middlesex North Registry of Deeds. (2005). *Lowell property sales for 2005.* Retrieved from: http://www.lowelldeeds.com/AnnSales/2005/lowell.pdf.

Middlesex North Registry of Deeds. (2009). *Lowell property sales for 2009.* Retrieved from: http://www.lowelldeeds.com/2009DataFiles/2009-12/low09-12.pdf.

Miller, J., & Decker, S.H. (2001).Young women and gang violence: Gender, street offending, and violent victimization in gangs. Justice Quarterly, 18(1), 115–140.

Mullins, C., Wright, R., & Jacob, B.A. (2004). Gender, retaliation, and street life. *Criminology, 42*(4), 911–940.

Sampson, R.J., & Laub, J.H. (2005). A life-course view of the development of crime. *Annals of the American Academy of Political and Social Science, 602*(1), 12–45.

Spergel, I.A. (1995). *The youth gang problem: A community approach.* New York, NY: Oxford University Press.

Thornberry, T.P. (1998). Membership in youth gangs and involvement in serious and violent offending. In R. Loeber & D.P. Farrington (Eds.), *Serious and violent juvenile offenders.* Thousand Oaks, CA: Sage Publications.

Thrasher, F. (1927). *The gang: A study of 1313 gangs in Chicago.* Chicago, IL: University of Chicago.

U.S. Census (2009). *City of Lowell, 2005–2009 American Community Survey, Five Year Estimates.* Washington, D.C.

Weisburd, D., & Braga, A.A. (2007). *Police innovation and crime prevention: Lessons learned from police research over the past 20 years.* Discussion paper presented at the United States National Institute of Justice Police Research Planning Workshop, Washington, D.C. Retrieved from http://www.ncjrs.gov/library.html.

Weisburd, D., & Eck, J.E. (2004). What can police do to reduce crime, disorder, and fear? *The Annals of the American Academy of Political and Social Science, 593*(1), 42–65.

Wilson, J.Q., & Kelling, G.L. (1982). Broken windows: The police and neighborhood safety. *Atlantic Monthly, 249*(3), 29–38.

Yablonsky, L. (1959). The delinquent gang as a near-group. *Social Problems, 7*(2), 108–117.

Chapter 7

Strategic Problem Analysis to Guide Comprehensive Gang Violence Reduction Strategies

Anthony A. Braga & David M. Hureau

Boston received national acclaim for its innovative approach to preventing youth violence in the 1990s (Butterfield, 1996; Witkin, 1997). The well-known Operation Ceasefire initiative was an interagency violence prevention strategy that focused enforcement and social service resources on a small number of gang-involved offenders at the heart of the city's youth violence problem (Kennedy, Piehl, & Braga, 1996). The Ceasefire strategy was associated with a near two-thirds drop in youth homicide in the late 1990s (Braga, Kennedy, Waring, & Piehl, 2001) and remained in place as the city's central gang violence reduction strategy until it was eventually discontinued in 2000 (Braga & Winship, 2006). Unfortunately, Boston subsequently experienced a very concerning resurgence in gang violence between 2001 and 2006 (Braga, Hureau, & Winship, 2008). The Operation Ceasefire strategy was soon revitalized and, once again, implemented as a key response to quell violence among Boston's gangs (Braga et al., 2008).

From its inception through its current incarnation, Operation Ceasefire has been framed as a problem-oriented policing enterprise that engaged a wide range of criminal justice, social service, and community-based partners. Among an array of policing strategies, problem-oriented policing has been suggested as a particularly promising way to prevent gang violence (Decker, 2002; Huff, 2002). While there are important parallels in gang activity across cities, such as the small participation of all city youth in gangs (Esbensen & Huizinga, 1993) and the expressive nature of much gang violence (Decker, 1996), the character of criminal and disorderly youth gangs and groups varies widely both within and across cities (Curry, Ball, & Fox, 1994). The problem-oriented approach facilitates understanding of local gangs and associated gang violence so responses can be logically linked to the nature of the problem. As Scott Decker (2003) suggests, one of the crucial factors in responding to gangs is how the problem is understood.

Properly addressing gang violence problems requires in-depth analysis of local gang dynamics. Unfortunately, research has demonstrated that problem analysis, as practiced in most local jurisdictions, is usually shallow (Cordner, 1998; Braga & Weisburd, 2006). The resulting problem-solving responses, therefore, tend to rely upon traditional or faddish responses rather than conducting a wider search for creative responses (Cordner, 1998). While there are many avenues through which problem analysis and response development can be improved, partnerships with academic researchers can be very helpful to criminal justice, social service, and community-based agencies in advancing problem analysis in local jurisdictions. Close partnerships with Harvard researchers have aided the Boston Police Department (BPD) and its partners in diagnosing the nature of sudden upswings in youth violence and developing appropriate responses to the gang dynamics that were driving these increases.

In this chapter, we first review the problem-oriented policing process and the research on the quality of problem analysis as practiced by most local jurisdictions. We then describe the Operation Ceasefire approach and locate the elements of the Ceasefire strategy within the Comprehensive Gang Model approach to gang violence reduction. Strategic problem analysis is critical in customizing the core elements of the model to local conditions and dynamics. We highlight the role that strategic problem analysis played in guiding the revitalization of Ceasefire and how ongoing problem analysis research serves to keep scarce enforcement, intervention, and prevention resources centered on high-risk gangs that need focused attention. We conclude that ongoing research on local gang violence problems is essential in controlling urban gang violence and in adapting the Comprehensive Gang Model to local conditions.

THE CHALLENGE OF PROBLEM ANALYSIS

Problem-oriented policing holds great promise for creating a strong local response to gang violence problems. Problem-oriented policing works to identify *why* things are going wrong and to frame responses using a wide variety of often-untraditional approaches (Goldstein, 1979; Eck & Spelman, 1987). Using a basic iterative approach of problem identification, analysis, response, assessment, and adjustment of the response, problem-oriented policing has been effective against a wide variety of crime, fear, and order concerns (Braga, 2008; Weisburd, Telep, Hinkle, & Eck, 2010). This adaptable and dynamic analytic approach provides an appropriate framework to uncover the complex mechanisms at play in gang violence and to develop tailor-made interventions to reduce gang-related victimization. The National Academy of Sciences' Panel on the Understanding and Control of Violent Behavior observed that sustained research on problem-oriented initiatives that modify places, routine activities, and situations that promote violence could contribute much to the understanding and control of violence (Reiss & Roth, 1993).

A number of jurisdictions have been experimenting with new problem-oriented frameworks to prevent gang and group-involved violence (Braga, Kennedy, & Tita, 2002). These new strategic approaches have shown promising results in the reduction of violence in Boston (Braga et al., 2001), Los Angeles (Tita, et al., 2003), Indianapolis (McGarrell, Chermak, Wilson, & Corsaro, 2006), and other U.S. cities. Pioneered in Boston, these new initiatives have followed a core set of activities to reduce violence (Kennedy, 1997; Braga et al., 2002). These activities have included the "pulling levers"-focused deterrence strategy, designed to prevent violence by and among chronic offenders and groups of chronic offenders; the convening of an interagency working group representing a wide range of criminal justice and social service capabilities; and jurisdiction-specific assessments of violence dynamics and perpetrator and victim characteristics. All these initiatives have been facilitated by a close, more or less real-time, partnership between researchers and practitioners. Solid problem analyses are the foundations upon which the interventions implemented by the interagency collaborations are built.

Problem analysis is the process of conducting in-depth, systematic analysis and assessment of crime problems at the local level (Goldstein, 1990). The role of problem analysis in problem-oriented policing is vital because it involves the in-depth examination of underlying factors that lead to crime and disorder problems for which effective responses can be developed and through which assessment can be conducted to determine the relevance and success of the responses. Given the variations in gangs and gang problems within and across jurisdictions (Curry, Ball, & Fox, 1994), problem analysis research is also critical to the appropriate framing of the comprehensive, collaborative strategies of the Comprehensive Gang Model. Problem analysis is action-oriented research that not only supports strategic interventions, but drives them as well. Unfortunately, as Boba (2003) observes, while problem-oriented policing has blossomed in both concept and practice, problem analysis has been the slowest part of the process to develop. In his twenty-year review of problem-oriented policing, Michael Scott (2000) concludes that problem analysis remains the aspect of problem-oriented policing that is most in need of improvement. The Police Executive Research Forum's national assessment of the U.S. Community Oriented Policing Services (COPS)-sponsored "Problem Solving Partnerships" program also found that problem analysis was the weakest phase of the problem-oriented policing process (PERF, 2000). We believe that these same problems would extend to action research projects implemented in support of the Comprehensive Gang Model.

Bynum (2001) suggests that police are generally good at identifying problems, but have difficulty clearly defining problems, properly using data sources, conducting comprehensive analyses, and implementing analysis-driven responses. Some officers skip the analysis phase or conduct an overly simple analysis that does not adequately dissect the problem or does not use relevant information from other agencies, such as hospitals, schools, and private businesses (Clarke, 1998). Based on his extensive experience with police departments implementing problem-oriented policing, Eck (2000) suggests that much problem analysis consists of a simple examination of police data coupled with the officer's working experience with the problem. In their analysis of problem-oriented initiatives in 43 police departments in England and Wales, Read and Tilley (2000) found that problem analysis was generally weak with many initiatives accepting the definition of a problem at face value, using only short-term data to unravel the nature of the problem, and failing to adequately examine the genesis of the crime problems. As a result, the responses of many problem-oriented policing projects rely too much on traditional police tactics, such as arrests, surveillance, and crackdowns, and neglect the wider range of available alternative responses. Read and Tilley (2000) found that officers selected certain responses prior to, or in spite of, analysis; failed to think through the need for a sustained crime reduction; failed to think through the mechanisms by which the response could have a measurable impact; failed to fully involve partners; formulated narrowly focused responses, usually on offenders; as well as a number of other weaknesses in the response development process.

As documented by Boba (2003), there are many ways through which the practice of problem analysis can be enriched, including the hiring and training of problem analysts within police departments, federal funding for problem-oriented projects and the publication and dissemination of problem-analysis activities, the participation of other city agencies in data sharing and analysis, and the encouragement and promotion of problem analysis by nonprofit and membership institutions such as the Police Foundation, Police Executive Research Forum, Vera Institute of Justice, and the International Association of Chiefs of Police. Academics also have much to offer in the advancement of problem analysis. In addition to providing training in analytic methods and concepts and developing a body of problem-analysis literature, academics can conduct problem analyses and high-quality action research evaluations in partnership with criminal justice agencies.

Partnerships between academics and police practitioners have been historically characterized by role conflicts, such as the classic example of researchers reporting the "bad news" that an evaluated program was not effective in preventing crime. For academic researchers, success or failure matters less than the commitment to the development of knowledge on what does and what doesn't work in preventing crime (Weisburd, 1994). For the police, this news could be interpreted as their personal failure, and the skepticism of academics can be viewed as irritating (Weisburd, 1994). In recent years, partnerships between police and academics have been much more collaborative and focused on working together in addressing crime problems. Unfortunately, the number of academics with the experience and expertise in working with police departments on problem analysis and response development is currently small (Boba, 2003). The challenge to the field is to increase these collaborations by educating police departments on the benefits of working with academics and to encourage uninvolved academics to learn more about and participate in problem analysis and problem-oriented policing projects.

Federally- and state-funded research and development programs, such as the U.S. Department of Justice Project Safe Neighborhoods initiative and the State of Massachusetts Shannon Grant initiative, have supported academic-practitioner partnerships to deal with serious violent crime problems. There are now many more examples of the productivity of these collaborative relationships. Problem analysis research is particularly important in adapting the general prevention strategies suggested by the Comprehensive Gang Model to local conditions. In this regard, the gang violence reduction efforts of a wide range of criminal justice, social service, and community-based partners become "problem-oriented." In this next section, we highlight the importance of ongoing academic-practitioner relationships in Boston in driving gang violence prevention strategies.

PREVENTING YOUTH VIOLENCE IN THE 1990s

The Boston Gun Project and Operation Ceasefire

Boston's appreciation for problem analysis today is grounded in their experience in the Boston Gun Project and subsequent problem analysis research exercises to address community violence. The Boston Gun Project was a problem-oriented policing enterprise expressly aimed at taking on a serious, large-scale crime problem—homicide victimization among young people in Boston. Like many large cities in the United States, Boston experienced a large sudden increase in youth homicide between the late 1980s and early 1990s. The Project began in early 1995 and implemented what is now known as the "Operation Ceasefire" intervention, which began in the late spring of 1996 (Kennedy et al., 1996; Kennedy, Braga, & Piehl, 1997). The Project was supported through a grant from the U.S. National Institute of Justice to a team of Harvard University researchers that allowed them to work with the BPD and its partners on problem analysis, response development, and evaluation. An interagency working group of law enforcement personnel, youth workers, and Harvard researchers diagnosed the youth violence problem in Boston as one of patterned, largely vendetta-like ("beef") hostility amongst a small population of chronic offenders, and particularly among those involved in some 61 loose, informal, mostly neighborhood-based groups. These 61 gangs consisted of between 1,100 and 1,300 members, representing less than 1% of the city's youth between the ages of 14 and 24. Although small in number, these gangs were responsible for more than 60% of youth homicide in Boston.

The Operation Ceasefire focused deterrence strategy was designed to prevent violence by reaching out directly to gangs, saying explicitly that violence would no longer be tolerated, and backing up that message by "pulling every lever" legally available when violence occurred (Kennedy, 1997). The chronic involvement of gang members in a wide variety of offenses made them, and the gangs they formed, vulnerable to a coordinated criminal justice response. The authorities could disrupt street drug activity, focus police attention on low-level street crimes such as trespassing and public drinking, serve outstanding warrants, cultivate confidential informants for medium- and long-term investigations of gang activities, deliver strict probation and parole enforcement, seize drug proceeds and other assets, ensure stiffer plea bargains and sterner prosecutorial attention, request stronger bail terms (and enforce them), and bring potentially severe federal investigative and prosecutorial attention to gang-related drug and gun activity.

Simultaneously, youth workers, probation and parole officers, and later churches and other community groups offered gang members services and other kinds of help. These partners also delivered an explicit message that violence was unacceptable to the community and that "street" justifications for violence were mistaken. The Ceasefire Working Group delivered this message in formal meetings with gang members (known as "forums" or "call-ins"), through individual police and probation contacts with gang members, through meetings with inmates at secure juvenile facilities in the city, and through gang outreach workers. The deterrence message was not a deal with gang members to stop violence. Rather, it was a promise to gang members that violent behavior would evoke an immediate and intense response. If gangs committed other crimes but refrained from violence, the normal workings of police, prosecutors, and the rest of the criminal justice system dealt with these matters. But if gang members hurt people, the Working Group concentrated its enforcement actions on their gangs.

The Ceasefire "crackdowns" were not designed to eliminate gangs or stop every aspect of gang activity, but to control and deter serious violence (Kennedy, 1997). To do this, the Working Group explained its actions against targeted gangs to other gangs, as in "this gang did violence, we responded with the following actions, and here is how to prevent anything similar from happening to you." The ongoing Working Group process regularly watched the city for outbreaks of gang violence and framed any necessary responses in accord with the Ceasefire strategy. As the strategy unfolded, the Working Group continued communication with gangs and gang members to convey its determination to stop violence, to explain its actions to the target population, and to maximize both voluntary compliance and the strategy's deterrent power.

A central hypothesis within the Working Group was the idea that a period of reduced youth violence might serve as a "firebreak" and result in a relatively long-lasting reduction in future youth violence (Kennedy et al., 1996). The Group reasoned that youth violence in Boston had become a self-sustaining cycle among a relatively small number of youth, with objectively high levels of risk leading to nominally self-protective behavior such as gun acquisition and use, gang formation, tough "street" behavior, and the like; behavior which then became an additional input into the cycle of violence (Kennedy et al., 1996). If this cycle could be interrupted, a new equilibrium at a lower level of risk and violence might be established, perhaps without the need for continued high levels of either deterrent or facilitative intervention.

A large reduction in the yearly number of Boston youth homicides followed immediately after Operation Ceasefire was implemented in mid-1996. A U.S. Department of Justice (DOJ)-sponsored evaluation of Operation Ceasefire revealed that the intervention was associated with a 63% decrease in the monthly number of Boston youth homicides, a 32% decrease in the monthly number of shots-fired calls, a 25% decrease in the monthly number of gun assaults, and, in one high-risk police district given special attention in the evaluation, a 44% decrease in the monthly number of youth gun assault incidents (Braga et al., 2001). The evaluation also suggested that Boston's significant youth homicide reduction associated with Operation Ceasefire was distinct when compared to youth homicide trends in most major U.S. and New England cities (Braga et al., 2001).

The Resurgence of Youth Violence in Boston, 2000–2006

As described extensively elsewhere, Boston's Operation Ceasefire strategy was discontinued in January 2000 (Braga & Winship, 2006; Braga et al., 2008). Soon after Ceasefire ended, the yearly number of youth homicides increased from 15 victims in 2000 to 26 victims in both 2001 and 2002, and then skyrocketed to 39 victims in 2006 (Figure 7.1). Between 2000 and 2006, Boston youth homicide had increased by 160%. As in the 1990s, firearms were the weapons of choice over the course of this new epidemic of youth violence. Eighty percent of the youth homicide victims during this time period were killed by firearms (166 of 207 youth victims). Fatal and non-fatal shootings also increased dramatically over this same time period (Figure 7.2). Similar to the trajectory of Boston youth homicides, the yearly number of shootings increased modestly between 2000 (162) and 2003 (177), followed by much larger increases in 2004 (268), 2005 (341), and 2006 (377). Between 2000 and 2006, the yearly number of shootings had increased by 133%.

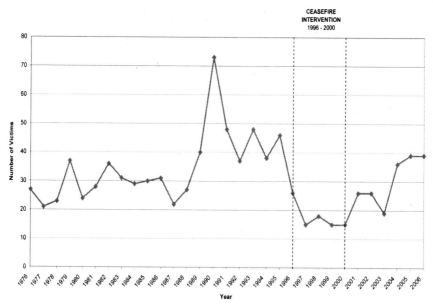

Figure 7.1.   Youth Homicide in Boston, 1976–2006 (Victims Ages 24 & Under)

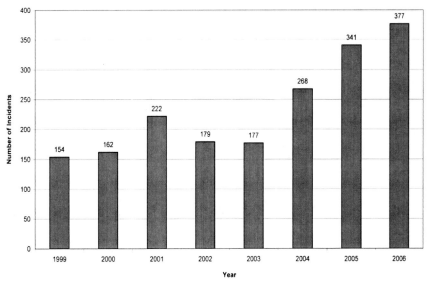

Figure 7.2.   Shootings in Boston, 1999–2006

Strategic Problem Analysis to Help Refocus Prevention Efforts

Boston's capacity to launch a strategic response to this new wave of youth violence was supported by the State of Massachusetts' Shannon Grant initiative. A core component of the Shannon Grant initiative was the Local Action Research Partnership (LARP) which provided funds for academic researchers to collaborate with practitioners to understand the nature of the local youth violence problem and to design, implement, and evaluate appropriate responses. With additional funds from U.S. Department of Justice Project Safe Neighborhoods (PSN) initiative and The Boston Foundation (TBF), Harvard researchers once again worked with the BPD and its partners in analyzing the resurgence of Boston youth violence.

The new strategic problem analysis research revealed that Boston's resurgence in youth violence shared many of the same characteristics of the youth violence epidemic of the late 1980s and early 1990s (Braga et al., 2008). Most of the shootings were concentrated in a small number of gun violence hot spots in Boston's disadvantaged, predominately minority neighborhoods of Dorchester, Mattapan, and Roxbury. These gun violence hot spots covered only 5.1% of Boston's 48.4 square miles, but generated nearly 53% (199) of the 377 fatal and non-fatal shootings in 2006 (Figure 7.3).

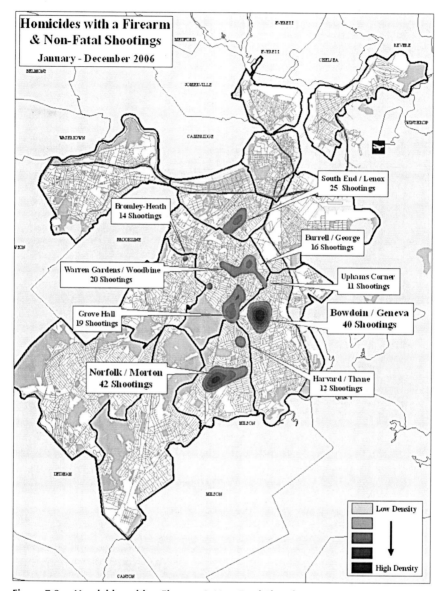

Figure 7.3.   Homicides with a Firearm & Non-Fatal Shootings, 2006

Youth homicide victims and youth homicide offenders shared essentially the same demographic characteristics—mostly male, largely from minority groups, and between the ages of 18 and 24 years old (Table 7.1). Boston youth homicide victims and youth homicide offenders were also very well known to the criminal justice system before each homicide

Table 7.1. Characteristics of Boston Youth Homicide Victims and
Youth Homicide Offenders, 2000–2006

	Victims, N=207		Offenders, N=121	
	N	%	N	%
Male	192	92.8	116	95.9
Female	15	7.2	5	4.1
Black non-Hispanic	156	75.4	87	71.9
White Hispanic	18	8.7	12	9.9
Black Hispanic	12	5.8	4	3.3
White non-Hispanic	11	5.3	8	6.6
Asian / Other	10	4.8	10	8.3
18–24 years old	159	76.8	96	79.3
17 and younger	48	23.2	25	20.7

event. 67% of youth homicide victims (139 of 207) and 86.8% of youth homicide offenders (105 of 121) had been arraigned at least once in Massachusetts State Courts before the homicide occurred. For those individuals who were previously known to the criminal and juvenile justice systems, youth homicide victims had, on average, 8.7 prior arraignments and youth homicide offenders had, on average, 7.1 prior arraignments. The prior criminal histories of both youth homicide victims and youth homicide offenders were characterized by a wide range of offense types including armed and unarmed violent offenses, illegal gun possession offenses, property offenses, drug offenses, and disorder offenses.

Youth homicide victims and youth homicide offenders had also been under some form of criminal justice system control before the homicide occurred. For youth homicide victims previously known to the justice system, 50.4% had been sentenced to serve time in an adult or juvenile correctional facility (70 of 139), 69.1% had previously been on probation before they were killed (96 of 139), and 30.9% were under active probation supervision at the time they were killed (43 of 139). Similarly, for youth homicide offenders previously known to the justice system, 55.2% had been sentenced to serve time in an adult or juvenile correctional facility (58 of 105), 57.1% had previously been on probation before they killed (60 of 105), and 25.7% were under active probation supervision at the time they killed (27 of 105).

Much of the increase in youth homicide was driven by a resurgence of gang violence in Boston (Figure 7.4). In 1999, the last full year of Ceasefire intervention, there were only 5 gang-related youth homicides. The number of gang-related youth homicides increased to 12 victims in 2000 and 14 victims in 2001, stayed relatively stable in 2002 and 2003, and then increased again to 23 victims in 2004, and peaked at 30 victims in 2006. Between 1999 and 2006, the number of gang-related youth homicides had increased six-fold. These gang-related youth homicides were personal and vendetta-like, with many homicides representing an event in a larger series of retaliations between feuding groups. Gang-related motives accounted for 76.9% of the 39 youth homicides in 2006. Boston gang members were also involved as either the perpetrator or victim in 70% of the shootings in 2006.

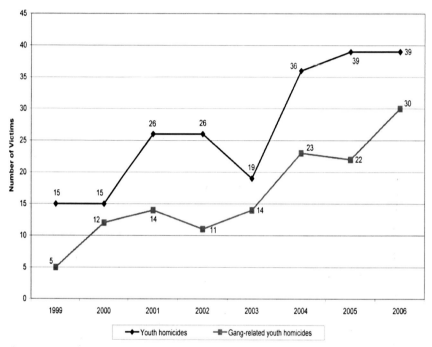

Figure 7.4.   Youth Homicide in Boston, 1999–2006 (Ages 24 & Under)

While a very small proportion of Boston youth participate in gangs, they generate a disproportionate share of homicide and gun violence. In 2006, Boston had 65 active street gangs with an estimated total membership of 1,422 youth. According to the 2000 U.S. Census, this represents only 1.3% of 113,715 youth ages 15 to 24 in Boston. In contrast to large and semi-organized gangs in Chicago and Los Angeles, Boston gangs were (and are) mostly small, informal, and loosely organized groups of youth. Gang membership was usually associated with a specific street, neighborhood, or housing project. Certain gangs were much more central to violence than others. For example, the Lucerne Street Doggz gang committed 30 shootings in 2006 (nearly 8% of all city shootings). The ten most violent gangs generated 32.4% of the citywide shootings in 2006 (122 of 377).

The strategic problem analysis research revealed strong parallels between the increase in youth homicide in the late 1980s and early 1990s, and the resurgence in youth homicide between 2000 and 2006. Once again, most of the violence was highly concentrated in a few places and among a few youth. These youth tended to be criminally active, gang-involved offenders who were well known to the criminal justice system and caught up in ongoing cycles of retaliatory street violence. The implication of this research was obvious: Boston needed to engage a comprehensive approach to its gang problem and revitalize the Operation Ceasefire strategy.

The BPD and its key partners started using the Ceasefire approach to quell outbreaks of gun violence among a very limited number of gangs over the course of 2006. Soon after Commissioner Edward F. Davis was appointed in December 2006, Operation Ceasefire was, once again, formally adopted by the BPD as its official citywide response to gang violence. Criminal justice, social service, and community-based agencies strongly desired a return to the violence reduction approach that worked during the 1990s and readily supported the BPD in expanding Ceasefire to a citywide initiative once again. The problem analysis research was very helpful in reaffirming the complex nature of Boston gang violence and the need to engage a comprehensive approach that blended strategic enforcement, community-based action, and social service and opportunity provision. The research was disseminated to law enforcement partners through a series of PSN meetings led by the BPD and U.S. Attorney's Office. The Shannon LARP initiative was very helpful in disseminating the research findings to social service and community partners and the funds from the broader Shannon grant initiative supported suppression and intervention actions in Boston. The "network of capacity" that undergirded Operation Ceasefire during the 1990s was, once again, properly focused on the problem of gang violence (Braga & Winship, 2006).

OPERATION CEASEFIRE AS A COMPREHENSIVE GANG MODEL

Building on the comprehensive approach recommended by Irving Spergel (1995), the U.S. Office of Juvenile Justice and Delinquency Prevention's Comprehensive Gang Model suggests gang violence reduction strategies should engage five complementary strategies: (a) organizational change and development, (b) community mobilization, (c) prevention, (d) intervention, and (e) suppression. Although Operation Ceasefire was a problem-oriented policing project centered on law enforcement interventions, the other elements of Operation Ceasefire that involved community mobilization, social intervention, and opportunity provision certainly supported and strengthened the ability of law enforcement to reduce gang violence. Beyond deterring violent behavior, Operation Ceasefire was designed to facilitate desired behaviors among gang members. As Spergel (1995) observes, coordinated strategies that integrate these varied domains are most likely to be effective in dealing with chronic youth gang problems.

Thus far, we have provided a general description of the Ceasefire strategy that highlighted the organizational change and development elements of the approach (interagency collaboration, focusing resources on high-risk individuals, innovative tactics, etc.). In this section, we locate the actions of the revitalized Operation Ceasefire working group within the Comprehensive Gang Model by highlighting its innovative suppression, social service and opportunity provision, and community mobilization elements (see also Braga & Kennedy, 2002).

Suppression

The typical law enforcement suppression approach assumes that most street gangs are criminal associations that must be attacked through an efficient gang tracking, identification, and targeted enforcement strategy (Spergel, 1995). The basic premise of this approach is that improved data collection systems and coordination of information across different criminal justice agencies lead to more efficiency and to more gang members being removed from the streets, rapidly prosecuted, and sent to prison for longer sentences (Spergel, 1995). Typical suppression programs include street sweeps in which police officers round up hundreds of suspected gang members, special gang probation and parole caseloads where gang members are subjected to heightened levels of surveillance and more stringent revocation rules, prosecution programs that target gang leaders and serious gang offenders, civil procedures that use gang membership to define arrest for conspiracy or unlawful associations, and school-based law enforcement programs that use surveillance and buy-bust operations (Klein, 1993).

These suppression approaches are loosely based on deterrence theory (Klein, 1993). Law enforcement agencies attempt to influence the behavior of gang members or eliminate gangs entirely by dramatically increasing the certainty, severity, and swiftness of criminal justice sanctions. Unfortunately, gangs and gang problems usually remain in the wake of these intensive operations. Malcolm Klein (1993) suggested that law enforcement agencies do not generally have the capacity to "eliminate" all gangs in a gang-troubled jurisdiction, nor do they have the capacity to respond in a powerful way to all gang offending in such jurisdictions. Pledges to do so, though common, are simply not credible to gang members. Klein (1993) also observed that the emphasis on selective enforcement by deterrence-based gang suppression programs may increase the cohesiveness of gang members, who often perceive such actions as unwarranted harassment, rather than cause them to withdraw from gang activity. Therefore, suppression programs may have the perverse effect of strengthening gang solidarity.

Beyond the certainty, severity, and swiftness of sanctions, the effective operation of deterrence is dependent on the communication of punishment threats to the public. As Zimring and Hawkins (1973) observed, "the deterrence threat may best be viewed as a form of advertising" (p. 142). The Operation Ceasefire Working Group recognizes that it is crucial to deliver a *credible* deterrence message to Boston gangs. Therefore, the Ceasefire intervention only targets those gangs who are engaged in violent behavior, rather than wasting resources on those who are not. Spergel (1995) suggested that problem-solving approaches to gang problems based on more limited goals, such as gang violence reduction rather than gang destruction, are more likely to be effective in controlling gang problems. Operation Ceasefire does not attempt to eliminate all gangs or eliminate all gang offending in Boston. Rather, Ceasefire is designed to focus almost exclusively on reducing serious gun violence by Boston gangs.

The Ceasefire-focused deterrence approach attempts to prevent gang violence by making gang members believe that consequences would follow any violent behavior and gun use and they would then choose to change their behavior. A key element of the strategy is the delivery of a direct and explicit "retail deterrence" message to a relatively small target audience regarding what kind of behavior would provoke a special response and what that response would be. In addition to any increases in certainty, severity, and swiftness of sanctions associated with acts of violence, the Operation Ceasefire strategy seeks to gain deterrence through the *advertising* of the law enforcement strategy, and the personalized nature of its application. It is crucial that gang youth understand the regime that the city is imposing. Beyond the particular gangs subjected to the intervention, the deterrence message is applied to a relatively small audience (all gang-involved youth in those target gangs in Boston) rather than a general audience (all youth in Boston), and operates by making explicit cause-and-effect connections between the behavior of the target population and the behavior of the authorities. Knowledge of what happens to others in the target population is intended to prevent further acts of violence by gangs in Boston.

In the communication of the deterrence message, the Working Group also strives to reach a common piece of shared moral ground with gang members. The Group wants gang members to understand that most victims of gang violence are gang members, the strategy is designed to protect both gang members and the community in which they live, and the Working Group has gang members' best interests in mind even if the gang members own actions required resorting to coercion in order to protect them. The Working Group also frames the process of communicating face-to-face with gangs and gang members to undercut any feelings of anonymity and invulnerability they might have, and that a clear demonstration of interagency solidarity enhances offenders' sense that something powerful is happening.

Social Intervention and Opportunity Provision

Social intervention programs encompass both social service agency-based programs and detached "streetworker" programs; opportunity provision strategies attempt to offer gang members legitimate opportunities and means to success that are at least as appealing as available illegitimate options (Curry & Decker, 1998; Spergel, 1995; Klein, 1995). Boston streetworkers are key members of the Operation Ceasefire Working Group and, along with the Department of Youth Services (juvenile corrections) case workers, probation officers, and parole officers in the group, add a much needed social intervention and opportunity provision dimension to the Ceasefire strategy.

In Boston, there are two primary streetworker organizations: Boston Centers for Youth and Families' (BCYF) streetworker program and TBF's StreetSafe Boston streetworker program. These streetworkers are charged with seeking out gang youth in Boston's neighborhoods and providing them with services such as job skills training, substance abuse counseling, and special education. Many Boston streetworkers are themselves former gang members. Some gang researchers suggest that meaningful gang crime prevention programs should recruit gang members to participate in the program as staff and consultants (Hagedorn, 1988; Bursik & Grasmick, 1993). Beyond their important roles as social service providers, streetworkers attempt to prevent outbreaks of violence by mediating disputes between gangs. Streetworkers also run programs intended to keep gang-involved youth safely occupied and to bring them into contact with one another in ways that might breed tolerance, including a Peace League of gang-on-gang basketball games held at neutral, controlled sites.

With these resources, the Ceasefire Working Group is able to pair criminal justice sanctions, or the promise of sanctions, with meaningful help and services. When the risk to drug dealing gang members increases, legitimate work becomes more attractive, and when legitimate work is more available, raising risks will be more effective in reducing violence. The availability of social services and opportunities are intended to increase the Ceasefire strategy's preventive power by offering gang members any assistance they need: protection from their enemies, drug treatment, access to education and job training programs, and the like.

Community Mobilization

Community mobilization strategies to cope with gang problems include attempts to create community solidarity, networking, education, and involvement (Spergel & Curry, 1993). The Ten Point Coalition of activist black clergy plays an important role in organizing Boston communities suffering from gang violence (see Winship & Berrien, 1999). In 1992, the Ten Point Coalition formed after gang members invaded the Morningstar Baptist Church where a slain rival gang member was being memorialized and attacked mourners with knives and guns. In the wake of that watershed moment, the Ten Point Coalition decided to respond to violence in their community by reaching out to drug-involved and gang-involved youth and by organizing within Boston's black community.

Boston Ten Point Coalition employs a limited number of streetworkers and works closely with the BCYF and TBF streetworker programs to provide at-risk youth with opportunities. Although the Ten Point clergy were initially very critical of the Boston law enforcement community during the early 1990s, they now have a strong working relationship. Ten Point clergy and others involved in this faith-based organization accompany police officers on home visits to the families of troubled youth and also act as advocates for youth in the criminal justice system. These home visits and street work by the clergy are incorporated into Operation Ceasefire's portfolio of interventions. Ten Point clergy also provide a strong moral voice at the gang forums in the presentation of Operation Ceasefire's anti-violence message.

The Boston Ten Point Coalition also plays a crucial role in framing ongoing discussions in Boston that makes it much easier to speak directly about the nature of youth violence in Boston. Members of the Ceasefire Working Group can speak with relative safety about the painful realities of minority male offending and victimization, "gangs," and chronic offenders. By serving as a respected intermediary body, the Ten Point clergy also make it possible for Boston's minority community to have an ongoing conversation with Boston's law enforcement agencies on legitimate and illegitimate means to control crime in the community. The clergy support Operation Ceasefire's tight focus on violent youth but will condemn any indiscriminate, highly aggressive law enforcement sweeps that put non-violent minority youth at risk of being swept into the criminal justice system. Before the Ten Point developed its role as an intermediary, Boston's black community viewed past activities of law enforcement agencies to monitor violent youth as illegitimate and with knee-jerk suspicion. As Chris Winship and Jenny Berrien (1999) observe, the Ten Point Coalition evolved into an institution that provides an umbrella of legitimacy for the police to work under. With the Ten Point's approval of and involvement in Operation Ceasefire, the community supports the approach as a legitimate youth violence prevention campaign.

The strategic problem analysis work used to guide Boston's Comprehensive Gang Model has now been institutionalized in the routine operations of the BPD's Boston Regional Intelligence Center (BRIC). The next section describes how the BRIC works with external research partners to focus Ceasefire and other gang violence prevention efforts.

Ongoing Strategic Problem Analysis to Guide Gang Violence Prevention Efforts

Established in May 2005, preceding the Shannon grant, the BPD's BRIC has maintained a collaborative relationship with the Harvard research team to assist the interagency collaboration in focusing Ceasefire prevention, intervention, and enforcement efforts on the violent gangs that most need this attention. The BRIC is a crime and intelligence analysis unit staffed by civilians and sworn personnel that produces strategic information products to support operational and investigative decision making. Over the course of 2008 and 2009, the BRIC institutionalized the collection, analysis, and dissemination of strategic information on gang-related fatal and non-fatal shootings. Briefly, on every weekday, the BRIC holds a morning phone conference call with BPD officers and detectives from its Youth Violence Strike Force (YVSF), Drug Control Unit (DCU), Homicide Unit, and its eleven policing districts. Violent crime incidents from the previous night are reviewed in detail, and on Mondays, the weekend's violent incidents are reviewed. BRIC analysts collect data from participating detectives and officers on the circumstances of shootings and, if the shooting involved gangs, the analysts request specific gang affiliation information for the shooting victim and suspected/arrested shooter.

The Harvard research team and the BRIC also conduct a detailed review of shooting incidents on a quarterly basis in each of the districts that experience shootings. Focus groups comprised of YVSF, DCU, homicide, and district detectives and officers discuss the details of each shooting incident and update the BRIC shooting database with the most recent intelligence. The BRIC and Harvard researchers create and continually update a "scorecard" that provides victimization and perpetrator counts of shootings for each Boston gang. The BPD command staff uses these scorecards in its routine Compstat and strategic investigation management meetings to ensure that its patrol and investigation divisions are appropriately focused on the most violent gangs. The citywide Ceasefire Working Group is also supported by smaller working groups via ongoing "Impact Meetings" in four police districts suffering from gang violence problems (B2, B3, C11, and D4). Intelligence and analytic products on violent gangs and gang members are disseminated to meeting participants in each of these districts; any new information developed in these meetings is collected by BRIC detectives and entered in the shooting database.

These data are also used by the interagency working group of criminal justice, social service, and community-based agencies to trigger the Operation Ceasefire intervention. As described earlier, in 2006, the Lucerne Street Doggz gang was the most violent gang in Boston. Figure 7.5 documents that the Lucerne gang perpetrated 30 shootings and were the victims of 7 shootings in 2006. This violent group was involved in approximately 10% of all shootings in Boston that year. Over the course of 2007, the revitalized Ceasefire interagency working group launched a coordinated set of enforcement, intervention, and prevention actions against the Lucerne gang. Figure 7.5 reveals that, as a result of this comprehensive attention, the Lucerne gang was only involved in four shootings in 2008. In this way, the ongoing problem analysis work not only serves to support strategic decision making but it also provides a mechanism through which performance of implemented responses to gang violence can be monitored.

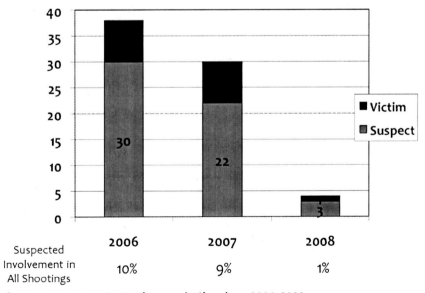

Figure 7.5. Lucerne St. Involvement in Shootings, 2006–2008

CONCLUSION

The broad lesson to be learned from this research is the considerable value added to the development of appropriate prevention and intervention strategies by in-depth problem analysis. For complex problems such as gang violence, a deep understanding of the nature of the problem is crucial in framing appropriate responses and ensuring that collaborative approaches, such as those framed by the Comprehensive Gang Model, are well focused on high-risk gangs and their violent dynamics. In Boston, strategic problem analysis revealed that criminally active gang members, who had ongoing disputes with rival gangs, were central to the city's homicide and gun violence problem in the 1990s and in the new millennium. Once again, the Operation Ceasefire focused deterrence strategy broadly fit the nature of the violence and was appropriately tailored to the nature of gangs and the operational capacities of law enforcement organizations, social service agencies, and community-based groups.

The problem analysis exercises described here benefited greatly from a solid working partnership between criminal justice practitioners and academic researchers. The research team essentially provided "real-time social science" aimed at refining the interagency working group's understanding of gang violence, creating information products for both strategic and tactical use, testing—often in elementary, but important, fashion—prospective intervention ideas, and maintaining a focus on outcomes and the evaluation of performance. None of the research described here was very sophisticated methodologically. But the ability to pin down key issues—such as who was killing and being killed and the role played by gangs and gang conflicts—kept the working group moving on solid ground, helped the participating agencies understand the logic of the proposed intervention (and the illogic of at least some competing interventions), and helped justify the intervention to the public.

Clearly, practitioner-academic partnerships add much value to the understanding of crime problems and the development of appropriate responses. Regrettably, such partnerships are uncommon. The challenge remains to encourage these collaborations through the education of practitioners and researchers in the principles and methods of strategic problem analysis and the benefits of working together. The Comprehensive Gang Model provides an important mechanism to promote practitioner-academic partnerships and facilitate strategic problem analysis. When armed with detailed information on the nature of gang violence, researchers can be very helpful to practitioners in ensuring that strategic enforcement, social opportunity and service provision efforts, and community-based actions are appropriately focused on the small number of people and places that generate the bulk of gang violence problems. In turn, partnering practitioners provide researchers with access to rich data on urban problems and the opportunity to use their analytical skills to make a difference in the "real" world of practice and policy development.

REFERENCES

Boba, R. (2003). *Problem analysis in policing.* Washington, D.C.: Police Foundation.

Braga, A. (2008). *Problem-oriented policing and crime prevention,* 2nd Ed. Boulder, CO: Lynne Rienner Publishers.

Braga, A., Hureau, D., & Winship, C. (2008). Losing faith? Police, black churches, and the resurgence of youth violence in Boston. *Ohio State Journal of Criminal Law, 6,* 141–172.

Braga, A., & Kennedy, D. (2002). Reducing gang violence in Boston. In W. Reed & S.H. Decker (Eds.), *Responding to Gangs: Evaluation and Research.* Washington, D.C.: U.S. Department of Justice, National Institute of Justice.

Braga, A., Kennedy, D., Waring, E., & Piehl, A. (2001). Problem-oriented policing, deterrence, and youth violence: An evaluation of Boston's Operation Ceasefire. *Journal of Research in Crime and Delinquency, 38,* 195–225.

Braga, A., Kennedy, D., & Tita, G. (2002). New approaches to the strategic prevention of gang and group-involved violence. In C.R. Huff (Ed.), *Gangs in America,* 3rd Ed. Thousand Oaks, CA: Sage Publications.

Braga, Anthony A., & Weisburd, D. (2006). Problem-oriented policing: The disconnect between principles and practice." In D. Weisburd & A. Braga (Eds.), *Police Innovation: Contrasting Perspectives.* New York: Cambridge University Press.

Braga, A., & Winship, C. (2006). Partnership, accountability, and innovation: Clarifying Boston's experience with pulling levers. In D. Weisburd & A. Braga (Eds.), *Police Innovation: Contrasting Perspectives.* New York: Cambridge University Press.

Bursik, R., & Grasmick, H. (1993). *Neighborhoods and crime: The dimensions of effective community control.* New York: Lexington Books.

Butterfield, F. (1996, November 21). In Boston, nothing is something. *The New York Times,* p. A1.

Bynum, T. (2001). *Using analysis for problem-solving: A guidebook for law enforcement.* Washington, D.C.: Office of Community Oriented Policing Services, U.S. Department of Justice.

Clarke, R.V. (1998). Defining police strategies: Problem solving, problem-oriented policing and community-oriented policing. In T. O'Connor Shelley & A.C. Grant (Eds.), *Problem-oriented policing: Crime-specific problems, critical issues, and making POP work.* Washington, D.C.: Police Executive Research Forum.

Cordner, G. (1998). Problem-oriented policing vs. zero tolerance. In T. O'Connor Shelley & A.C. Grant (Eds.), *Problem-oriented policing: Crime-specific problems, critical issues, and making POP work.* Washington, D.C.: Police Executive Research Forum.

Curry, G.D., Ball, R., & Fox, R. (1994). *Gang crime and law enforcement recordkeeping.* Washington, D.C.: National Institute of Justice, U.S. Department of Justice.

Curry, G.D., & Decker, S. (1998). *Confronting gangs: Crime and community.* Los Angeles: Roxbury Press.

Decker, S. (2003). Policing gangs and youth violence: Where do we stand, where do we go from here? In S. Decker (Ed.), *Policing gangs and youth violence.* Belmont, CA: Wadsworth Publishing Company.

Decker, S. (2002). A decade of gang research: Findings of the National Institute of Justice gang portfolio. In W. Reed & S. Decker (Ed.), *Responding to Gangs: Research and Evaluation.* Washington, D.C.: National Institute of Justice, U.S. Department of Justice.

Decker, S. (1996). Gangs and violence: The expressive character of collective involvement. *Justice Quarterly, 11,* 231–250.

Eck, J. (2000). *Problem-oriented policing and its problems: The means over ends syndrome strikes back and the return of the problem-solver.* Unpublished manuscript. Cincinnati, OH: University of Cincinnati.

Eck, J., & Spelman, W. (1987). *Problem-solving: Problem-oriented policing in Newport News.* Washington, D.C.: National Institute of Justice, U.S. Department of Justice.

Esbensen, F., & Huizinga, D. (1993). Gangs, drugs, and delinquency in a survey of urban youth. *Criminology, 31,* 565–587.

Goldstein, H. (1979). Improving policing: A problem-oriented approach. *Crime and Delinquency, 25,* 236–258.

Goldstein, H. (1990). *Problem-oriented policing.* Philadelphia: Temple University Press.

Hagedorn, J. (1988). *People and folks: Gangs, crime, and the underclass in a rustbelt city.* Chicago: Lakeview Press.

Huff, C.R. (2002). Gangs and public policy: Prevention, intervention, and suppression. In C.R. Huff (Ed.), *Gangs in America,* 3rd Ed. Thousand Oaks, CA: Sage Publications.

Kennedy, D. (1997). Pulling levers: Chronic offenders, high-crime settings, and a theory of prevention. *Valparaiso University Law Review, 31,* 449–484.

Kennedy, D., Braga, A., & Piehl, A. (1997). The (un)known universe: Mapping gangs and gang violence in Boston. In D. Weisburd & J.T. McEwen (eds.), *Crime mapping and crime prevention.* New York: Criminal Justice Press.

Kennedy, D., Piehl, A., & Braga, A. (1996). Youth violence in Boston: Gun markets, serious youth offenders, and a use-reduction strategy. *Law and Contemporary Problems, 59,* 147–196.

Klein, M. (1995). *The American street gang: Its nature, prevalence, and control.* New York: Oxford University Press.

Klein, M. (1993). Attempting gang control by suppression: The misuse of deterrence principles. *Studies on Crime and Crime Prevention, 2,* 88–111.

McGarrell, E., Chermak, S., Wilson, J., & Corsaro, J. (2006). Reducing homicide through a "lever-pulling" strategy. *Justice Quarterly, 23,* 214–231.

Police Executive Research Forum. (2000). *PSP National evaluation final report.* Washington, D.C.: Police Executive Research Forum.

Read, T., & Tilley, N. (2000). *Not rocket science? Problem-solving and crime reduction.* London: Policing and Crime Reduction Unit, Home Office.

Reiss, A., & Roth, J. (Eds.). (1993). *Understanding and preventing violence.* Washington, D.C.: National Academy Press.

Scott, M. (2000). *Problem-oriented policing: Reflections on the first 20 years.* Washington, D.C.: U.S. Department of Justice, Office of Community Oriented Policing Services.

Spergel, I. (1995). *The youth gang problem: A community approach.* New York: Oxford University Press.

Spergel, I. & Curry, G.D. (1993). The national youth gang survey: A research and development process. In A. Goldstein & C.R. Huff (Eds.), *Gang intervention handbook.* Champaign-Urbana, IL: Research Press.

Tita, G., Riley, K.J., Ridgeway, G., Grammich, C., Abrahamse, A., & Greenwood, P. (2003). *Reducing Gun Violence: Results from an Intervention in East Los Angeles.* Santa Monica, CA: Rand Corporation.

Weisburd, D. (1994). Evaluating community policing: Role tensions between practitioners and evaluators. In D. Rosenbaum (Ed.), *The challenge of community policing: Testing the promises.* Thousand Oaks, CA: Sage Publications.

Weisburd, D., Telep, C., Hinkle, J., & Eck, J. (2010). Is problem-oriented policing effective in reducing crime and disorder? Findings from a Campbell systematic review. *Criminology & Public Policy, 9,* 139–172.

Winship, C., & Berrien, J. (1999, Summer). Boston cops and black churches. *The Public Interest,* 52–68.

Witkin, G. (1997, December) Sixteen silver bullets: Smart ideas to fix the world. *U.S. News and World Report,* 67.

Zimring, F., & Hawkins, G. (1973). *Deterrence: The legal threat in crime control.* Chicago: University of Chicago Press.

Chapter 8

Impact of the Shannon CSI: Challenges and Observations from a Multisite Evaluation

JACK MCDEVITT & RUSSELL WOLFF

This chapter serves two purposes: to describe major findings from a series of impact evaluations conducted during the first three years of the Shannon Community Safety Initiative (SCSI) and secondly to locate the challenges encountered within a broader discussion of the multisite evaluation methodology. In particular, we will highlight issues that demonstrate the extent of variability found among the grantee sites as they implement the Comprehensive Gang Model recommended by the Office of Juvenile Justice and Delinquency Prevention. We believe that discussing the findings and our methods within this context will help illuminate important issues not only for SCSI going forward but for researchers and practitioners involved in evaluations of multisite interventions.

Briefly, our perspective comes from our work as the Statewide Youth Violence Research Partner (SYVRP), a contract to work with the Massachusetts Executive Office of Public Safety and Security (EOPSS) on SCSI. The role of the SYVRP is multifaceted. More formally, the SYVRP, in cooperation with EOPSS, is responsible for organizing and hosting regular technical assistance sessions for grantees, including such topics as crime mapping and workforce development. The responsibility most germane to this chapter and the most substantial undertaking of the SYVRP is the annual evaluation of the impact of SCSI.

Our chapter discussion is organized in five steps: first, we locate SCSI within the context of multisite evaluations and address the goals of SCSI and the anticipated challenges with their assessment; second, we describe the characteristics of the communities participating in SCSI with particular attention to their variability; third, we discuss several conceptual and data collection issues related to the evaluation of SCSI; fourth, we describe our methods and present findings from the evaluation; finally, we tie the findings and our experience conducting the evaluation together with some suggestions for how others might proceed under similar circumstances in terms of the evaluation environment.

A MULTI-SITE EVALUATION

The assessment of SCSI can be clearly identified as a multisite evaluation. The term multisite evaluation broadly refers to "an evaluation in which two or more sites engage in a coordinated effort to address a core set of study questions" (Straw & Herrell, 2002, p. 10). At one end of a continuum is the multicenter randomized clinical trial of an intervention with standardized indicators to collect and analyze. As one travels along the continuum, the degree of variation in program model, intervention, population, and other conditions increase. Straw and Herrell (2002) identify meta-analysis as the opposing pole. Like any evaluation method, multisite evaluation offers potentially significant benefits while posing a number of methodological challenges. The overall advantage to this method is the capacity "to accelerate the development of knowledge in a program area" (Rog, 2010, p. 211). Variation in the location, population demographics, or other factors may increase the program's generalizability to other circumstances and groups (external validity). Statistical power may be enhanced through access to greater sample sizes relative to evaluations within single sites. Also, implementing a program in numerous sites may provide information on important differences in the program environments (contextual effects) or uncover a greater number of internal implementation issues that would not otherwise be identified.

However, there are also substantial challenges to multisite evaluation. Increasing the number of implementation sites inherently increases the amount of variation in how the program is implemented in each site. While variation in site implementation can be beneficial to overall program success, especially when the program or intervention is tailored to the needs of a particular site, the number of challenges grows when the program elements are allowed to vary across sites. In the SCSI context, the evaluation was unable to obtain many of the potential quantifiable benefits noted above because of the tension between the needs for comparable indicators across sites and the desire to have sites tailor interventions to their specific needs. Based on the Comprehensive Gang Model, SCSI is structured with the understanding that community problems and local characteristics will differ, necessitating approaches that take such contingencies into account. As a result, many comparable quantitative indicators were not available for each site.

Although challenging to evaluation efforts, the high level of variability is arguably one of SCSI's greatest programmatic strengths. SCSI employs as a program model the Office of Juvenile Justice and Delinquency Prevention's (OJJDP) Comprehensive Gang Model to guide the emphases of a site's strategy, including prioritizing comprehensiveness and a greater focus on non-enforcement interventions. This model, developed, implemented, and evaluated in different locations over the last 20 years, is based in large part on the finding that communities will experience the most success combating their gang problems through tailoring their responses based on local conditions, as discussed in earlier chapters. It should be noted that the level of variation associated with SCSI is not altogether uncommon, at least not in the criminal justice context (see Skogan & Lurigio, 1991), and there is ample empirical research supporting highly tailored approaches to severe social problems. In addition to individual site evaluations of the Comprehensive Gang Model (Spergel, 2007; Spergel, Wa, & Sosa, 2001; 2002), evidence has supported this approach in several national initiatives such as the Strategic Approaches to Community Safety Initiative (SACSI) (e.g., Decker, Curry, Catalano, Watkins, & Green, 2005), Project Safe Neighborhoods (PSN) (McGarrell, Corsaro, Hipple, & Bynum, 2010), and Weed and Seed (Dunworth, Mills, Cordner, & Greene, 1999; Trudeau, Barrick, Williams, & Roehl, 2010).

In addition to the challenges of methodological issues described above, the administrative decisions regarding SCSI have also affected evaluation efforts. Measurement of standardized outputs was challenged because SCSI was originally funded as a one-year program; quarterly reports developed by the state did not require sites to capture consistent data; for example, on the number of youth served by programs. Because of original expectations that SCSI would be a short-term program and ongoing challenges to its continuation, longer term evaluation strategies were not feasible. The vicissitudes of the state legislative funding process and troubled economy continue to insert a degree of uncertainty into SCSI operations. Originally starting as a supplemental budget item, SCSI funding has remained an ongoing question during the budget approval cycle each fiscal year. It has on occasion been "zeroed out" only to be revived through lobbying efforts on the part of grantees and law enforcement agencies across the state. Although for the first 3 years funding was ultimately allocated and awarded (approximately $11 million in each of the first two years and approximately $13 million in year three), the survival of SCSI has continually been in question. In the following section, we describe with greater specificity the variability across the communities and grantee sites in order to further contextualize this project's evaluation and to offer insight into complex multisite evaluations more generally.

CHARACTERISTICS OF THE GRANTEE COMMUNITIES

Not only do gang histories, membership, activity, involvement in criminal offending, and other characteristics vary from place to place, community histories, demographics, relationships among groups, local economics and political environments, and specific reactions to gangs and gang activity in the past also vary dramatically by jurisdiction. Although earlier chapters have described the elements of SCSI, it will be helpful to note some of the program's characteristics during its first three years, especially in terms of framing later discussions of its impact. This section focuses on demographic variability to illustrate the point.

Starting in 2006, there were originally 15 grantees referred to as "sites" in this chapter. These grantees were made up of one or in some cases more than one community, totaling 37 communities involved in SCSI during the first year. Grantees initially had to have a population threshold of 100,000 to qualify for funding, which resulted in smaller communities collaborating for grant purposes. In year two, 16 sites representing 39 communities received funding. Year three saw an increase to 17 sites composed of 41 municipalities. In the initial year of funding, 9 sites had one jurisdiction, with the number of jurisdictions ranging from two to nine in the remaining 6 sites. Little changed since then; in year three, 10 sites involved a single community with the other 7 ranging from two to ten communities per site. Cities and towns in multijurisdictional sites typically are contiguous. Every participating jurisdiction includes the local police department as a partner, but the number of partner agencies including faith-based organizations, government agencies, arts and recreation-based programs, or other entities has differed and continue to differ by site. EOPSS prefers a municipal entity serve as the lead agency for a site and gives that agency the authority to allocate funds to other agencies within the site.

Of the 41 cities and towns comprising the 17 sites in year three, populations range from 3,504 (Essex) to 617,594 (Boston) (see Appendix for a complete list of populations). Table 8.1 helps put community differences into perspective by showing the range, average, and median figures for a number of demographic indicators (U.S. Census Bureau, n.d.). Clearly, residents in many of the SCSI communities have different daily experiences from one another in terms of their racial and ethnic backgrounds, educational careers, and financial standing.

Table 8.1. SCSI Grantee Community Demographics

Indicator	Low End of Range	High End of Range	Average	Median
Percent Hispanic/Latino	0% (Essex)	71% (Lawrence)	13%	8%
Percent African American	0% (Essex)	36% (Randolph)	7%	4%
Percent Asian	0% (Essex)	21% (Quincy)	5%	3%
Percent not U.S. citizens	1% (Norton)	29% (Chelsea)	9%	7%
Percent ages 5–17 in families in poverty within school district	4% (Melrose)	39% (Holyoke)	15%	13%
Percent residents 25 and older with highest education level high school diploma	12% (Cambridge)	40% (Revere)	30%	31%
Median household income last 12 months	$32,337 (Lawrence)	$97,500 (Ashland)	$58,282	$56,782

Percentages are based on U.S. Census Bureau Small Area Income and Poverty Estimates (SAIPE) count data. Figures for ages 5–17 in families in poverty within the school district were divided by the total figures for ages 5–17. Data for Essex are not included in the calculations, as it is the only one of the SCSI communities to be part of a regional school district. The partner municipality (Manchester) is not part of SCSI.

One might well ask why a community at the higher end of this median household income range is involved in SCSI. Originally, in order to submit a proposal for funding under SCSI, an applicant had to reach a certain threshold of population served. This resulted in some combinations of communities that may have included jurisdictions with very minor gang problems, but helped the application meet the population threshold.

The City of Boston possesses both the most sophisticated set of tools with which to address issues of gang and youth violence as well as the largest number of gang related incidents, with a population and incidence of gang violence much higher than the next largest cities, Worcester (181,045) and Springfield (153,060). Crime statistics cited in these sites' applications for SCSI year four funding are illustrative. In Boston in 2008, 33 of 49 gun homicides (67%) and 198 of 273 nonfatal shootings (73%) were identified as gang-related. Further, 122 gangs were identified, with police sources noting the involvement of approximately 3,500 individuals. Worcester's application states that in 2008 the city had 24 gangs with over 1,000 members. Of the six homicides reported that year, three were indicated as having taken place within a major hot-spot, suggesting gang involvement. Springfield, although possessing a populace approximately 15% smaller than that of Worcester, reported 14 homicides in 2008, noting that from 2000–2008, 31% of the city's homicides were identified as gang-related. Twenty-eight gangs were identified with approximately 2,500 individuals involved or affiliated.

It is not surprising that these differences and the demographic variation noted above have led to the implementation of significantly different strategies. This also illustrates the complexity of the gang definition problems, including whether incidents are categorized as gang-related or gang motivated, and we further discuss those problems as they relate to evaluation later on in this chapter.

CONCEPTUAL AND DATA COLLECTION ISSUES

In this section, we now turn to data collection and analysis issues resulting largely from the variability discussed and the characteristics of the program model.

Strategies, Activities, and Reporting Requirements

The Comprehensive Gang Model's emphasis on customizing solutions to local needs results in enormous variation across sites in terms of the specific population targeted, services offered, goals pursued, and indicators measured. In the first year, for example, SCSI funds were used to support wholly or in part 819 separate gang and youth violence reduction programs. Combined with the initial lack of any mandate for sites to report specific types of outcome indicators, such as gang-related incidents, this variability represented an enormous challenge to the evaluation. Although changes have been made to EOPSS's reporting instruments and requirement since then, sites are required to report on the indicators related to their specific strategies and activities only.

Evaluating Sites Versus Jurisdictions

A major issue both conceptually and practically concerns the level of analysis on which to focus. The site (n=17) initially would appear to be the logical unit of analysis, since administratively SCSI funds sites and the regional focus of multi-jurisdictional sites is a major goal of the program. However, numerous indicators, for example, crime incidents, are classified by individual jurisdictions, necessitating a community-level analysis as well as a site-level assessment. Crime-related topics are more readily addressed by individual communities, whereas cross-agency collaboration can be discussed across sites as well as communities.

Attributing Effects to SCSI

Even where positive change may be observed, the lack of systematically-collected baseline data makes it nearly impossible to attribute these effects to SCSI. In most communities the intervention was focused on the neighborhoods with most of the gang violence, and this left few comparable neighborhoods to use as comparison sites. Thus, the prospect of conducting a quasi-experimental design that might allow for statistical conclusions to be drawn about SCSI's effects has been unfeasible.

Moreover, it is clear that in many communities SCSI is one of numerous efforts targeted at gang violence, directly or indirectly. The larger jurisdictions in particular have long experience with the federal and state grant-making infrastructures for such initiatives as Weed and Seed and Project Safe Neighborhoods on the federal level as well as Safe Neighborhoods Initiative resources provided by the Commonwealth of Massachusetts. Many of these initiatives are targeted to the same neighborhoods and the same youth, further complicating the ability to evaluate one SCSI site's direct impact on violence.

Despite the challenges to doing a full cross-site evaluation discussed above, we have attempted to analyze what happened during the first three years of SCSI funding. This analysis is more descriptive than evaluative, but it does offer a picture of what occurred as a result of the SCSI in Massachusetts and is useful to other evaluators who face the same problems.

DATA SOURCES

To describe SCSI activities and assess the initiative's impact, we primarily use three sources of data to conduct the analysis: surveys of law enforcement and service provider agencies; interviews with personnel from select sites; and materials submitted by sites to EOPSS (e.g., quarterly programmatic reports and applications for grant funding). Each source is described below.

Surveys

The year one evaluation consisted primarily of interviews with site representatives. It was thought that during the first year of SCSI, funding changes in major outcome indicators (e.g., reduced gang crimes) would not be observable in such a short time frame. Additionally, as noted earlier, it was unclear whether SCSI would be renewed. When funding was allocated for a second year, 2 survey questionnaires were designed to measure program partners' experience and perceptions of numerous issues related to youth and gang violence and implementation of SCSI grant programming. One survey targeted each law enforcement agency serving an SCSI community and a second survey was administered to each service provider agency working on the grant from each SCSI community. The law enforcement instrument addressed broad areas of agency policy, gang characteristics and activity, extent of collaboration, strategies and tactics employed, training provided, as well as any challenges that developed over the first 3 years of SCSI. The service provider agency questionnaire addressed many of the same topics but also addressed the goals and organization of these agencies. In year three, similar questionnaires were used with some minor revisions. Survey instructions for the law enforcement survey asked for the chief or the highest ranking individual within the agency who has the most experience investigating gang-related activity within the community to complete the questionnaire. Actual respondents include the range of ranks as well as civilian personnel in a few cases. The service provider survey instructions asked for either the agency director or the individual at the agency with the most experience working with gang-involved youth to complete the questionnaire. Again, respondents include a range of staff members of these organizations. We report here on the results of the year three survey, which had a response rate of 80% for police departments (33 of 41 departments) and 72% for service providers (111 of 154 organizations).

Case Studies and Interviews

As noted above, in the first year of the grant, we conducted "case studies" of each of the 15 original sites. These consisted of semi-structured interviews with project representatives to obtain insight into their implementation of SCSI and learn more about their challenges and accomplishments. Interviewees included the project director and representatives from law enforcement and service provider agencies. In subsequent years interviews were also conducted to supplement the data collected from the law enforcement and service provider surveys to learn additional details about programs implemented in a site or the perceived impact of various initiatives. The interview sites were selected based on several factors, including the originality of the intervention, regional diversity, and whether the site was composed of a single municipality or was multi-jurisdictional. Northeastern and EOPSS conducted interviews with program directors, law enforcement personnel, service providers, and other site partners in six sites during year two and five sites during year three.

For each SCSI site additional materials were also used to inform evaluation efforts. These include quarterly progress reports and applications for grant funding. Each SCSI site is required to document their quarterly programmatic activities to EOPSS. These reports include information on program activities, partnerships, and program successes and challenges. Sites also have the option of including other measures and outputs that better reflect the progress of their activities.

FINDINGS

In this section we discuss findings from the evaluation of SCSI. The findings relate to gang-related violence and gang characteristics, anti-gang programming, and collaboration. First, however, we provide a brief rationale for presenting these findings in particular. Clearly, an anti-gang program must attempt to reduce gang-related crime and violence. Previously, we have described some of the challenges in measuring gang-related crime and provide a fuller discussion of those here and report on the proxy measures employed. Especially in the first year but also in subsequent funding periods, it has been informative to identify the number and types of programs supported by SCSI funds. These are important outputs because they reflect the direction and strategy pursued by the sites when interpreting the Comprehensive Gang Model. Finally, collaboration represents a critical aspect of the spirit of the Comprehensive Gang Model and its expression through SCSI. The heart of the model is the recognition that gang crime and violence are the results of underlying community processes that have developed over a long period of time and are extremely resistant to change. For this change to take place, the nature of interagency interactions must shift toward a more collaborative approach. Through our data collection efforts we try to determine the extent to which this may be happening in the early years of the SCSI program.

Gang-Related Violence and Gang Characteristics

Ultimately the critical outcome of SCSI is the change in violence committed by gang members in the grantee communities. However, it is not currently possible to say with any certainty whether gang-related crime rates have changed in SCSI communities. Setting aside for the moment the question of how long of a lag time should be expected between a site's attempt to alter historical and organizational processes contributing to gang violence, obtaining meaningful data on gang-related crime and violence is an ongoing challenge not only in Massachusetts, but across the United States. Findings from the 2009 National Youth Gang Survey indicate that, "with the exception of graffiti offenses, nearly half of [responding law enforcement agencies reporting gang activity] as a matter of practice do not record *any* local crime as gang related" (Egley & Howell, 2011, p. 2, italics in original).

Although we obtained juvenile and adult incident data on violent crime from the grantee communities during preparation of the second annual report, ultimately these data were not used in the impact analysis. First, the data represent the aggregated incidents for each community, whereas SCSI efforts in many communities are focused on specific locations. Further, while national research has shown that gangs are responsible for a disproportionate number of homicides, this tends to be the case for larger cities. Homicide is a rare event in most communities, with gang-related murders being even rarer. Howell (2006, p. 3) notes that "more than 80% of gang-problem agencies, in both smaller cities and rural counties, recorded zero gang homicides" in 2004. Similarly, although for the largest cities in the United States gang violence may represent half of the total violent crime (Egley & Ritz, 2006), it is the case for most communities that incidents involving gang members or motives will usually represent a small percentage of the total number of incidents (Greene & Pranis, 2007). Using city-wide figures of undifferentiated offenses (i.e., without determining whether an offense is gang-related) in pre-post tests of SCSI's impact on gang crime does not have the precision necessary to measure if gang-related crime has been reduced; this is in fact what we found. Further narrowing the analysis parameters to account for specific geographies and ages of participants may achieve better estimates but still do not necessarily address gang-specific events.

Additionally, several jurisdictions also still do not appear to have a set of gang-related definitions specifying how "gangs," "gang crimes," "gang members," or incidents (gang-related or gang-motivated) are identified within the organization. Even where such data are available, there are practical considerations rendering this information extremely difficult to obtain. Gang databases, where implemented, have tended to make information on individuals involved in or suspected of associating with gangs swiftly available for approved members of the agency; the same cannot be said for incident data. If a police officer suspects gang motivation in an incident, the officer can run the suspect's name through the gang database and see if a match is found. This process works operationally but does not generally include a step where the officer updates the original incident report to add information on gang affiliation. This likely represents a serious loss not only to evaluation efforts but to the agencies and communities themselves.

Finally, using crime data can be additionally problematic as an outcome indicator when smaller jurisdictions with very low incidence of total crime, let alone gang crime, are considered partners within multijurisdictional sites. This is particularly so for two sites involving nine and ten jurisdictions each. Simply averaging incident rates or another measure of central tendency would clearly offer an inappropriate and misleading measure of gang crime either across one of these site's communities or of the site as a whole. Multi-jurisdictional SCSI sites explicitly pursue the goal of regional information sharing and collaboration, which may require assessing a somewhat different set of outcome indicators or perhaps suggest that changes in gang crime be analyzed only in the larger participating jurisdictions as both a direct measure for those cities as well as an indirect or proxy measure for surrounding areas affected by gangs in different ways (e.g., vandalism, low attachment to school, and academic success).

In light of these limitations, we asked respondents to the law enforcement and service provider surveys to self-report their perceptions of changes in gang-related crime since the beginning of the grant. The National Youth Gang Survey conducted annually by the National Gang Center since the mid-1990s also uses an agency self-report procedure to obtain information on gang crime and characteristics. While self-report methods are open to challenges of subjectivity and bias, we were encouraged by the range of responses. For example, the police did not universally report decreased gang violence as one might expect if agencies were trying to demonstrate their effectiveness. See Table 8.2 for aggregate responses from SCSI police departments in year three.

The counts and percentages do not sum to the total number of responding agencies (n=33) and 100%, respectively, because responses of "unsure" and "N/A" are not reported here.

Since SCSI was intending to address the causes of gang violence, it appeared useful to ask survey respondents both about what gangs are

Table 8.2. Police Perceptions of Changes in Gang-Related Crime since the Beginning of SCSI (n=33)

Offense	Perceived Decrease	No Perceived Change	Perceived Increase
Gang-related homicide	9 (27%)	9 (27%)	4 (12%)
Gang-related robbery	8 (24%)	9 (27%)	8 (24%)
Gang-related aggravated assault	10 (30%)	7 (21%)	11 (33%)
Gang-related violence in schools	11 (33%)	15 (46%)	3 (9%)
Gang-related violence involving gang members from outside the community	6 (18%)	15 (46%)	10 (30%)

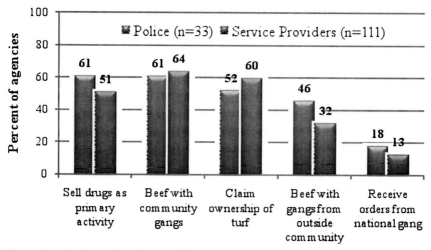

Figure 8.1.   Police and Service Provider Perceptions of Activities Characterizing Gangs in the Community

doing (see Figure 8.1) and how their characteristics might be changing since the beginning of SCSI (see Table 8.3). Obtaining information on perceived changes in gang characteristics and community dynamics that might provide incentives for gang involvement offers several potential benefits. In terms of gang activities, both police and service providers reported that gangs in their community were most often involved in drug sales and ongoing conflicts or "beefs" with other gangs in the community, either due to actions viewed to be disrespectful or turf ownership claims (see Figure 8.1). National Youth Gang Survey results suggest that these are important factors facilitating gang violence in communities nationally (Egley & Howell, 2011).

Identifying these activities and perceived changes in gang characteristics may provide a current snapshot on attributes and activities across the grantee communities. It may also speak to changes in gang-related crime

Table 8.3.   Police Perceptions of Changes in Gang Characteristics since the Beginning SCSI (n=33)

Characteristic	Perceived Decrease	No Perceived Change	Perceived Increase
Number of gangs	3 (9%)	17 (50%)	7 (21%)
Number of members in the most active gangs	6 (18%)	11 (33%)	14 (42%)
Average age of gang members	10 (30%)	20 (61%)	1 (3%)
Number of female gang members	4 (12%)	17 (52%)	10 (30%)

when shifts occur and, ideally, help alert communities to the likelihood of a shift in gang behavior. Levels of collaboration and referrals to services are likely to be tied to such changes.

It should be noted that the research literature does identify community population size as being associated with gang characteristics and activities (see Egley and Howell, 2011; Maxson, Curry, & Howell, 2002; Miller, 2001). While we did analyze our findings by population, the site/community tension makes drawing conclusions about correlations with size problematic. In particular, regional approaches make it difficult to ascertain whether a finding should be scrutinized as a possible community or site-based effect.

Anti-Gang Programs

During the preparation of the evaluation report following the first year of funding, it was recognized that outcomes related to changes in gangs and gang crime were unlikely to emerge after one year of implementation. Although targeted law enforcement actions may exert a specific deterrence effect on particular individuals in the short term (but, as noted above, this remains challenging to measure), the Comprehensive Gang Model also specifically targets community capacity and individual risk factors for involvement in gangs and violence. Given the complexity of such issues, the mitigation of these factors may not result in immediately observable results on either gang-related crime itself. What was readily apparent, however, was that SCSI had provided support for a large number of programs. Analysis of the original funding year activities identified that within the 15 sites (including 37 individual cities and towns) originally funded, SCSI supported wholly or in part 819 gang and youth violence reduction programs, with each site working on average with 16 new or existing partners. This total figure includes one-time events such as conferences or meetings, summer trips, or cultural enrichment events. Table 8.4 categorizes these programs into the five Comprehensive Gang Model categories.

Table 8.4.   SCSI Programming in Year One by OJJDP Strategy Area

Strategy Area	Total Programs Identified	Percent of Total Programs
Social Intervention	321	39%
Opportunity Provision	221	27%
Suppression	120	15%
Organizational Change	81	10%
Community Mobilization	76	9%
Total	819	100%

The most common strategy implemented across the sites was social intervention followed by opportunity provision. Street outreach, educational support activities, anti-gang education programs, and after school and weekend enrichment programs were among the most common social intervention activities funded in the first year of SCSI. Among the most frequently used opportunity provision programs were job skills development programs, employment referral programs, and a large number of employment opportunities, including both summer jobs and year-round employment. The third most common strategy area was suppression.

The most common suppression activities included directed "hot spot" patrols targeting gang members or gang neighborhoods, as well as joint (federal, state, and local or multiple community) investigations.

This represents a success for the program, since from the beginning of SCSI the leaders at the funding agency had stressed that SCSI was not a suppression-only program and that communities needed to implement a comprehensive strategy to reduce gang violence, not simply a traditional suppression-based approach. Often gang violence reduction programs take the form of police overtime to patrol known gang areas; SCSI sites actively sought to minimize suppression-focused strategies and embrace a more comprehensive approach. This was particularly compelling since the local police department has often been either the official grant recipient in a site or the official point of contact listed. In one community, although the local police department was the recipient of the grant they decided that only a limited amount of funds from the initial grant were to go to police department activities. The data from year one as illustrated in Table 8.4 strongly suggest that most communities heard and embraced a comprehensive approach as envisioned by the program's founders.

It is one thing to initially spread the resources to multiple agencies involved in different levels of programming, but an open question existed if this kind of comprehensive approach could be sustained over time. If the first three years of SCSI funding are examined according to the OJJDP Comprehensive Gang Model categories (Table 8.5), communities continued to support programs in very similar ways with social intervention

Table 8.5. SCSI Spending by Strategy Area

Strategy Area	Year One	Year Two	Year Three
Social Intervention	40%	41%	44%
Suppression	33%	33%	29%
Opportunity Provision	25%	24%	26%
Organizational Change	1%	1%	1%
Community Mobilization	1%	1%	1%
Total	100%	100%	100%

programs and opportunity provision program being allocated nearly two-thirds of the funding while suppression programs remained stable at about one-third of the overall funding. For reasons discussed below, organizational change and community mobilization activities were allocated a small amount of the total SCSI dollars.

This initial analysis suggests that from the beginning, SCSI sites enjoyed several significant achievements. First, the grant supported a large number of programs. Second, sites appear to have taken a comprehensive approach to reducing youth involvement in gangs and violence as envisioned by the original SCSI legislation. This approach differs from the types of suppression-based initiatives often implemented in communities across the country (see Greene & Pranis, 2007). Ironically, the argument that a community is a unique environment has long been used by criminal justice agencies to justify organizational insularity (Skogan & Lurigio, 1991) whereas this notion increasingly supports data-driven collaborative problem-solving approaches. Similarly, sites allocated the majority of grant resources toward social intervention and opportunity provision programming, as opposed to primarily suppression-based actions. This contrasts with other national anti-gang violence initiatives. For example, the Weed & Seed initiative now mandates that at least 40% of site funds be used for "seeding," up from 23% originally provided for such activities; however, at least 50% of funds are still mandated to be spent on enforcement-related "weeding" activities (with up to 10% allocated for administrative costs) (Trudeau, et al., 2010). By comparison, between 65% and 70% of SCSI funding overall is going toward the provision of nonprofit and human services programming versus about one-third of funding toward suppression activities of local law enforcement.

Collaboration

The Comprehensive Gang Model suggests that one of the major factors leading to the prevention of gang violence is collaboration among agencies and other stakeholders. While we have shown that funds were distributed in support of more comprehensive approaches, a question remains as to how truly collaborative these agencies were in attempting to reduce gang violence. The SCSI legislation and requests for proposals specifically state preferences for projects involving "regional, multi-jurisdictional strategies." Thus, an important part of the evaluation of SCSI is to measure the extent to which collaboration among a wide variety of sites' partner agencies has changed following the implementation of SCSI activities. During the original year of SCSI, most site partners reported that they increased collaboration with agencies with which they had existing relationships. This allowed many groups to get their initiatives moving quickly.

Importantly, this was also a first step in overcoming inter-agency distrust, competition for resources, or other conflicts. Particularly in sites composed of multiple jurisdictions, task forces developed that crossed a number of these historic boundaries. As discussed later in this section, organizational change and community mobilization efforts are challenging initiatives to implement, requiring institutional change and sustained focus (e.g., Gebo, Boyes-Watson, & Pinto-Wilson, 2010). However, as many sites continued to build upon their ongoing efforts during years two and three, these are becoming more of a reality.

Surveys conducted in years two and three allowed us to obtain details about individual communities as well as the sites in which they participate. Here it became necessary to mix units of analysis (i.e., agency, community, site) in order to obtain as much information on collaboration in particular. We discussed earlier that each participating community involved the local police department. Service providers often serve youth across jurisdictions and cannot be analyzed at the community level in many cases.

The surveys have provided feedback on the level of collaboration among project partners; however, without further explication "collaboration" can be a vague term, meaning different things to different stakeholders and likely does not allow for direct inference of the quality of a relationship (see Thomson & Perry, 2006, for a concise discussion of collaborative processes and distinctions between collaboration and other similar terms such as cooperation and coordination). Although our survey instruments did not specifically define collaboration, to get at the issue of the quality of inter-agency interactions we asked respondents about their perceptions of the effectiveness of various partnerships vis-à-vis accomplishing SCSI goals. The service provider questionnaire also asked for perceptions of changes concerning a concrete action critical to an agency's operations—the number of referrals provided by various types of agencies. We briefly describe these findings below.

Police agencies most often report that collaboration with other police departments has significantly increased since SCSI began (see Figure 8.2). However, almost half of responding police agencies also report significant increases in collaboration with service providers during this time. More than half of responding agencies in year three report that collaboration with service providers has been extremely effective (15%) or effective (42%) in reducing gang violence.

We also asked service providers for their perspective regarding the collaboration of SCSI partners. One of the most striking findings is the increased collaboration service providers report with the police. In year three, 60% of service providers say they significantly increased their collaboration with police since the beginning of SCSI (see Figure 8.3). More than 20 percentage points separate this finding from the next source of

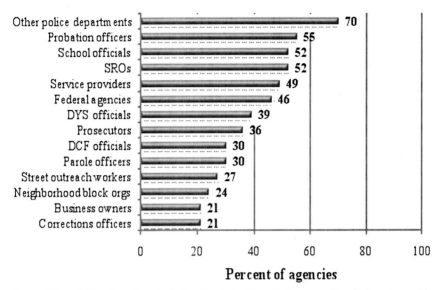

Figure 8.2. Police departments indicating "significantly increased" collaboration with the following agency types since the beginning of SCSI (n=33)

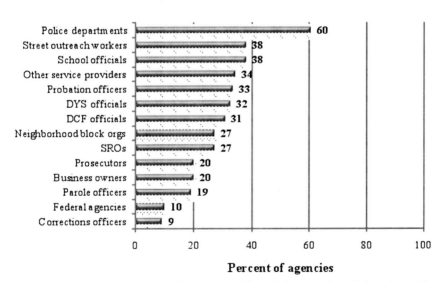

Figure 8.3. Service providers indicating "significantly increased" collaboration with the following agency types since the beginning of SCSI (n=111)

collaboration. Regarding the effectiveness of collaborating with law enforcement agencies, almost three-quarters of responding agencies in year three rate these collaborations as extremely effective (38%) or effective (36%) in addressing gang-involved or at-risk youth.

Service providers have also benefited from breaking down prior communication barriers. Many sites have reported that a silo mentality has historically operated in the non-profit service community as agencies frequently competed with other agencies over the limited pool of grants and other resources available to fund their efforts. Although the provision of SCSI funding has been an instrumental part of getting agencies to the table, the collaborative emphasis of SCSI has helped agencies see more effective ways of working with youth that includes other program partners. Results of the year three survey show that 34% of responding agencies see collaboration with other service providers having significantly increased during this period (see Figure 8.3). It appears that during the first three years of SCSI support there has been a substantial increase in the number of service providers that are working more collaboratively.

Another question that could be asked about this increased collaboration involves its impact. If more collaboration does not result in additional benefits for at-risk youth, why are we collaborating? One of the most significant results of the SCSI is that for a number of reasons including increased collaboration, more at-risk youth are being referred for services. While collaboration may mean different things to different people, referrals are a more concrete reflection of partnership. One-quarter or more of service providers report seeing a significant increase in the number of referrals they have received from law enforcement (37%) and the schools (33%) since the beginning of the SCSI. More than one-quarter indicate significant increases in referrals from community members (28%), other service providers (28%), and street outreach workers (27%). This is one of the most promising outputs of the SCSI to date. The facts that (1) police and schools are referring more at-risk youth to services and (2) agencies are referring at-risk youth to other agencies that may be providing more appropriate services mean that one of the original goals of SCSI—getting at-risk youth to services—is being met. While referrals represent program "outputs" rather than youth "outcomes," they are encouraging findings. Certainly, assessing quality of services provided and following up with youth subsequent to service provision must also be addressed.

DISCUSSION

As our findings suggest, there is evidence that SCSI has benefited the grantee communities involved. It is also clear that conclusions about the program's impact on gang violence are difficult to draw for several reasons. First, SCSI addresses longstanding community practices, such as insufficient interagency collaboration and piecemeal or primarily enforcement-oriented interventions that are likely influencing gang dynamics; these take time to change. Second, there are methodological issues that continue to challenge any evaluation efforts. Appropriate law enforcement data on gangs and gang-related incidents are rarely collected by local police departments, and we continue to develop ways to glean cross-site lessons despite inter-site differences.

Many of the issues we have encountered when trying to assess SCSI are not unique to a multisite evaluation, but the extent of their challenge may be exacerbated in this context. Other challenges stem directly from the nature of a multisite program. With the greater emphasis on tailoring initiatives to the local context, multisite evaluations of programs such as those based on the Comprehensive Gang Model will require much greater effort to take advantage of several methodological benefits that occur in more tightly controlled multisite projects with experimental research designs. In addition to requiring cooperation with evaluation efforts into site contracts, Mowbray and Herman (1991) identify several practices they built into their multisite evaluation of mental health programs that might be helpful to interventions with substantial variation:

> Acting as grant managers, state program specialists with expertise in providing services to individuals who are homeless and mentally ill are required to review quarterly reports, make site visits, and provide hands-on technical assistance to ensure that interventions are being implemented as intended. An evaluation specialist is available to review data submissions and analysis and make site visits to help ensure the quality of the evaluation component.

In this discussion, we suggest a number of factors that are important for practitioners and evaluators to be cognizant of when involved in the implementation and assessment of the Comprehensive Gang Model, and a multisite evaluation in particular.

Planning for Phased Implementation and Evaluation Processes

As we have noted, it has taken years and in some cases generations to develop the entrenched gang culture that exists in some communities. Whether identifying or strengthening programmatic and community resources, activities supported through SCSI funding have contributed to solidifying a foundation for addressing youth gang violence and the entrenched gang culture. We should not expect to eliminate this culture in one or even three years. The effect of a site's efforts rests in part on the ability of each community involved to change entrenched agency practices. Over the course of the SCSI grant, sites have reported a number of changes in the way their communities approach their gang problems. We suggest that these changes reflect progress toward community mobilization and organizational change, which are the more structural and thus challenging aspects of the Comprehensive Gang Model and, ironically, perhaps the least dependent on funding dollars. When we speak of a site's evolving approach to gangs, we have begun to speak of a specific type of "evolution," by which we refer to when communities are not only doing more programming but are establishing new community expectations, implementing more effective organizational arrangements, and sustaining these practices. Evaluation and implementation of the Comprehensive Gang Model elsewhere will also want to attend to the quantity and quality of outcomes based on the number of OJJDP strategies put into practice as well as the dosage of each strategy. While SCSI requires grantees to follow the Comprehensive Gang Model, it is the case that sites place different emphasis on each of the five strategies. Some may continue to rely predominantly on suppression-based activities while others more fully implement the Comprehensive Gang Model. More work must be done to specify how the Comprehensive Gang Model can be fine-tuned to the unique characteristics of sites and communities. Gebo, Boyes-Watson, and Pinto-Wilson (2010) suggest an alternative way of conceptualizing the five strategy areas, with organizational change and development and community mobilization playing important foundational roles:

> These two strategies work as parallel structures to create social intervention and provide opportunities to the community. For true, lasting organizational change to occur, the organizational strategy must be the foundation upon which other strategies, including suppression, exist. Community mobilization is a part of the organizational strategy, not separate from it (Gebo et al., 2010, p. 168).

It may be useful then to view community mobilization in particular as occurring on a continuum or at least as having an initial phase and a later phase. A subsequent mobilization, one that builds on having important partners at the table, is required to maintain efforts over the long term. Perhaps another way of thinking is that as communities come together, the development of relationships makes organizational change—and the sustainability of efforts—possible. While it is difficult to say so definitively, the observations made by Northeastern and EOPSS based on systematic qualitative data collection and interactions with grantee partners appear to indicate that this transition is in motion in most SCSI sites.

There are also issues within local political and economic environments that are important to consider in developing implementation and evaluation strategies. In at least one site, the initial SCSI partnership was purposefully made available to any agency desiring involvement. This was done to overcome longstanding agency territoriality resulting largely from competition over scarce funding. As a result, the original implementation plan was based on an existing partnership rather than one specifically engineered to structure the development of a partnership. Although this may appear to be an overtly political tactic that squanders limited resources, this approach may in fact have made it possible for any partnership to get off the ground and lay the foundation for subsequent, more efficiently targeted efforts. More time may be needed to devote to stakeholder and agency partner involvement in the planning process and to efforts to determine whether this can be mitigated or at least transformed as the project matures. These observations strongly suggest the need for a purposefully phased approach at the multi-site level to both implementation and evaluation.

Sustaining Efforts

Communities are motivated to apply for SCSI funding for a variety of reasons. A violent gang-related incident may be the impetus for communities to push for new policies and programs to make the streets safer and provide programs to keep youth out of gangs. Whatever the reason for this initial mobilization, there is no guarantee that partners stay motivated or significantly alter their previous strategies for addressing gangs. As Decker and Curry (2002) observe, the demise of such partnerships is the norm rather than the exception. Through an emphasis on action research, the SCSI has sought to help sites build a strong foundation that embraces continual reassessment of gang and youth violence problems over the long term and keeps partners active and working together. While this focus on reassessment and sustainability is an important factor in sites' success, project partners in many sites continue to worry about the likelihood of maintaining their advances without funding predicated on the Comprehensive Gang Model strategies. As state dollars allocated to programs like SCSI continue to decline, collaborations that have been developed over the initial three years will experience strains. As some agencies have their funding discontinued, will they remain part of the anti-youth violence orientation of the community? This will be a particularly important challenge for SCSI communities and threatens to undo much of the very strong collaboration building efforts that have gone on to date. One concern Northeastern and EOPSS continually heard during interviews after the drastic reduction in SCSI funding for year four was that the project partners "don't want to look back five years from now and say, 'remember when we all used to regularly meet and work together to address gang and youth violence issues?'"

The action research process and the Comprehensive Gang Model emphasize a high level of participation among grantee partners. Participatory evaluation models, which have been shown to encourage more use of evaluation products and involvement in the process (Toal, King, Johnson,

& Lawrenz, 2009), become more challenging and are qualitatively different in multisite contexts. Whereas participation in a single site program
often can be achieved through frequent face-to-face meetings and other
interpersonal interactions with each partner (that is, individual stakeholders), in multisite evaluations the "participant" or stakeholder can
become increasingly associated with the overall site project rather than
the individuals comprising it (Toal et al., 2009). Lawrenz and Huffman
(2003, p. 472) describe the fundamental difference.

> [In single-site programs] these people may all be familiar with each other
> and the important issues. . . . A participatory approach is feasible in that the
> various stakeholders can all contribute to decisions about how the evalua-
> tion should operate. In the large, multi-site evaluations . . . however, there
> are many different layers of stakeholders, there is wide diversity, and each
> site is often unfamiliar with the others. Furthermore, the sites were selected
> because of their success in a competitive grant process, not because they
> would facilitate the program evaluation in general, let alone a multi-site
> participatory evaluation. Each "site" is also a combination of sites, each with
> its own stakeholders, and is a complex, expensive project funded for many
> thousands to millions of dollars.

If participation is an impetus for site partners to use evaluation products, then this is also critical in terms of communicating evaluation information to policy makers and other important stakeholders influencing
funding allocation.

The decision of Massachusetts's policymakers to invest in a comprehensive approach to reduce gang violence appears to have begun to yield
positive results. Communities involved report increased collaboration between law enforcement and service provider agencies and among service
providers. This increased collaboration is viewed by participating agencies as a more effective approach to reducing gang violence than previous
efforts. Additionally, it appears that more youth are being referred to programs in SCSI communities, which was an original intent of the program.
By describing our findings and challenges within the multisite evaluation
context, we have provided a perspective through which to understand
the progress of SCSI grantee efforts and information useful to others who
may be engaged in such work.

REFERENCES

Decker, S., & Curry. G. D. (2002). "I'm down for my organization": The rationality
of responses to delinquency, youth crime, and gangs. In A. R. Piquero & S. G.
Tibbetts (Eds.), Rational *Choice and Criminal Behavior: Recent Research and Future
Challenges* (pp. 197–219). New York: Routledge.

Decker, S. H., Curry, G. D., Catalano, S., Watkins, A., & Green, L. (2005). *Strategic Approaches to Community Safety Initiative (SACSI) in St. Louis*. Research report prepared for the U.S. Department of Justice.

Dunworth, T., Mills, G., Cordner, G., & Greene, J. (1999). *National evaluation of Weed & Seed: Cross-site analysis*. Washington, D.C.: U.S. Department of Justice, National Institute of Justice.

Egley, Jr., A., & Howell, J. C. (2011). *Highlights of the 2009 National Youth Gang Survey*. Washington, D.C.: U.S. Department of Justice, Office of Juvenile Justice and Delinquency Prevention.

Egley, Jr., A., & Ritz, C. E. (2006). *Highlights of the 2004 National Youth Gang Survey*. Washington, D.C.: U.S. Department of Justice, Office of Juvenile Justice and Delinquency Prevention.

Gebo, E., Boyes-Watson, C., & Pinto-Wilson, S. (2010). Reconceptualizing organizational change in the Comprehensive Gang Model. *Journal of Criminal Justice, 38*, 166–173.

Greene, J., & Pranis, K. (2007). *Gang wars: The failure of enforcement tactics and the need for effective public safety strategies*. Washington, D.C.: Justice Policy Institute.

Howell, James C. (2006). *The impact of gangs on communities*. Washington, D.C.: U.S. Department of Justice, Office of Juvenile Justice and Delinquency Prevention.

Lawrenz, F., & Huffman, D. (2003). How can multi-site evaluations be partnerships? *American Journal of Evaluation, 24*, 471–482.

Maxson, C. L, Curry, G. D., & Howell, J. C. (2002). Youth gang homicides in the United States in the 1990s. In W. L. Reed & S. H. Decker (Eds.), *Responding to Gangs: Evaluation and Research* (pp. 107–137). Washington, D.C.: U.S. Department of Justice, National Institute of Justice.

McGarrell, E. F., Corsaro, N., Hipple, N. K., & Bynum, T. S. (2010). Project Safe Neighborhoods and violent crime trends in U.S. cities: Assessing violent crime impact. *Journal of Quantitative Criminology, 26*, 165–190.

Miller, W. B. (2001). *The growth of youth gang problems in the United States: 1970–98*. Washington, D.C.: U.S. Department of Justice, Office of Juvenile Justice and Delinquency Prevention.

Mowbray, C. T., & Herman, S. E. (1991). Using multiple sites in mental health evaluations: Focus on program theory and implementation issues. In R. S. Turpin & J. M. Sinacore (Eds.), *Multisite Evaluations* (pp. 45–57). San Francisco: Jossey-Bass, Inc.

Rog, D. J. (2010). Designing, managing, and analyzing multisite evaluations. In J .S. Wholey, H. P. Hatry, & K. E. Newcomer (Eds.), *Handbook of Practical Program Evaluation* (pp. 208–236). San Francisco: Jossey-Bass.

Skogan, W. G., & Lurigio, A. J. (1991). Multisite evaluations in criminal justice settings: Structural obstacles to success. In R. S. Turpin & J. M. Sinacore (Eds.), *Multisite Evaluations* (pp. 83–96). San Francisco: Jossey-Bass, Inc.

Spergel, I. A. (2007). *Reducing youth gang violence: The Little Village Gang Project in Chicago*. Lanham, MD: AltaMira.

Spergel, I. A., Wa, K. M., & Sosa, R. V. (2001). *Evaluation of the Bloomington-Normal Comprehensive Gang Program*. University of Chicago.

Spergel, I. A., Wa, K. M., & Sosa, R. V. (2002). *Evaluation of the Mesa Gang Intervention Program*. University of Chicago.

Straw, R. B., & Herrell, J. M. (2002). A framework for understanding and improving multisite evaluations. In J. M. Herrell & R. B. Straw (Eds.), *Conducting Multiple Site Evaluations in Real-World Settings* (pp. 5–15). San Francisco: Jossey-Bass, Inc.

Thomson, A. M., & Perry, J. L. (2006). Collaboration processes: Inside the black box. *Public Administration Review, Special Issue,* 20–32.

Toal, S. A., King, J. A., Johnson, K., & Lawrenz, F. (2009). The unique character of involvement in multi-site evaluation settings. *Evaluation and Program Planning, 32,* 91–98.

Trudeau, J., Barrick, K., Williams, J., & Roehl, J. (2010). *Independent evaluation of the national Weed and Seed strategy: Final report.* Washington, D.C.: U.S. Department of Justice, Community Capacity Development Office.

U.S. Census Bureau. *American Community Survey* (2005–2009 estimates for Hispanic/Latino, African American, and Asian populations and median household income). Retrieved from http://factfinder.census.gov/home/saff/main.html?_lang=en.

_____. *American FactFinder* (2010 census population figures for Massachusetts cities and towns, 2000 census figures for educational attainment). Retrieved August 23, 2011 from http://factfinder2.census.gov/faces/nav/jsf/pages/index.xhtml.

_____. *Small Area Income and Poverty Estimates (SAIPE)* (2009 estimates for family poverty in school districts). Retrieved August 23, 2011 from http://www.census.gov/did/www/saipe/index.html.

APPENDIX

Table 8.6. SCSI Cities and Towns by Population (U.S. Census Bureau, 2010)

City or Town	Population	City or Town	Population
Boston	617,594	Attleboro	43,593
Worcester	181,045	Everett	41,667
Springfield	153,060	Salem	41,340
Lowell	106,519	Leominster	40,759
Cambridge	105,162	Fitchburg	40,318
New Bedford	95,072	Holyoke	39,880
Brockton	93,810	Beverly	39,502
Quincy	92,271	Chelsea	35,177
Lynn	90,329	Randolph	32,112
Fall River	88,857	Gloucester	28,789
Lawrence	76,377	Melrose	26,983
Somerville	75,754	Saugus	26,628
Framingham	68,318	Danvers	26,493
Haverhill	60,879	Gardner	20,228
Malden	59,450	Marblehead	19,808
Medford	56,173	Norton	19,031
Taunton	55,874	Winthrop	17,497
Chicopee	55,298	Ashland	16,593
Revere	51,755	Swampscott	13,787
Peabody	51,251	Essex	3,504
Methuen	47,255		

Chapter 9

Learning from Community Responses to Gangs

Brenda J. Bond & Erika Gebo

The stories introduced in this book offer a glimpse into the implementation of the Comprehensive Gang Model (CGM) across a number of urban communities in Massachusetts. The value of this collection can be understood in several ways. First, the CGM is recognized as a promising practice and has been promulgated by the national Office of Juvenile Justice and Delinquency Prevention; therefore, we expect that knowledge about how these practices are implemented will grow, providing a clearer road map for adoption and implementation of this initiative. Such a roadmap can also inform other comprehensive community initiatives. Existing research on CGM outcomes is limited, as is knowledge about the implementation of the CGM (Spergel, 1995). This latter issue is critical, as the activities and associated challenges of implementation are crucial to realizing successful outcomes in comprehensive community initiatives. This is especially true as these types of multi-agency arrangements are complex and involve various and diverse entities, such as the government, non-profit organizations, residents, neighborhood groups, and community leaders. Research partners can help bring to light those often unknown and unpredictable implementation challenges assisting communities in addressing the challenges of working together, inputting best practices, and evaluating outcomes (Lasker & Weiss, 2003). The Massachusetts partnership between practitioners and researchers resulted in equal attention to implementation processes and outcomes, an essential component of understanding the real-time dynamics of CGM implementation.

In this summary chapter we highlight several themes from across the collection of stories. While each chapter discusses the CGM in a different community and through a different lens, there are notable themes across chapters which can inform our understanding of gang violence and comprehensive community initiatives such as the CGM. These themes are the dynamic nature of gang and gang violence; the quality of data to understanding and directing decision-making; the importance of the ecological context; and the reality that complex problems such as gang violence require complex solutions. We discuss these themes and the implications for gang violence reduction research and practice and note where there are lessons for other comprehensive community initiatives.

GANGS AND GANG VIOLENCE ARE DYNAMIC

Gangs and gang violence are dynamic, meaning there are significant variations and constant shifts in which gangs are active and for what reasons, across time and place (Maxson, et al., 1985). The constitution of gangs and gang membership in a small community differs from that in a large, urban metropolis. Gang motivations and relationships between gangs also vary; some small gangs, sometimes called crews, operate locally and are motivated by neighborhood turf, while other national gangs operate criminal enterprises (Curry, Ball, & Fox, 1994). Given these variations, prevention, intervention, and suppression solutions may work with one gang in one location at one time, but may not work in another location at another time. Moreover, research explicitly points out that a very small percentage of offenders are responsible for the majority of criminal behaviors troubling a community (Campbell Collaborative, n.d.; Greene & Pranis, 2007). For these reasons localized gang and community knowledge must be generated and combined with relevant research to create the most appropriate, relevant, and effective interventions (Klein & Maxson, 2006).

Contributors to this volume illustrate this theme quite well. While the five core CGM strategies were fundamental to the problem-solving approach, how each strategy was implemented varied by data-driven decisions about what parts of the problem needed attention. For example, Braga and Hureau (Chapter 7) illustrate this idea in comparing the first rendition of Operation Ceasefire, developed in response to youth violence in the mid-1990s to Ceasefire 2, based on violence in Boston in the early 2000s. A specific model of interventions and suppression was created in the 1990s as a result of in-depth and thorough analysis of the nature of gang motivations and techniques at that time (Kennedy, Braga, & Piehl, 1996).

When faced with a growing and concerning increase in gang violence in the early 2000s, Boston partners reflected on the lessons of the 1990s, utilizing a strategic problem analysis framework to uncover the contemporary dynamics of gangs and gang activity. They learned that these elements differed from those of the earlier days. Further, government and social service provider actors also changed from those who took part in the original Ceasefire, resulting in a very different organizational context in which these interventions and suppression activities took place. Given these different dynamics, it was inappropriate to force the early Operation Ceasefire model onto the challenges facing Boston in the latter part of the century. What was needed was a strategic analysis of Boston's gang problem then and there.

Other contributors point to the relevance of changing gang dynamics in their accounts. Gebo and Tobin (Chapter 4) illustrate the difficulty of developing a gang risk assessment instrument in part due to the fact that gang and gang activity is a moving target and there are varied understandings of what constitutes a gang and gang member in the community. Similar accounts are presented by Ross and Foley (Chapter 3). Both chapters connect the need to capture the dynamic nature of gangs and gang membership to inform intervention.

Boyes-Watson (Chapter 2) moves beyond the products of gangs and gang violence, to show that the lenses through which people view gangs and gang violence have significant effects on the types of strategies employed to address gang violence and how those strategies are implemented. Her chapter emphasizes the need for people of color to be equal partners in any crime initiative, particularly if such initiatives are to address the difficult tasks of organizational change and community mobilization. Finally, McDevitt and Wolff (Chapter 8) identify the challenges of evaluating these large scale comprehensive community initiatives, in part due to the dynamicity of gangs.

While the idea of a "model" program or "promising practice" may have immediate appeal to law enforcement practitioners and service providers in the field, it is imperative that those implementing these types of inter-agency approaches recognize the dynamic nature of gangs and gang membership in the identified context. Foregoing the strategic analysis of the nature and characteristics of local gang activity is likely to lead to incongruous, insufficient, and ineffective resource allocation (Schnieder, 2000).

QUALITY DATA SHOULD DRIVE DECISIONS

Research shows that effective prevention, intervention, and suppression efforts must result from a thorough and in-depth analysis of relevant data (Goldstein, 1990). In addition, data are used to continuously analyze and examine how a strategy such as the CGM is implemented (process), and with what effect (outcomes) (Goldstein, 1979). In the CGM context, qualitative and quantitative data can be found in crime reports (e.g. number of offenders, nature of relationship between offender and victim), community interview data (e.g. perceptions of safety), and observational accounts of programs or activities (e.g. diversity of youth participants). These types of data form the basis for CGM implementation. As suggested, the strategic analysis approach discussed by Braga & Hureau (Chapter 7) is grounded in the collection and analysis of quality data to uncover the dynamic nature of gangs. Yet, a real-time challenge facing practitioners is that collecting and analyzing quality data is a meticulous, relentless and complicated activity (Boba, 2003), especially in inter-agency comprehensive arrangements like the CGM.

Data collection and analyses affect how the CGM is constructed and how participating partners allocate financial and human resources. One notable theme across chapters relative to data use is the phenomena of subjectivity and its role in understanding the gang problem. Ross and Foley (Chapter 3) underscore the different perceptions of different implementation actors (e.g. law enforcement or social service providers), based on their understanding of the role of different individuals (e.g. victims, offenders). Their work revealed that prevention and intervention services are more freely given to those considered lower risk, while those that are most in need of services and most involved in gangs are typically ignored. Their analysis provided an opportunity to assess needs and service gaps as part of a more comprehensive understanding of a community, yet those decisions came from the divergent roles and values of CGM partners. Similarly, Gebo and Tobin (Chapter 4) chronicle the struggles of developing a gang assessment instrument when multiple partners are a part of the process, many of which hold very different perspectives. Therefore, what data were collected and how it was interpreted was subject to individual perceptions.

In another example of how data quality issues confront practitioners, Bond, et al. (Chapter 6) illustrate how a CGM partner recognized the shortcomings of their own data to understanding their local gang problem. In the task of defining and measuring retaliation, partners identified critical disconnects in capturing data in the field. The authors found that not only do police incidents take on different meanings and documented differently depending on which police officer responds to a call, but also that various community partners define the problem differently; therefore they allocate their resources differently depending on these divergent perceptions. Different training and field experiences fostered different understandings amongst patrol officers as well as law enforcement and social service providers. The task of defining and measuring retaliatory gang violence revealed critical definition gaps that were impeding their ability to conduct a thorough analysis of the gang problem in their city. Such problems have been recognized as part of the complex landscape of work done in natural settings, as opposed to tightly controlled laboratory or field experiments (Martin, 1975).

Researchers often push communities to collect quality data for analysis, so that accurate descriptions of the problem and identification of the most effective solutions can occur (Klein & Maxson, 2006). Moreover, there is an increased pressure on practitioners to adopt evidence-based practices (Sherman, 1998); yet, the dilemma faced is that the dynamics of the implementing environment, along with the idiosyncratic configuration of key agencies and actors doing such work make it difficult to match the contextualized local problem and partners to narrowly constructed evidence-based practices (Bond & Gebo, in press). For example, Boyes-Watson (Chapter 2) describes the changing relationships between a local police chief who partners with the mayor to broaden the scope of gang reduction activities; while Varano & Wolff (Chapter 5) describe the gang outreach workers who address the needs of bereaving family members. How do existing evidence-based practices for these types of approaches help implementing actors? The stock of knowledge on the human capital portion of what works is not yet sufficient to issue directives about implementation (NCCD, 2009). Another set of questions that address data arise. Do agencies have the capacity to not only collect data in the field or access and tailor evidence-based practices? Does the capacity exist to ensure that subjectivity, definitions, and data collection disconnects are addressed before data are analyzed and utilized?

What is needed is a genuine attempt by researchers and practitioners to collect quality data about implementation and the perceived impact of these tailored strategies for future decisions. Stakeholders must recognize that quality data and the use of evidence are an important foundation for implementation, but inadequacies should not stifle comprehensive approaches to community challenges. There is a need to be careful with best practice adherence, as agencies and grass-roots organizations, particularly in the most underserved and minority neighborhoods where gangs flourish, may be the most vulnerable to being axed (Clear, 2010).

Data collection is not often a principal goal of practitioners, especially when community expectations about service need increase yet resources remain scarce (Bond & Aydnwylde, 2010). Most funding is directed toward providing services, not collecting data for research purposes. These, however, are not mutually exclusive goals. It is incumbent upon researchers to show the value of quality data collection and analysis (Chapter 7), for practitioners who can use it to make data-driven decisions, and for policymakers who use it to make funding decisions. It is also important for researchers working with communities to be a resource and provide support to practitioners (Weisburd, 1994). As data collection needs change in the implementing environment, and as pressures continue regarding data collection and evidence-based practices, researchers can assist practitioners and organizations to move the thinking of an agency towards 'quantifying' their work as a valuable process, not a one-time, burdening event.

IMPORTANCE OF ECOLOGICAL CONTEXT

Stepping back from the specificity of the nature of gangs and how we understand them, practitioners and researchers must also consider the economic, political, social, and institutional context of the implementing community when adopting the CGM, as well as other comprehensive community initiatives. Factors that impact the community broadly, such as a high unemployment rate or a popular mayor, also impact the implementation of comprehensive community initiatives (Bond & Gebo, in press). These environmental conditions should be considered at the outset and during implementation of these types of comprehensive initiatives as part of a community's problem analysis. The CGM encourages a flexible approach to the implementation of its various components, and this was seen throughout the various stories presented in this book. Indeed, the model suggests that local context and data should drive the model adopted by local communities.

Bond & Gebo (in press) compare and contrast three of these Massachusetts CGM sites to illustrate how different ecological factors, categorized into Matland's (1995) typology of program implementation, including such things as the prominence of local actors, historical relics, and political elements, resulted in different implementation strategies of the CGM. Their article illustrates that communities capitalized on the most influential ecological factors when implementing the CGM, and arguably all other, comprehensive initiatives.

This theme was suggested in several chapters of this book. For example, at least one community experienced shifts in economy that resulted in changes in CGM implementation. Specifically, Varano & Wolff (Chapter 5) document the very real problems of responding to the immediacy of gangs and gang violence when outreach workers' funding was reduced, resulting in less time on the street conducting outreach. Braga and Hureau (Chapter 7) speak about implementation at two different points in time to deal with Boston's gang violence problem. In this discussion they suggest that not only has the gang problem changed between decades, but so too have institutional and community partners who must participate in the strategy.

Implementing actors must embrace these changing ecological dynamics to ensure appropriate and effective implementation (Decker, 2003).

An additional contextual influence of note is the role and influence of local implementation participants, be they partners or program participants. Several contributors noted local actors as influential to implementation. In the Tri-City's implementation of the CGM (Boyes-Watson, Chapter 2), local community actors were critical to the inclusion of non-whites as equal partners. This occurred through the implementation of peace circles, a forum for emphasizing equality and understanding of diverse viewpoints. Similar challenges were discussed relative to Worcester (Chapter 5) where the community and official government actors held divergent perceptions about the needs and delivery of service within the broader community. Gebo and Tobin (Chapter 4) introduce the Gang Assessment Instrument, which serves as a tool for gauging needs and services amongst the population of interest. In both instances, the perceptions of local actors not only influence the types and levels of services offered, but decisions about which populations are most in need of services. This point seems particularly important given that gangs and gang activities are dynamic and do not present themselves according to static, narrow, or clear-cut criteria.

In another instance, the Lowell Police Department (LPD) took the lead in acknowledging the need to more fully understand the retaliatory violence problem, and they were the first to open up their organization and allow researchers to access their data as part of that investigation. LPD administrators were forthright in recognizing the shortcomings of their own data and led the way for other partners to undertake similar analyses in pursuit of a better understanding of the problem (Bond, et al., Chapter 6).

An interesting challenge that results from the intersection of implementation and its environment is that initiative goals and outcomes must and will vary across implementation sites, as McDevitt and Wolff discuss in Chapter 8. While the critical elements of the CGM must be adhered to by implementation sites, there is a need to uncover contextual elements that are beyond the identification of five strategy areas (organizational change, community mobilization, social intervention, opportunities provision, and suppression) as potential contributors to success. Given that comprehensive community initiatives occur in natural settings that cannot be tightly controlled, it is imperative that the features that affect implementation and the results, both intermediary (output) and long-term (outcome) be identified and recognized. What is affected by implementation also means that while some key evaluative factors should be universal across sites (i.e. gang reduction; gang violence reduction), other evaluation measures must be tailored to the specific goals of individual communities.

SOLUTIONS ARE COMPLEX AND
REQUIRE COMPREHENSIVENESS

Implementation of the Comprehensive Gang Model in Massachusetts has solidified the broader understanding that social and public policy issues within urban communities are complex and require thoughtful and engaging participation of diverse partners. Contributions here reveal that solutions to gang problems are beyond the realm of criminal justice alone, influenced by idiosyncratic localized dynamics that not only point to the nature and characteristics of existing problems, but also what the solution should look like. Indeed, partners include individuals, organizations, and the community. Collaboration across non-traditional entities, such as police, outreach workers, and hospitals (Varano & Wolff, Chapter 5) and faith-based institutions (Braga & Hureau, Chapter 7) are essential ingredients to tackling community challenges. In reality, bringing diverse individuals and partners together, who may have divergent perspectives and priorities is a challenge (Decker, et al., 2008). Yet, the stories within suggest it also offers an opportunity to collectively confront the problems that plague communities and impact residents' quality of life.

The specific stories and the common themes tell us that implementation is influenced by economic conditions, institutional, social, and cultural factors, and family dynamics, as discussed in Chapter 1. Specified problems identified at the local level are a fundamental element of tackling problems such as gang violence; models such as the CGM should be considered and tailored to the context in which the gang problem exists. Researchers, practitioners, and policymakers must be willing to face the often frustrating, dynamic nature of gangs and gang violence. They must seek to understand their implementing environment. They must look at how 'best practice' strategies fit into a flexible framework, within an idiosyncratic context, and then continually update their knowledge and concomitant strategies through a quality data-based decisions (Bond, et al., Chapter 6). There is a need to focus as deliberately on the process of implementation as well as the outcomes of implementation, as it is in that process where critical success elements may be found. Lastly, from this specified strategy comes a more tailored evaluation that considers the existence and intersection of various contextualized factors (McDevitt & Wolff, Chapter 8).

Research tells us that targeting the small percentage of violent, hardcore offenders and providing them a choice of a carrot (services to help meet their needs) or a stick (suppression if further violence occurs) is effective (Kennedy, 1997). But that is only part of the solution. There needs to be more work done on how communities can work together effectively to engage in quality coordination and proven and creative programming in a way that is sustainable over time. The CGM provides a framework for getting to that. The Massachusetts experience demonstrates challenges, successes, and lessons of implementation of a comprehensive community initiative that works toward lasting, sustainable change to reduce gang violence.

REFERENCES

Boba, R. (2003). *Problem analysis in policing.* Washington, D.C.: Police Foundation.

Bond, B., & Aydnwylde, G. (2010). *Facing the economic crisis: Challenges for Massachusetts police chiefs.* Boston, MA: Pioneer Institute for Public Policy Research.

Bond, B., & Gebo, E. (in press). Comparing implementation policies of a best practices crime policy across cities. *Administration and society.*

Campbell Collaboration (n.d.). *The Campbell Collaboration: What helps? What harms? Based on what evidence?* Retrieved November 27, 2011 from http://www.campbellcollaboration.org/.

Clear, T. (2010). Policy and evidence: The challenge to the American Society of Criminology: 2009 presidential address to the American Society of Criminology. *Criminology, 48,* 1–25.

Curry, G., Ball, R., & Fox, R. (1994). *Gang crime and law enforcement recordkeeping.* Washington, D.C.: National Institute of Justice, U.S. Department of Justice.

Decker, S. (2003). Policing gangs and youth violence: Where do we stand, where do we go from here? In S. Decker (Ed.), *Policing gangs and youth violence.* Belmont, CA: Wadsworth Publishing Company.

Decker, S., Bynum, T., McDevitt, J., Farrell, A., & Varano, S. (2008). *Street Outreach Workers: Best Practices and Lessons Learned.* Boston: Northeastern University.

Goldstein, H. (1979). Improving policing: A problem-oriented approach. *Crime and Delinquency, 25,* 236–258.

Goldstein, H. (1990). *Problem-oriented policing.* Philadelphia: Temple University Press.

Greene, J., & Pranis, K. (2007). *Gang wars: The failure of enforcement tactics and the need for effective public safety strategies.* Washington, D.C.: Justice Policy Institute.

Kennedy, D., Piehl, A., & Braga, A. (1996). Youth violence in Boston: Gun markets, serious youth offenders, and a use-reduction strategy. *Law and Contemporary Problems, 59,* 147–196.

Kennedy, D. (1997). Pulling levers: Chronic offenders, high-crime settings, and a theory of prevention. *Valparaiso University Law Review, 31,* 449–484.

Klein, M., & Maxson, C. (2006). *Street gang patterns and policies.* New York: Oxford.

Lasker, R., & Weiss, E. (2003). Broadening participation in community problem solving: A multidisciplinary model to support collaborative practice and research. *Journal of Urban Health, 80,* 14–47.

Martin, J. (1975). Controlled vs. natural setting: Some implications for behavioral analysis and change in classroom situations. *Alberta Journal of Educational Research, 21*(1), 39–45.

Matland, R. (1995). Synthesizing the implementation literature: The ambiguity-conflict model of policy implementation. *Journal of Public Administration Research and Theory, 5*(2), 145–174.

Maxson, C., Gordon, M., & Klein, M. (1985). Differences between gang and non-gang homicides. *Criminology, 23,* 209–222.

National Council on Crime and Delinquency (2009). *Developing a successful street outreach program: Recommendations and lessons learned.* Oakland, CA: National Council on Crime and Delinquency.

Schnieder, S. (2000). Organizational obstacles to participation in community crime prevention programs. *International Criminal Justice Review, 10,* 32.

Sherman, L. (1998). *Evidence-based policing.* Washington, D.C.: Police Foundation.

Spergel, I. (1995). *The youth gang problem: A community approach.* New York, NY: Oxford University Press.

Weisburd, D. (1994). Evaluating community policing: Role tensions between practitioners and evaluators. In D. Rosenbaum (Ed.), *The challenge of community policing: Testing the promises.* Thousand Oaks, CA: Sage Publications.

Index

action research partnerships, 133, 148, 153, 177, 181; *See also Local Action Research Partnerships*

best practices, 47–49, 83, 106, 181, 184
Boston Gun Project. *See Operation Ceasefire*

CGM. *See Comprehensive Gang Model*
collaboration cross-agency, 6–8, 88, 102, 141, 161, 168–170; challenges with, 72, 76, 100–102, 167–168; faith communities, 2, 145; strategies for, 26; success with, 55–56, 70, 72, 184–185; collective efficacy, 18–21
communities of color, 17; disproportionate representation as victims and offenders, 37–38; relationships with government actors/agencies, 27, 31–32, 51–52, 71, 76
community mobilization, 17, 26, 145, 165–166, 172
community policing, 22, 169

Comprehensive Gang Model, 9–10, 39–40, 106, 130, 141, 155, 177
crews, 25, 74

data, 154–155, 158–159; decision-making assistance, *See problem analysis and refinement*; quality of, 73–75, 110, 119, 121, 123, 162–163, 180–182

gangs: assessment instruments for, 61–63, 67–69; chronic, 25; databases, 64; definitions, 2–3, 65–66, 71, 74, 110–111, 158, 162; dynamic nature of, 178–179; emergent, 25, 140; etiology, 4, 105; formal social control of, 1; gun violence and, 43–44, 136–137, 147; informal social control of, 2; reification, 67–68; retaliation, 108–109, 113, 115, 140, 164; risk factors, 39–40, 67, 138–139; risk versus need, 41–42, 71; LARP. *See Local Action Research Partnerships*

About the Contributors

Brenda J. Bond, Ph.D., is Assistant Professor in Suffolk University's Sawyer Business School, Institute for Public Service. Her interests are in the management of the police organization, Compstat, Crime Analysis, and Police Research and Development practices, comprehensive approaches to community safety, and the quality and utilization of crime and community data. She works with police leaders across the nation on a variety of policy initiatives. Brenda received her Ph.D. from the Heller School for Social Policy and Management at Brandeis University.

Carolyn Boyes-Watson, Ph.D., is Professor of Sociology and founding director of the Center for Restorative Justice at Suffolk University. She has published numerous articles on restorative justice, focusing on the role of the community, conflict with the state, and implications for organizational development. Her most recent publications include *Bringing Justice Home: Peacemaking Circles and Urban Youth* and *Heart of Hope: A Guide for Using Peacemaking Circles to Develop Emotional Literacy, Promote Healing and Build Healthy Relationships* with Kay Pranis.

Anthony A. Braga, Ph.D., is Professor in the School of Criminal Justice at Rutgers University and Senior Research Fellow in the Program in Criminal Justice Policy and Management at Harvard University's John F. Kennedy School of Government. He is the current President of the Academy of Experimental Criminology and a former Visiting Fellow at the U.S.

National Institute of Justice. He received his M.P.A. from Harvard University and his Ph.D. in Criminal Justice from Rutgers University.

Ellen Foley, Ph.D., is an Assistant Professor of International Development and Social Change in the department of International Development, Community, and Environment at Clark University. She earned her Ph.D. in medical anthropology from Michigan State University. Her research explores the intersection of global health policy, national health reform, and access to health care in West Africa, with a particular focus on HIV/AIDS policy and reproductive health. She has conducted community-based research on health disparities in Philadelphia, PA and Worcester, MA.

Erika Gebo, Ph.D., is an Associate Professor of Sociology and co-director of the Center for Crime and Justice Policy Research at Suffolk University in Boston. Her publications and expertise are in the areas of juvenile justice, community interventions, family violence, and crime policy and evaluation. She has worked on the Massachusetts Shannon Community Safety with the cities of Springfield and Boston and Tri-city area of Fitchburg, Leominster, and Gardner. Prior to a return to academia, she held various positions in the social service and law enforcement fields.

David Hureau, M.P.P., is a doctoral student in Social Policy and Sociology at Harvard University and a Research Fellow at the Harvard Kennedy School's Program in Criminal Justice Policy and Management. Prior to joining Harvard's doctoral program, David earned his M.P.P. from the Harvard Kennedy School with a concentration in Criminal Justice Policy and worked for several years researching the dynamics of violent crime in Boston with Anthony Braga. David's research interests include urban sociology and neighborhood effects, gangs, crime, and ethnography.

Jack McDevitt, Ph.D., is the Associate Dean for Research in the College of Social Studies and Humanities at Northeastern University. Dean McDevitt is the co-author of three books and numerous articles addressing the issues of hate crime, racial profiling, human trafficking, and gang violence. His work attempts to understand the intersection of race/ethnicity and the criminal justice system. For the past five years, Dean McDevitt has led a group of researchers who served as the Statewide Research Partner for the Shannon Community Safety Initiative in Massachusetts.

Erin K. McLaughlin, M.P.A./M.S.C.J.S., graduated from Suffolk University in 2010 with a dual Master's degree in Public Administration and Crime and Justice Studies. She also received a Bachelor of Arts degree in Criminology from Stonehill College in Massachusetts. Erin has experience as a researcher of public safety programs and has worked in the area of urban youth employment. She currently works for the Massachusetts State Police.

Nicole Rivers-Kustanovitz is Associate Director of the Moakley Center for Public Management and an adjunct instructor for the Institute for Public Service at Suffolk University. Nicole has fourteen years of professional experience in a variety of areas including project management, program development, group facilitation, strategic planning, policy analysis, and research methods. Nicole currently teaches graduate level courses in quantitative analysis and program evaluation/policy analysis.

Laurie Ross, Ph.D., is an Assistant Professor of Community Development and Planning in the Department of International Development, Community, and Environment at Clark University. She received her Ph.D. in public policy from the University of Massachusetts-Boston. Ross engages in collaborative research with community partners on issues such as tobacco advertising, youth and gang violence, and youth worker professional development. Ross coordinates the HOPE Coalition, a youth-adult partnership in Worcester.

Kim Tobin, Ph.D., co-authored "Gangs and Delinquency in Developmental Perspective," recipient of the 2003 Hindelang Award, and authored "Gangs: An Individual and Group Perspective." She has also engaged in evaluation research for local communities. Since 1998, Kim has worked at Westfield State University, first as a faculty member in its Criminal Justice Department before becoming Dean of Graduate and Continuing Education in 2008. She received her Ph.D. in sociology from the University of New York at Albany.

Sean P. Varano, Ph.D., is an Assistant Professor in the School of Justice Studies at Roger Williams University. His research interests include juvenile justice policy, violent crime reduction strategies, gang violence, police technology, and program evaluation. His recent publications involve the effects of gang membership on recidivism, police responses to citizen initiated calls for service, and the effects of the changing landscape of public safety for large scale sporting events in the wake of 9/11.

Russell Wolff, M.S., served as project manager for the Shannon statewide research partnership for Northeastern University and as a member of the Shannon local action research partnership with New Bedford. He was a senior research associate at the Center for Criminal Justice Policy Research and is currently a Ph.D. student in Criminology and Justice Policy at Northeastern. His research focuses on policing; organizational change, collaboration, and governance; and gang and youth violence.